Net Law:
How
Lawyers
Use the
Internet

Paul S. Jacobsen

Lawyers Use the Internet

bsen

Published by Songline Studios, Inc. and O'Reilly & Associates, Inc., 101 Morris Street, Sebastopol, CA 95472

Editor: Stephen Pizzo (707) 829-6512 steve@songline.com

Printing History: January 1997:   First Edition

Songline Guides is a trademark of Songline Studios, Inc.

Many of the designations used by manufacturers and sellers to distinguish their products are claimed as trademarks. Where those designations appear in this book, and Songline Studios, Inc., was aware of a trademark claim, the designations have been printed in caps or initial caps.

Specific copyright notices and restrictions for software included on the CD-ROM accompanying this book are included on that CD-ROM. All of the specification documents and programs described in this book and provided by vendors for inclusion on the CD-ROM are subject to change without notice.

While every precaution has been taken in the preparation of this book, the publishers take no responsibility for errors or omissions, or for damages resulting from the use of information in the book or the CD-ROM.

This book is printed on acid-free paper with 85% recycled content, 15% post-consumer waste. The publishers are committed to using paper with the highest recycled content available consistent with high quality.

ISBN: 1-56592-258-1

Cover Design: Edie Freeman
Production Services: Thomas E. Dorsaneo

Contents

Foreword

J.G. Ballard, the English novelist, wrote, "Science and technology multiply around us. To an increasing extent they dictate the languages in which we speak and think. Either we use those languages, or we remain mute."[1] His words are relevant to the need for lawyers to become familiar with the Internet. It is not advisable for anyone to remain silent in the face of the enormous technological change now occurring, but for the legal profession in particular it can be potentially devastating for our clients, our practice, and our profession.

Even the most able litigator, negotiator, and judge enters the world of cyberspace for the first time with some trepidation. We have all heard about the wealth of information that pours through modems from the Internet. This tremendous volume of information is precisely the problem: the sheer quantity itself seems to dissolve information into an indistinguishable mass that conceals the smoking gun in the midst of the irrelevant. Additionally, for many who watched cautiously from the sidelines as the "techies" played in this virtual world and began giving birth to a global community in cyberspace, the change has hit like a bolt of lightning. Almost overnight, we must come to understand and work with emails that have no post office, windows that are not attached to homes but to home pages, search engines that have no vehicles, hits that require no physical contact, and chat rooms that have no physical space.

There are many reasons why lawyers need to enter into this virtual world, some philosophical and some practical. Lawyers are knowledge workers. Knowledge is the raw material that lawyers shape into workable solutions and compromises that form the norms of, and bring order to, our society. The Internet has internalized the local flavor of each user and transformed it into a sense of "global village." Like any institution in its infancy, this new virtual community needs guidance even if it has a general direction. This is the New Frontier; there is a certain Wild West quality about the Internet. The laws are a little fuzzy and no one is quite sure who is the sheriff, marshall, or

[1] J. G. BALLARD, CRASH, Introduction

mayor in town. Lawyering is the art of organizing and communicating the ideals, mores, and philosophies of society (the virtual global society in this case) into acceptable norms that do not unduly burden any segment. I can think of no better place for creative and visionary lawyers to turn their attention than this new frontier.

On a more practical level, the Internet provides wonderful opportunities for networking, client development, efficiency, and standardization. Email is perhaps the most important communication tool since the telephone, and it provides one added advantage—affordability. Email provides practitioners with a cost effective and extremely efficient method of communicating with clients, potential clients, other attorneys, and experts in a variety of fields from around the globe.

This new global village is pushing globalization of the law. It is rapidly drawing attorneys into international venues and introducing them to clients who live and work outside the U.S. The Internet knows no physical boundaries, time zones, or sovereign territory and requires no compatible hardware. Tourists and business travelers alike are welcomed without the need for passports or visas.

This open quality of the Internet has led to another important development—democratization of the legal profession. It offers a more collegial system that places solo practitioners on a more level playing field with large law firms. Here, the solo and small firm practitioners not only have the same opportunity to market, network, and attract clients, but they also have the same potential for researching cases. Up-to-the-minute information can be the deciding factor in litigation and negotiation. Legal research on the Internet is quickly coming into its own. Although still not a complete resource, the Internet contains a host of free information resources for lawyers, and that body of information continues to expand. We must all become familiar with and knowledgeable about this new technology, because, rest assured, the days of electronic filing and other more efficient paperless methods of practicing law are fast approaching.

Neither progress nor the law is ever a finished product. Rather, they are both an endless process of evolution. Like a chameleon, progress has the uncanny ability to change color and direction as the need arises; curiously, it not only survives, but regains force and vitality with each transformation. Today, we measure progress by the wide strides taken by the child prodigy we call "the information revolution"—the Internet. If progress has once again dusted off its coat and entered center stage with incredible force, let the lawyer stay a step ahead and greet her at the door.

Paul Jacobsen has written a very useful and readable book—particu larly for those new to the Internet. More importantly, he has captured the relaxed, informal, seemingly carefree, yet very deliberate and precise aura of the Internet. I encourage my colleagues in the legal profession to bring your motherboards and learn to surf, not on water, but on the information superhighway.

CU there :-)

Robert A. Stein
Executive Director and Chief Operating Officer
American Bar Association

About the Author

Paul Jacobsen practices law in Minnesota, and lives near Brainerd, Minnesota. Until 1995, he was a partner at Briggs & Morgan, a 130-lawyer law firm in Minneapolis/St. Paul. His legal practice has covered a wide variety of subjects, with a concentration in construction law, insurance, and litigation.

For several years, he was an adjunct professor of law at William Mitchell College of Law, teaching Legal Writing and Government Contracts. In addition to his law practice and his teaching, he has published articles in law reviews.

He holds a J.D. from the University of Minnesota Law School and a B.A. in economics from St. Olaf College. Paul and his wife, Sally, have three young children, with whom he enjoys spending his free (?) time.

Acknowledgments

Sometimes this can be overdone, so I'll try to keep it short. Initially, I'd like to thank those legal colleagues who, over the past 12 years, have taken the time to explain things to me, from long ago showing me how to draft a complaint, to more recently telling me how to configure a modem. Without their willingness to teach, I would never have been able to teach others what I've been (slowly) learning over the years.

In writing this book, I must thank Mark and Steve at Songline for bringing this project to my attention and helping move it quickly through the publication process. I also thank them for their comments on the manuscript, in addition to the comments of Samuel Lewis and Karna Berg. And, of course, I continue to appreciate (and dread) those who generously help me co-exist with computers. Without their help, I would have long ago attached a boat anchor to my computer and condemned it to a watery grave.

Last, but most importantly, thanks to my wife, Sally, and to my children, Elisabeth, Pete, and Luke. You are my motivation; without you, I would have little reason to get *anything* done.

Paul Jacobsen
jacobsen@brainerd.net

Introduction

Why would a lawyer care about the Internet? Since you picked up this book, you must have been at least toying with the idea. But is the Internet a useful tool for lawyers? Or just a time-wasting high-tech gadget? Like any tool, the Internet is only as effective as the person using it. One of the law firms featured in this book has its own answer. They report over 40,000 visits a week to their Web site, 6,000 subscribers to their Internet-distributed newsletter and, after just a few years, fully two-thirds of their business is attributable to their Web site.

Of course, your experience may differ. But clearly the Internet has matured into a useful business tool that, like the telephone and fax before it, is being integrated into the legal profession's day-to-day business. And like those earlier technological tools, those who wait too long to adopt them will find it increasingly difficult to compete. If you're still sitting on the sidelines, then consider *Net Law* your wake-up call.

- ▶ Is This the Internet Book for You?
- ▶ Where Are We Now and Where Are We Going?
- ▶ How to Use *Net Law*

IS THIS THE INTERNET BOOK FOR YOU?

This book not only tells you how to get *on* the Internet, but it also shows you *what* to do when you get on it. And rest assured, you're in good company. Some lawyers are using it regularly, but most are only now getting online. This means that there's still time for you to catch up with your colleagues who are already "Net-lawyers." By the time you finish this book you will be able to harness the power of the Internet.

And this book is for you if you like to learn things after most of the bugs have been worked out. Although the Net isn't insect-free (and never will be), it's a lot easier to use than just a few years ago. You won't be forced to learn by trial and error, often getting lost like an explorer slogging through a foreign jungle without a local guide. With this book, dozens of legal guides—all lawyers or other legal professionals experienced in using the Internet—will explain from first-hand experience what's useful and not useful about the Net. Using their experiences, you'll not only learn how to get online, but also learn the best ways to use the Internet in your legal practice.

And if you're not yet on the Internet, *now* is the time to do it. The Internet revolution is where the PC computer revolution was ten years ago. With that revolution winding down, PCs are now found in virtually every law office. But it took over ten years for it to happen. The Internet revolution is different, because if the PC revolution was running on diesel, the Internet revolution is running on jet fuel. You don't have ten more years to learn about the Net. The revolution is moving fast—for some, *way* too fast.

If you're still not sure that *now* is the time to get on the Net, read on. You don't have much more time to waste.

WHERE ARE WE NOW AND WHERE ARE WE GOING?

First, the statistics. Some estimates put up to 30 million people on the Internet today, but it's really not a number that anyone can prove. Certainly the number of people who have *access* to the Net is at least that large. An American Bar Association survey released in July of 1996 reports 58% of small law practices have access to the Internet, up from just 14% one year prior. But not all lawyers with *access* to the Internet actually *use* it. Bill Skeels, an attorney with Lawsight (*http://www/lawsight.com*), estimates that by the end of 1996, 15-20%

of all lawyers will regularly *use* the World Wide Web portion of the Internet in their professional practices, up from around 5% a year earlier. Regardless of the numbers, however, these statistics show that lawyers' access and use of the Net has more than tripled in 1996 alone.

Although the numbers are impressive, they shouldn't come as a surprise when we look at the Internet in its historical context. You'll probably take this as pure hyperbole, but many contemporary thinkers rank the Internet alongside the invention of the printing press in 1440.

That is a pretty big claim, but maybe not such an exaggeration. The Gutenberg printing press allowed the widespread distribution of information to the masses. But despite its accomplishments, the printing press wasn't—and its successor printing presses still aren't—the perfect means of communication. Attorney Stephen J. McGarry, in a paper he presented at the Global Forum in Paris, said the following:

> *Though revolutionary in its day, the printed production of information suffers from the same impediments as it did almost 500 years ago: the high cost of collection, production, and distribution to the provider which then must be passed to the user. The user is faced with three problems: (1) the printed product rapidly becomes dated; (2) there is often no search mechanism other than a table of contents or an index; and (3) storage. The active distribution cost borne by the user is quite high.*

Books and other paper-based material still have to be printed and distributed. There is a cost to accessing information on a paper-based medium, and it's a cost that increases with each additional page printed. Presenting more information costs more money. In the jargon of the economist, there is a marginal cost for each printed page. And because there is such a cost, there is an inherent barrier to the type and quantity of information that makes it to the printed page.

But the Internet is different. Once on the Net, information is available to everyone at virtually no increased cost of production. There are no publishers, warehouses, or bookstores that each have to make a profit at every step along the distribution chain. The information can be immediately updated for the one-time cost of revising the source material. Millions can then access the latest version and read or download the information. In other words, information on the Net has a marginal cost of virtually zero. And because it's so easy to place information on the Internet, the barriers to publishing information are slight. Virtually anything and everything is on the Net, which is simultaneously its greatest virtue and its greatest vice.

Of course, a person must have some basic hardware to get on the Internet in the first place—a computer, a modem, and an Internet connection. But many law offices already have most of this basic hardware in place. Once a person has the hardware, the cost to access information is no more than the cost of an Internet connection, which can run as low as $15 a month. Public access to the Net has outpaced business access. Once access to the Net becomes like owning a TV set or radio (there are plans of integrating Internet access with future TVs using high-speed cable modems) the Internet will bring to fruition the original promise of the printing press.

Hyperbole, maybe. But even Judge Dalzell, in ruling that the Communications Decency Act of 1996 was unconstitutional,[2] seemed awed by the Internet's potential (I don't know about you, but I've never before awed a federal judge):

> It is no exaggeration to conclude that the Internet has achieved, and continues to achieve, the most participatory marketplace of mass speech that this country—and indeed the world—has yet seen. The plaintiffs in these actions correctly describe the "democratizing" effects of Internet communication: individual citizens of limited means can speak to a worldwide audience on issues of concern to them. Federalists and Anti-Federalists may debate the structure of their government nightly, but these debates occur in newsgroups or chat rooms rather than in pamphlets. Modern-day Luthers still post their theses, but to electronic bulletin boards rather than the door of the Wittenberg Schlosskirche. More mundane (but from a constitutional perspective, equally important) dialogue occurs between aspiring artists, or French cooks, or dog lovers, or fly fishermen.

The Internet is about as close as we'll get to achieving the widespread and cheap distribution of information. There'll always be a use for books—that laptop computer isn't very cozy in front of a fire. But when you need quick information or communication at your fingertips, the Internet beats the printed page hands down.

But does this revolution mean anything to the practice of law? If law had nothing to do with information, you could safely answer that the Internet was of little value. But so much of law is simply getting information in some form—caselaw, statutes, regulations, and the like. Can lawyers avoid using the best tool yet devised to distribute

[2] *A.C.L.U. v Reno*, 929 F. Supp. 824 (E.D. Pa 1996)

information? Lawyer T. K. Read, in the article *Pushing the Advertising Envelope: Building Bill Boards in the Sky Along the Information Super-highway,* said:

> The one thing agreed upon by both proponents and antagonists alike is that the Internet is as significant a technological development as the car, phone, or TV, and that it will change the world as we know it. Consequently, if global change is on the way, then a corresponding change in the practice of law is also imminent and the beginnings of this change can be seen from observing how lawyers today are currently utilizing the Net.

I invite you to read the rest of this book to learn how lawyers are currently utilizing the Net. Use their experiences as your stepping stone into the world of Cyberlaw.

HOW TO USE NET LAW

Like an intense foreign language course, this book will immerse you in the tools and culture of the Internet. Read it, and you'll learn from Internet trailblazers what the Internet can (and cannot) do for your law practice.

You may jump around in the book if you want. But you may find it useful to read the first few chapters if you're not familiar with the language of the Net. So you know what's ahead and where you may want to go, here's a quick overview of *Net Law:*

In **Chapter 1**, we overview why the legal profession is on the Internet. You'll learn why other lawyers have become Net-literate, and what they faced when they did.

Chapters 2 and **3** introduce you to the basics of the Internet: how to get online and, once you are, the basic tools you will learn how to use. If you're already familiar with some of the basics, you can skim this fairly quickly.

In **Chapter 4**, we learn how other legal professionals are using electronic mail ("email") to strengthen their law practices and make their professional lives easier and more efficient. Other lawyers will explain the security concerns facing all forms of communication, including email, and the ways you can solve the problems. The chapter will also give you a few pointers about how to use email and not be instantly spotted as an Internet "newbie" once you begin your forays on the Internet.

The next two chapters introduce you to the vast storehouse of information on the Internet. In **Chapter 5**, you'll learn how the Internet can save time and money for legal research. With the help of experienced Net-lawyers, the chapter will tell you where to find the most comprehensive information, introduce you to ways to search for information, and discuss how to cite the information once you find it. In **Chapter 6**, we explore other valuable uses of the Net, such as discussion groups, getting CLE credits online, doing discovery on the Internet, and finding a new job through cyber-ads.

In **Chapters 7** and **8** we delve into Web pages. First, using the experiences of many other lawyers, we review the reasons to have a Web site and what results you can expect. Next, we talk about how to plan and build your Web site, whether you do it yourself or hire someone else. With tips from other lawyers who have had Web sites for years, you'll learn what's important in building a site that creates legal business for you.

Finally, **Chapter 9** looks ahead and attempts to spot the legal trends being fueled by the Internet. You'll see how other legal professionals are innovatively using the Net to streamline their legal practices. You'll also hear about some of the latest technology and other trends that are just down the pike.

Why the Law Profession Is on the Internet

When I began discovering the vast resources of the Internet, I thought of Arlo Guthrie's "Alice's Restaurant." And, in fact, I wanted to make sure I correctly remembered the first few lines of the song. Within a minute of plugging the words "Alice's Restaurant" into a search engine, I was at a Web site about Arlo Guthrie's songs. Not only did it include the song's lyrics, but much more about Mr. Guthrie and his life.

"You can get anything you want at Alice's Restaurant." And that nearly sums up the Internet. Because the Net is a vast storehouse of information, it is natural for lawyers to be on it. As attorney Steve McGarry writes: "While almost all businesses require information, law *is* information." Why shouldn't the legal profession be leading the way in a technology that personifies information?

The law profession is realizing that there are many practical reasons to be on the Internet. In this chapter, we'll fly over NetWorld, and get an overview of its many uses. In the following chapters, we'll land and take a closer look at some of those uses. But first, the tour by air:

- ▶ Why Lawyers Are on the Net—The Carrots
- ▶ Why Lawyers Are on the Net—The Sticks
- ▶ You're Not in Kansas Anymore…

WHY LAWYERS ARE
ON THE NET—THE CARROTS

The Internet excels in communication, research, and marketing. These should be enough to motivate every lawyer to pay attention.

COMMUNICATION

Our profession cannot operate without effective communication. First, it was the mailed letter, then the phone, then overnight mail, then voice mail, and now the fax. Although the fax machine is the bane of many lawyers longing for simpler days, lawyers quickly embraced it because it provided something clients wanted.

Communication on the Internet takes the fax—and the letter and the phone call—a giant leap forward.

The Net allows many forms of communication. Ignoring the fine distinctions, there are essentially three: first, email and its variants, such as mailing lists and discussion groups; second, real-time communication, such as chat groups and audio or video conferencing; and third, remote information retrieval, such as downloading information from a Web site. Even a federal judge recently recognized that the "Internet is therefore a unique and wholly new medium of worldwide human communication."[1]

The most common variant of Net communication is electronic mail, or email. Email is quickly becoming ubiquitous as one of the most effective communication tools ever devised. It can combine the best of the phone, the fax, and the written letter.

Because of its advantages, lawyers such as Bob Cumbow of Seattle are seeing a "growing reliance on email as the communication medium of choice for many clients. It's fast, cheap, and user-friendly, combining the best features of letter writing and phone calling." And its attributes go beyond those of the letter or phone. With email, you can communicate worldwide for very little cost. And, with the proper setup, you can send a message to thousands of people for the same effort it takes to send one message. You can't do that with the phone, fax, or regular mail service.

[1] *ACLU v. Reno, 929 F. Supp 824 (E.D.Pa. 1996)*

Colorado attorney Joseph Hodges, Jr., runs a solo probate practice, and email saves him both time and money while allowing him to keep up with his many activities:

PERSONAL ACCOUNT
Joseph Hodges, Jr.
Solo practitioner
jghodges@usa.net

> *These activities require that I be able to communicate with the other people working on these projects at all times during the day, not to mention the fact that I need to be able to respond to several of these people at the same time. Short of carrying around a portable telephone all of the time, not to mention spending a fortune on long distance conference call charges and suffering through the hassle of trying to call everyone at a time during the day when they all can be on the line at the same time but in four different time zones, I would not be able to effectively communicate with these people were it not for the Internet. Now I can simply download and read my emails at any time and from virtually any location (as I do have a portable cellular telephone, primarily so I can dial into the Internet for my emails from any good U.S. cell location), compose responses to the same, and instantly send those responses back to the senders (as well as copies to other people), all for a fraction of the cost of using the normal telephone lines, and free of the hassles of trying to fax the same document to a group of people.*

> *In essence, the Internet and my portable PC and cellular phone have allowed me to become essentially a "virtual lawyer" whenever I care to be. That capacity alone will, I feel, allow me to remain not only competitive with but ahead of the curve as lawyers and our computer-literate clients move into the 21st century.*

Lawyers are discovering the advantages of email not only for sending messages, but also for sending documents. With a common email function, you can send a perfect electronic copy of a document with a few clicks of a computer mouse. Washington lawyer John Maxwell, Jr., talks about this use of email:

PERSONAL ACCOUNT
John Maxwell, Jr.
Meyer, Fluegge, & Tenney, P.S.
http://www.wolfenet.com/ ~maxjd/genmft.html
maxjd@wolfenet.com

> *The neat thing about email is attachments. You can attach anything to an email message as long as it is a file on your computer. Therefore, instead of faxing a cover letter with some documents for your client's approval you could email the client with a message and attach the word processing files. Currently there are still advantages to the standard fax machine if you're sending a lot of external documents and pictures that would otherwise take longer to scan. But if the document, picture, or other file is already on your machine, nothing beats the speed of email.*

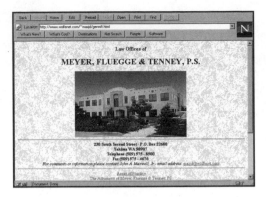

FIGURE **1-1**

And with variants of email, you can communicate with thousands of others through mailing lists, or read postings at a newsgroup with related software. Lawyers rely on communication. Without email, you're missing one of the most effective means of doing it.

RESEARCH

Using the Net for research has come into its own. In the past couple of years, the information on the Internet—particularly that portion of it known as the World Wide Web—has reached the critical mass it's needed to become a valuable research tool for the legal profession. Also, free online search engines can be used to cut through the clutter and find specific information.

This book devotes an entire chapter to research on the Net, featuring the experiences and tips of legal professionals now using it for research. Some lawyers use the Internet because it saves them thousands of dollars; they've been able to cancel their expensive contracts with Westlaw and Lexis. Other lawyers use the Net for research because it has more varied resources than these legal databases. For example, at no cost to you, you can get daily syllabi of U.S. Supreme Court decisions the day they are issued. With a few keystrokes, you can get by return email a full-text copy of any decision you request.

PERSONAL ACCOUNT

Jeremy March
Deputy Legal Counsel for the Southern California Association of Governments
march@scag.ca.gov

California attorney Jeremy March writes how the Internet has saved him both time and money for research:

In the spring of 1993, when I was being interviewed for my current position as Deputy Legal Counsel for the Southern California Association of Governments (a regional transportation and environmental planning agency), I was asked by the woman who was to become my boss whether I knew anything about computer-driven legal research. "No, but that's all right," I assured her. "I enjoy going down to the law libraries and conducting research the old-fashioned way, by hand." Eighteen months, innumerable subway rides to the L.A. County Law Library, and perhaps two thousand dollars in Xeroxing and Lexis and Westlaw fees later, however, I had somehow lost my passion for "old-fashioned" legal research.

Our office has a rudimentary law library containing West's annotated California and U.S. Codes and a few other sources which we use every day. This arrangement worked fine for my purposes except when I had to run a subject search through state or Federal law or when I had to consult a source (say, the California Jurisprudence legal encyclopedia, or some of the more obscure titles of the Code of Federal Regulations) which we did not use frequently enough to justify the cost of a subscription. We would have to pay for a Lexis or Westlaw search whenever a subject or word search had to be done through the Codes.

If the search was inadequate (for example, because I hadn't used the best possible search terms), I had to pay for another search. Whenever I needed to consult a source not in the office, I had to take a not-very-fast subway ride down to the L.A. County Law Library, pore over the source in question, and then Xerox the needed pages at fifteen cents per copy. At a time when funds to government agencies were beginning to be cut, this "old-fashioned" approach to research was not just aggravating, but prohibitively expensive.

Things began to change one night in August of 1994, when I went into the Horseshoe Coffeehouse in the San Fernando Valley for a milkshake. After overhearing my disparaging remark about how useless the "information superhighway" seemed to be, a teenaged girl named Lara came over to my table, grabbed my arm, and dragged me over to a coin-operated terminal with Internet access. Over the next two hours, Lara (who dressed entirely in black and had a shaved head, tattoos, a ring through her nose, and a kind of amused contempt for lawyers) explained to me how to use Gopher, the World Wide Web, email, and various other Internet tools.

It began to dawn on me that the Internet (particularly the Web) might have applications for legal research, and I followed up this first lesson with a very useful seminar entitled "Use of the Internet for Attorneys" given by California attorney Jerome Mullins. At the seminar, and through subsequent experimentation, I discovered a number of useful Web sites which contain word-searchable versions of the California and U.S. Codes and at least some of the materials which I could previously examine only at the County Law Library.

Like many attorneys, Jeremy March became frustrated with researching on the Net when it contained archaic search engines relying on confusing, text-based commands. But like the difference between a Macintosh and DOS computer, the Internet—with the Web and its hyperlinks—has become much easier to navigate. Not long ago, researching on the Net was like trying to find gold nuggets buried in a mountain: you had to sift through a lot of dirt before you stumbled upon a nugget. Today, MegaSites and search engines (which we'll discuss in Chapter 5) are making the prospecting much easier. In fact, many attorneys find that even when they have the printed resources right in their offices they still use the searchable Net to find what they need.

Research on the Net is now one of its greatest virtues and one of the primary reasons lawyers are flocking to the Internet. In addition to communication and research, the legal profession has found the Net because it helps the bottom line: it's a place to market their services.

MARKETING

To some lawyers, marketing may still be a dirty word and seen as below the dignity of the profession. But most accept it as necessary in our competitive legal world. And with that realization in hand, lawyers simply cannot ignore the new world on the Internet.

New York attorney Peter W. Martin, in the article "Five Reasons for Lawyers and Law Firms to Be on the Internet," explains why:

> *A virtual New York and Paris (with equivalent population) was how* The New York Times *piece put it—with coffee houses, towers of commerce, romantic hideaways, etc. Now a community of that size and vibrancy must be chock-full of potential business for lawyers. And, indeed, clients and potential clients are there.*

And it's not just clients on the Net. Keeping visible in the legal community is another reason to be on the Internet. Peter Martin continues:

> *Think of the Net again as a burgeoning city—a new marketplace or market access point for legal services. You would expect lawyers to move in and for successive entrants to locate their offices in places where potential clients might look for legal services. For all the reasons that law offices cluster, that yellow page listings (on the one hand) and Martindale-Hubbell listings (on the other) are not to be ignored—not to speak of both subtler and more aggressive outreach efforts—lawyers find it important to be visible among other lawyers.*

FIGURE 1-2
*Pederson & Freedman's
site clearly communicates
that immigration law is
their specialty*

Being visible has little advantage in and of itself. But even in its infancy, the Internet is proving to be a very effective way to attract clients. You'll hear many more experiences later in this book, but attorney and Web page consultant Bruce Hake gives a few examples:

I've heard many impressive stories. Here are some details:

- *One firm has been hired by 20 new clients, all professionals (mainly foreign physicians) in about six months (http://ilw.com/pederson).*

- *My own solo practice is averaging about one good new client per month from my simple Web site (http://ilw.com/hake). I refer away about 80 percent of the queries that come to me, picking the cases most to my interest.*

- *One law firm in Ohio told us they're averaging about one new client a week (http://ilw.com/fleischer).*

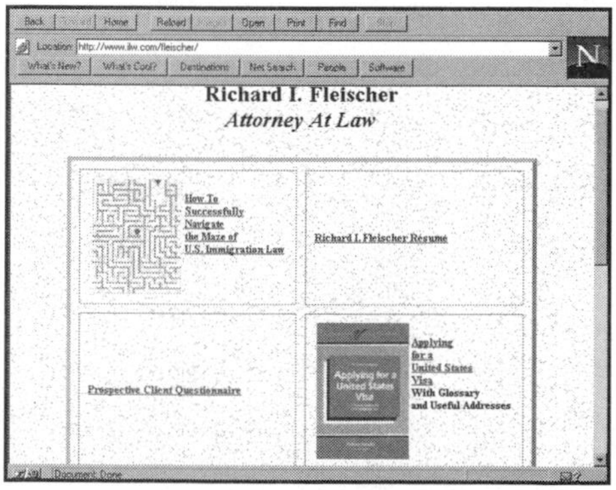

PERSONAL ACCOUNT
Bruce Hake
President, Hake Internet
Projects, LLC
http://ilw.com
bruce@hake.com

FIGURE 1-3

FIGURE 1-4
Counsel Connect's Web site connects clients and lawyers

The Internet is also being used as a way for clients to find lawyers directly. For example, at Counsel Connect's Web site (*http://www. counsel.com*), laypeople can send an email outlining their needs to a lawyer. Counsel Connect will forward the message to those of its members who are qualified for the work.

Lawyers are on the Net because of the many advantages it can offer— for communication, research, and marketing. But if those reasons aren't enough, many other lawyers are using the Internet because they realize they have no choice if they want to be effective lawyers in the future.

WHY LAWYERS ARE ON THE NET—THE STICKS

Like taking a class in law school only because it's on the bar exam, you may get on the Internet only because you feel you have to. It's been reported that in November of 1994, only five law firms had home pages on the Web. In mid-1996, more than 350 law firms were linked to Washburn University's Web site alone, and it's believed there are thousands of lawyer Web sites. Matthew Gray of the Massachusetts Institute of Technology reports that the size of the Web is currently doubling every six months. Within the very near future,

FIGURE 1-5
The Net knows no borders and increasingly neither does the legal profession, as the Solberg Web site demonstrates

having a Web site will be expected of most law firms, just like having a fax machine or being listed in the Yellow Pages.

Being on the Net is more than having a Web site. Being able to use its communication and research tools is also important for any lawyer hoping to stay competitive.

Norman Solberg is an American lawyer practicing international law in Japan. He reports that Japanese lawyers are behind their American colleagues in using computers and the Internet. Yet he still felt the need to familiarize himself with the Net in order to keep up with the competition:

> I am admitted to practice in Japan as a Gaikokuho Jimu Bengoshi (Gaiben) or foreign legal advisor. As such, my practice is limited to foreign and international law, not Japanese law, so I work closely with Japanese lawyers, or Bengoshi, on matters which involve both areas.
>
> My kind of lawyer absolutely must offer fresh ideas and access to timely, state-of-the-art information. If I don't, despite my wide experience in international and corporate practice, I won't be perceived as offering anything different from other American lawyers whom such clients might consult. Finding the right information is, of course, a key skill element in the practice of law. I apply my skills to understand exactly what information is available and what is of value to the clients. However, I now must also know how and where to find such information efficiently in a new medium, the Internet. In that regard, the learning experience, while painful, is essential to this kind of practice.

That learning experience can come at your own pace, or hit you like a ton of bricks. Intellectual property attorney Bob Cumbow learned that a whole new body of law was quickly being created and that he had to learn about it:

> In the fall of 1994, when I was still just a workaday trademark attorney, I was advising a client who wished to register its trademark for an online information service. The guy I was talking to was more interested in trademark law than most clients. He even took me to lunch and asked questions about the ins and outs of trademark protectability. He also explained his business to me, and gave me an online demonstration that included my first look at Usenet and the World Wide Web.

One day he sent me an issue of the magazine Wired, *noting a particular article he thought would interest me as a trademark attorney. The article, of course, was the now legendary "Billions Sold," by Joshua Quittner.*

Using his own registration of the domain name mcdonalds.com as a point of focus, Quittner wrote about the myopia of corporate America in not getting their trademarks and key product names registered as domain names. Disputes had already begun to arise as major companies and organizations woke up and found that someone not connected with them had "taken" their name as an Internet domain name. Sometimes it was just cute; sometimes it was the deliberate action of either a gold-digger who hoped to get rich selling the name "back" when the company got wise, or a competitor attempting to divert business. The latter was the case in Kaplan v. The Princeton Review, where TPR had registered the domain name kaplan.com—they said it was a joke, but Net users who accessed the site, possibly thinking they were getting information from Kaplan, a major competitor of TPR, found a table comparing TPR's services to Kaplan's, with Kaplan coming in second-best on every point. (The case eventually went to arbitration, and TPR reportedly surrendered the domain name to Kaplan for a case of beer.)

Not one week after my client had sent me the Quittner article, I got a call from another client. "One of our competitors has registered our trademark as a domain name! What can we do?" Because that first client had made sure I knew that the cutting edge of trademark law was in the area of Internet domain name registrations, I knew what the second client was talking about, and was able to help them. In addition, a light bulb went on over my head, and that was the beginning of my "Internet law practice."

Now, you may not want to develop an "Internet law practice" like Bob Cumbow. But does that mean you can ignore the Net? As we learned in law school, doesn't every lawyer have to know at least enough so that he or she can spot the key issues? And, if your clients starts talking about domain name disputes, or contracts with ISPs, or flaming on the Net, don't you at least want to know what they're talking about?

In some instances, being Net-savvy is already required to practice law. For example, you have to be on the Internet if you're handling one of the maritime asbestos cases in the Northern District of Ohio. The 400 involved attorneys *must* file all pleadings electronically through the Internet. It's the only practical way that the court can manage the 500,000 docket entries every year. It's also convenient, because it allows the attorneys to electronically view and obtain all case documents and dockets from their offices.

If you don't want to get on the Net, you may simply realize you have to. Stephen McGarry, President of Lex Mundi, states it this way:

> *Though the Internet will transform the legal profession, different parts of the profession will find different components to be the most beneficial to them. While most will win by the creation of efficiencies, there will be losers. The losers will be those who do not immediately grasp the concept and who seek to maintain the inefficient obsolete systems.*

Like lawyers who thought they could get by without a fax in the '80s, some lawyers still think they can skate by without using the Internet. Think again. To put it bluntly, you don't really have a choice.

YOU'RE NOT IN KANSAS ANYMORE...

If you've realized (even begrudgingly) that you must learn this new technology, welcome! Although much on the Internet will not ruffle the trained cynicism of the legal professional, cyberspace is a different world. Like Oz was to Dorothy, it will be both familiar and strange at the same time.

Attorney Bob Cumbow gives an example of how cyberspace is not always what you expect:

> *A client, a developer of video and computer game software, called to complain of a site on which an Internet user had published interactive games infringing a number of my client's copyrighted characters and registered trademarks. Trouble was, we had only the infringer's email address—no name, address, or other identification. Now, customarily when an act of infringement is uncovered, the trademark/copyright owner's attorney will send a demand letter by certified mail.*
>
> *This demand letter comes in one of three flavors:*
>
> *1. You probably didn't know what you were doing, but we have to ask you to stop.*
>
> *2. You should have known better, but please stop now.*
>
> *3. You knew damn well what you were doing, stop at once or be sued.*
>
> *This case clearly called for letter 2 or 3, since the use of my client's game characters could not have been accidental or coincidental. We opted for letter 2. The question then was, how do we send it? I suggested sending the infringer an email. Shock. Horror. This had never been done before. The demand letter is a time-honored institution in intellectual property*

protection. But a demand email? No one had ever heard of such a thing! But email can, after all, be traced and marked for return receipt, I noted; and besides, it's all we've got, so we might as well try it. The client agreed. "One of two things is likely to happen," I told the client. "Either we'll get someone who will back off quickly, or we'll get one of these freemen netizens who will mail-bomb us back into the 19th century."

About an hour later, I got a reply to my demand letter. Here it is, in its entirety: "Sorry, I'm only 11."

Later I talked by phone with both the boy and his mother. Bright kid. Needless to say, we resolved the dispute amicably—as they say in litigation circles.

There's a well-known cartoon showing two dogs on a computer with the tag line, "On the Internet, no one knows you're a dog." You may not find yourself dealing with dogs or 11-year-old trademark infringers, but you *will* find surprises around many Net corners. This book will try to lessen some of those surprises.

Connecting to the Internet

2

The next two chapters are a map that will help you navigate this virtual universe called the Internet and get you where you want to go.

Those readers who are more advanced may choose to skip these two chapters. If you decide not to read these chapters in detail right now, at least skim them quickly to learn some of the Net vocabulary we'll be using in the rest of this book. And if your law office already has an Internet connection, some of this chapter may not be of interest to you. So read what you need of the next two chapters, but don't get bogged down in the fine print you don't need right now.

What does the Internet look like? How many ways are there to connect to the Internet? How do lawyers get the Internet into their offices to make it go to work for them? In this chapter, we answer these questions to help you better understand how to make this book work for you.

▶ What *Is* the Internet?

▶ How Do I Connect? Let Me Count the Ways...

▶ What's a LAN, and Does Our Office Need One?

▶ Should I Get My Own Domain Name?

WHAT *IS* THE INTERNET?

To understand what the Internet is, think of a technology that lawyers already use and could not live without.

Plain Old Telephone Service (POTS) extends all over the world. When you pick up your phone and dial another phone, the phone company automatically routes your call through the available phone lines until the phone on the other end rings. As long as the phone you are calling is connected to the phone system, you can reach it.

Now, instead of a phone, imagine a computer at each end. By analogy, that's the Internet. It's hundreds of thousands of computers, all over the world, connected in a way that lets other computer users call them up and access them. In most cases, the computers use the same phone lines the phone system uses, so connections get routed through available lines automatically. If your computer is connected to the Internet, you can reach any other computer currently connected to the Internet. You can view and retrieve any information on any computer that someone has made available to other computers.

But where did the Internet infrastructure come from? The Internet had its start in late 1960s with the U.S. Department of Defense's ARPANET. By design, it did *not* use a central hub to transfer information. Instead, information could always go through multiple routes on the assumption that portions of the network would go down during a nuclear war (remember the Cold War?).

It took decades for the Internet to grow, but once it started, it grew exponentially. In 1981, fewer than 300 computers were linked to the Internet, and by 1989 it was fewer than 90,000 computers. But by 1996, nearly 10,000,000 were connected. The recent Internet hype has resulted, not by the Internet's creation, but by the recent critical mass of computers that has caused the Net to go almost everywhere and be useful to the common person.

In essence, then, the Internet is nothing more than a whole lot of computers communicating with each other. Each computer stores a variety of information and makes some or all of it available to other computers on the Net. If you have an Internet connection, you have access to every publicly accessible computer on the Net. If you choose to set up your computer as an Internet server, other computers also have access to whatever you make publicly available.

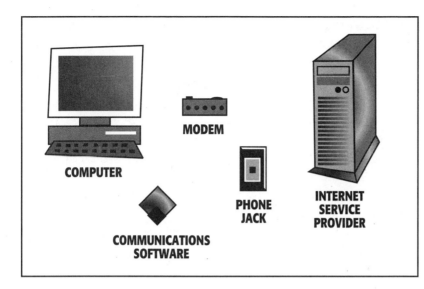

FIGURE **2-1**
*What you need to
connect to the Internet*

HOW DO I CONNECT? LET ME COUNT THE WAYS...

Making your initial connection to this collection of connected computers seems a daunting task. Although there are whole books on the subject, generally there are two ways to connect to the Internet: either through a dial-up connection or through a direct connection. If you're not a computer whiz, you'll want to do it the first way—through a dial-up connection.

DIAL-UP CONNECTIONS

This refers to connections where you use your computer, a modem, and a phone line to dial another computer that connects you to the Net. Once a modem is installed in your computer, certain software on your computer (called a dialer—see Chapter 3) tells your modem to dial another modem. When that other modem answers, the two modems will "talk" to each other and, if everything has been properly set up, let you connect to the Internet.

There are several types of dial-up accounts.

Multipurpose commercial provider

This category includes enterprises such as Prodigy, CompuServe, and America Online. These services all started out as closed systems; when you dialed in, you connected to their computers and stayed

Modem

A modem allows computers to communicate with each other over a phone line. Currently, modem speed or baud rate ranges from 2400 to 33,600 bytes per second (33.6 kbps), but manufacturers have announced the release of 56 kbps modems for sometime in 1997. The faster the modem, the more it will cost. Modem prices range from around $50 to over $300. The faster the modem, the faster it will transmit data. Faster modems do cost more, but can save you money in the long run if you pay hourly for your connect time. And faster modems will allow you to access more easily the graphic-heavy World Wide Web portion of the Internet. Currently most consultants recommend at least a 28.8 kbps modem.

there. With the growth of interest in the Internet, all of these online services now provide access to the Internet.

You can think of these types of services as gated communities: someone has selected the materials for the system, keeping out materials they consider unsuitable or that won't attract a substantial audience. They contain a range of materials such as newspapers, chat forums, stock prices, etc. You can choose to leave the gated community and enter the diverse world of the Internet. The commercial services also provide more guidance and often easier-to-use tools than many other providers. They will also provide you with all of the software you need to get online, along with help if you need it. Using one of these services is great for someone who has no previous online experience. But, if you're online a lot, these services can become expensive since you pay a monthly fee for a set number of hours for your account and then pay for each additional hour online. (This may be changing, as America Online now offers a flat monthly rate for unlimited use.) These services will give you software to get online; for example, by calling 800-316-6633, America Online will send you all the necessary software.

Full-service Internet providers

There are companies that offer one-stop Internet access, known as Internet Service Providers (ISP). They provide all you need to connect to the Net, including an integrated software package that contains communication software, a browser, an email program, and other tools.

These services can vary widely. Some of them require you to use only their software. Others let you use your choice of software. (For example, you may have to use their email product, but can use Netscape instead of the browser they provide.) Since you can usually get a free month on one of these services, it may be worthwhile for you to try some and see which you prefer. Again, you generally pay by the hour after a set number of hours per month. This integrated service is usually as simple to set up as a commercial account.

Local or national Internet provider

This type of account is more for the do-it-yourselfer than either of the above. In this bare-bones scenario, the Internet Service Provider only provides connectivity. They usually provide instructions on how to connect to their service computer and how to obtain the software you need for your account. (Public domain software is free, but usually lacks the technical support of commercial products.) Some ISPs may send you a disk containing the software or just tell you where to download it from the Net. They may provide a little or a lot of help in getting your system configured. You can, in many cases, upgrade to commercial versions of the software, but you do it yourself. Their service may be great, mediocre, or lousy. In other words, you have to do more homework to get one of these accounts up and running. We discuss how to find an ISP in the next section.

So why would you bother with this type of provider? The main reason is cost. Many of these ISPs offer a varying range of options, including an option of unlimited connect time. Fees can range from $5 a month for a few hours of connect time to $30 a month for unlimited connect time. If you are comfortable solving your own computer problems, you may want to explore this option. This may all change now that the traditional long distance and local phone companies are jumping into the ISP business. Service may improve and prices drop as AT&T, Sprint, and MCI duke it out for your ISP business.

Within this category, you may have the choice of two types of dial-up accounts: a shell account or a PPP/SLIP account. Unless you have a very old machine or very slow modem, plan to go with the PPP or SLIP account. A shell account will have no graphics, but the PPP and SLIP accounts will let you use all the graphical functions on the Net.

A SLIP (Serial Line Internet Protocol) or PPP (Point-to-Point Protocol) account is the most common type of dial-up Internet connection. SLIP connections were the earliest connection used to accommodate graphical Web browsers and even they are being replaced by PPP accounts. Using a suite of communication protocols called TCP/IP (Transmission Control Protocol/Internet Protocol), dialing up with a SLIP or PPP account essentially makes your computer a "node" on the Net. You can use all the graphical Internet tools, and can upload and download files directly from the Net to your computer.

Finding and choosing an ISP

So, how do you find a good ISP? You can look in your local paper or check the phone book, but the best source of ISPs is online. (I know, it's like telling a person to drive the car to a driving school for lessons, but it points out how quickly the Net is becoming a source of important resources and information.) Because the market is changing so fast, any printed list of ISPs is out of date by the time it makes it into your hands. Assuming you find a way to get online (find a colleague who's on the Net or go with a commercial provider for a while), check out POCIA (*http://www.celestin.com/pocia*) or "thelist" (*http://thelist. iworld.com*). POCIA has about 1,000 providers, while "thelist" boasts of nearly 3,000 ISPs. Also, "thelist" allows you to search for a provider by name, state, country, and even area code, which comes in handy if you're looking for a local provider that won't hit you with long distance or 800 connect charges.

Although going with a local company ensures a local (toll-free) number, some attorneys believe that a national ISP is the way to go so they can have easy access wherever they may be. This is fine as long as the ISP provides an 800 or local number for your use. A national provider may be best if you frequently travel and need to reach your ISP from all over the country.

Local or national, probably the most reliable method of finding an ISP is by asking around and getting references. Ask other attorneys you know who are already on the Net what they think of their ISP. Do they receive busy signals when they try to connect? Do they have frequent hang-ups while connected? Do they receive late email? Even good providers will occasionally get snowed under and serve up a busy signal, but it should be the exception, not the rule.

Once you've narrowed your list of ISPs, call customer service and ask questions. A good first question to ask is the location of the telephone connection you will use with each service. If it is anything other than a local call, you should definitely hesitate before signing up for the service. If you are a frequent traveler and care about checking your email while on the road, you might also inquire about the provider's provision of dial-in connections across the country.

Other things to ask: Do you provide software or must I find my own? Besides the monthly fee, are there other charges? Do any of the fees include server space for my own Web site? How many megabytes of space does the monthly fee include? How many modems do you have, and at what speeds do they run? With the answers, narrow down your choices and sign up with one.

DIRECT CONNECTION

If you're a single user thinking about getting online, a dial-up connection is the way to go. But when you start thinking about getting an entire law office online, you'll need to start researching your direct

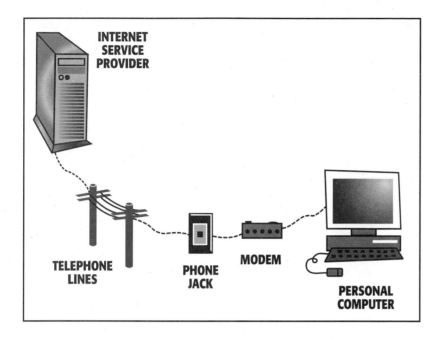

INTERNET SERVICE PROVIDER

TELEPHONE LINES

PHONE JACK

MODEM

PERSONAL COMPUTER

FIGURE **2-2**
For a dial-up connection, all you need is a modem, a telephone jack, a computer, some software (see disk in the back of this book), and an Internet Service Provider or commercial service (also included with the disk)

connection options. Oftentimes a direct connection which uses digital rather than analog phone lines will provide you with more *bandwidth*; this means the line allows more traffic to go over the wires than regular phone lines. Some common bandwidth terms you might hear are ISDN, T1, and T3. These refer to how much data can flow through the lines at one time. However, you can also have a direct connection through a 28.8 kbps modem and an analog phone line. This may be enough to put a small office online as long as the office rarely uses the connection for more than email.

A direct connection or dedicated line allows you to leave your computer or a local area network (LAN) (e.g., an office network) connected to the Internet all the time. With a direct connection you are continuously connected. This is an important option to consider if you want more than a few connections for your office or if you intend to maintain your own Web server.

Some ISPs will lease all the services needed to maintain a direct connection. But if users' email accounts and Web pages reside on servers at your office, a direct connection requires that a technical person maintain and troubleshoot that system at your office rather than at the ISP. While this situation gives you more control over your network and the ability to use the Net to its full potential, it does require more staff and resources, which are additional costs.

Bandwidth

The capacity to carry data. The more bandwidth the more data can go through the network at once. If you have a lot of bandwidth, more people can be online simultaneously.

Server

A computer whose main purpose in life is to provide service to other computers. For example, lawyers can access files on a server, putting them on their computer only when they need them. This system places fewer demands on individual computers.

In the long run, if you're planning to have multiple users on the system, a direct connection can save you money by using fewer phone lines and modems. You also won't need to pay a service provider a monthly fee for each new account. However, the initial cost of installing the network and other equipment can be high, though increased competition has eroded the cost significantly in recent months, particularly for ISDN services.

Don't automatically be frightened away from a direct connection by the initial costs. In the chapters ahead, you'll see that a small office can do quite a lot with a simple and cheap dial-up connection. But for larger offices and those with more ambitious plans, a direct connection allows more people in your law office to use Internet resources simultaneously.

READ THE FINE PRINT

I shouldn't have to remind lawyers of this, but the service contract is rarely read by those who are eager to connect. Often the agreement is shared in extremely small print on an envelope or on the computer's screen. It is tempting to skip over this document and move on to the installation or the connection. In most cases, the act of opening and installing constitutes acceptance of the terms. Take the time to read and consider what you are accepting.

What type of services and technical support does the ISP offer? Some people swear by the small local Internet Service Providers, claiming that they offer far better face-to-face support and assistance than any of the large corporate providers and better deals. Others swear *at* them! It is impossible to generalize. ISPs are just about as friendly and reliable as dry cleaners or auto mechanics. It all depends upon the individuals. If they are dedicated, earnest, friendly, and skilled, you have the best of all worlds. If they are rude, overwhelmed, disorganized, and arrogant, you will regret the relationship.

No matter which type of provider you select, you should ask plenty of questions about technical support services before you sign up for a long-term relationship.

WHAT'S A LAN, AND DOES OUR OFFICE NEED ONE?

A local area network (LAN) connects computers and other peripheral equipment (such as printers) to each other in a small area, usually a building or a set of adjacent buildings. This type of connection will make it easy to send files back and forth. A LAN usually has a server that allows users to share CD-ROM drives, printers, and other peripherals. By using a dedicated connection to connect the LAN to the Internet, lawyers in the office can access the Internet simultaneously without the firm purchasing many modems and installing several phone connections. Having a LAN and a dedicated line may have a higher initial cost, but is less expensive and more efficient than installing a separate phone line and modem for each computer.

A HYBRID SOLUTION: DIAL-UP GATEWAY (ALSO KNOWN AS NETWORK MODEM)

If you have a LAN, but don't have the funds to tackle a large scale direct connection, there is an emerging option called a dial-up gateway or network modem. Using a specialized piece of equipment that combines the functions of a modem and a router, you can use a single phone line to make contact with your ISP and have the dial-up connection provide Internet connectivity to all machines on your local area network.

This approach works best with small groups of five to seven machines, and can allow for various simultaneous sessions. Simultaneous World Wide Web sessions should be done with automatic loading of graphics turned off; otherwise, the system will slow to a crawl. Some of the newer boxes allow more than one phone line, thus doubling the effective speed of the connection. They also allow for upgrading to higher speed transmission methods, such as ISDN, frame relay and fiber optic cable, when they become available. Check with your ISP. They will ultimately be the ones who will have to make it work, and will therefore be most familiar with the equipment available and in use in your area. At the time of this writing, this type of modem costs around $1,000.

Router
A piece of hardware that transfers data between two or more networks. A router acts like a postal clerk sorting mail into appropriate mailboxes.

TIP

When you start publishing on the Web, people, as you had hoped, begin visiting your site. The more people who access the site, the more bandwidth they will use, cutting down on the bandwidth available to the users in your office. (In other words, your office network will slow down.) You can solve this problem by limiting access to your site or by putting your pages on a server outside your network, such as an ISP's server.

SHOULD I GET MY OWN DOMAIN NAME?

As we'll discuss in more detail in the next chapter, the "domain name" is one part of the "Internet address" for Web sites and email. Oftentimes, the domain name signifies a computer directly connected to the Internet. On the other hand, the owners of many domain names do not have their own computer directly connected to the Internet. Instead, these owners simply lease computer space from someone else. In other words, you don't have to maintain an Internet server to own a domain name.

Yes, even lawyers can have their own domain name. For example, the Minneapolis/St. Paul law firm of Briggs & Morgan has the domain name of *briggs.com*. It's like your street address on the Net.

Even sole practitioners and small law firms should seriously think about getting a domain name. The InterNIC (part of Network Solutions, Inc.) is the registration authority in the United States. The InterNIC fee is $100 in advance for the first 2 years of maintenance and $50 for every year thereafter. If you're going to run a Web site, it's a small investment when looking at the big picture.

PERSONAL ACCOUNT

Samuel Lewis
Romanik Lavin Huss & Paoli
http://www.CompLaw.com
slewis@CompLaw.com

Attorney Samuel Lewis talks about getting his own domain name after creating his first Web site:

> *The last step was to find a domain name for the Web site. This was really an optional step. Since the Web server was running on my company's network, it could very well have taken the name assigned by the company. I decided that I wanted to keep the server separate from the company, and so I obtained a form to register a domain name with InterNIC. This is the same*

primary domain that I run today. After a few queries on the InterNIC "whois" database, I found that one of my choices wasn't already in use. Thus, I registered the domain name CompLaw.com. At this point, I was well on my way to creating something special.

If it's not required, why should you bother with your own domain name? First, it gives you brand identity on the Internet. Think of your domain name as your Net trademark. Second, a familiar domain name (for example, your law firm name) is easy to remember, so you'll be easy to find on the Net.

A third reason is that it gives you portability. What happens if you become dissatisfied with your ISP or the company that rents you space for your Web site? If you move, you'll have to change the addresses for your email and your Web site. This can be worse than changing your street address or your phone number. Unless you pay for forwarding, once you leave your old site, anyone using your old address will get their email to you returned and will get an error message when looking for your Web site. But if you have your own domain name, you can move to a new Internet server without anyone knowing that it occurred. It's like having one of the new "1-500" phone numbers that follows you wherever you go. With your own domain name, you won't be stuck with an ISP that gives you poor service or that just doubled its rates.

Another good reason to apply for your own domain name is to grab that piece of valuable cyber-real estate before someone else does. Thousands of domain names are being registered every week. Wait and you may never be able to get a domain name that has any meaning or relation to who you are. In fact, some lawyers recommend that you register every possible domain name that you think you may ever use. The cost, $50 a year per name, is low enough to make it worthwhile if you really want to protect certain domain name combinations.

You can check domain name availability at *http://www.synaptic.net/ domain.html* or *http://www.rawspace.com* (If these Web addresses don't make any sense to you now, read the next chapter and then come back to them later.) You can register a name through InterNIC, which can be reached at (703) 742-4777, email at *hostmaster@rs.internic.net* or on the Web at *http://rs.internic.net*.

Basic Internet Training

3

To get the most out of your Internet connection, you have to develop some basic Net skills. As you spend more time online, you'll find a host of other resources and tools you can adopt. But for now, you should focus on the core skills required to get you on your way.

We've briefly talked about email and the Web. In this chapter, we'll discuss just how they work and how to use them. We'll also discuss two other key Net tools, the Web browser and the newsreader. For those who like interaction with their prospective Net-clients, we'll explain IRC, or Interactive Relay Chat. And finally, we'll briefly talk about actually constructing and publishing your own Web pages. In later chapters, you'll see how legal professionals use these tools in their practices.

If you've already been on the Net, much in this chapter may be of little interest to you. But if you've never seen a Web page, you may feel frustrated by all the new terminology. If you're new to the Net, you may need to re-read a section of this chapter or come back later to look up a term. Don't let this discourage you, as you'll soon get the hang of it all once you're on the Net.

- ▶ Choosing Your Tools
- ▶ Nuts and Bolts of Email
- ▶ Joining Mailing Lists
- ▶ Newsgroups
- ▶ Interactive Communication Tools
- ▶ Using the World Wide Web
- ▶ Web Publishing

CHOOSING YOUR TOOLS

There are many sources for Internet tools. Some are available for free online, others may come with an Internet account or be purchased as a kit. For example, Eudora is a favorite email program, and Netscape is the most popular Web browser. You can download versions of these programs off the Net as well as purchase commercial versions (that come with end-user support) in software stores.

Here are some other ways you can connect to the Internet and get the tools you need:

- A commercial online service such as America Online or Compu-Serve provides Internet access and an integrated set of tools for using email and browsing the Web.
- A local Internet provider will provide instructions for you to connect to their service and download free versions of tools.

In other words, there are many different tools for accessing the Internet, but all share a common set of basic functions. The purpose of the following tutorial is to introduce you to these basic functions.

AN OVERVIEW OF INTERNET SOFTWARE TOOLS

These tools provide you with the ability to communicate online:

Dialer (or dial-up networking)

This program, required only with dial-up Internet accounts, establishes a connection to an Internet Service Provider. Once you have the connection, your computer is on the Internet and you can use the programs described in this section. The dialer is used to make the connection as well as terminate it when your Internet session is completed. Windows 95 comes with a built-in dialer that works with its own Internet Explorer Web browser or other browsers like Netscape's. If you don't have a dialer on your computer already, most ISPs will provide you with a freeware dialer program.

Email (electronic mail) program

An email program is a software tool for sending and receiving email messages. When you get an Internet account, you get an email address that anyone online can use to send you mail. In order to send a message, you need to know the email address of the person you want to communicate with online.

Two of the most popular mail programs are Eudora and Pegasus. You can download the freeware Eudora Light for Windows or Mac (*http://www.qualcomm.com/quest/products.html*) or Pegasus Mail for Windows or DOS (*http://www.pegasus.use.com/*). Both are free for non-commercial use, although QualComm also sells a more full-featured version of Eudora called Eudora Pro. And many browser programs (see next) contain an integrated email program.

World Wide Web browser

A Web browser is used to retrieve the pages from Web servers and display them on your computer screen. (A Web server is a computer on the Internet using a common programming language). Most Web pages today include graphics and text, with an increasing amount of multimedia data as well (audio, animation, and video). The pages usually contain hyperlinks to other documents or images. In addition, a Web browser can get information from other types of servers, including FTP for downloading files and programs. Many ISPs will give you a freeware Web browser, which will get you online. The most popular browser is Netscape Navigator, which can be downloaded at *http://www.netscape.com* once you're online.

Others are Microsoft's Internet Explorer and NCSA's Mosaic. Netscape integrates other tools into its Web browser so that you can use it for email and as a newsreader.

Newsreader

Usenet newsgroups provide yet another way for people on the Internet to communicate with each other by posting news on a distributed bulletin board system. "News" is a vast collection of daily postings on almost every subject imaginable. At last count, the number of individual newsgroups was approaching 20,000. You can subscribe to various subject-specific newsgroups and read the news in each group using a newsreader. You can also use the newsreader to create your own postings.

Hyperlinks
Also known as hypertext links or simply "links," hyperlinks connect a given document to information within another document. The links are usually represented by highlighted words or images. When the user mouse clicks on the highlighted link, the user automatically connects to the linked document.

Netscape Navigator provides a newsreader, as does GNN, but most other newsreaders are public domain programs that use command line interfaces rather than a graphical interface. We'll deal in depth with newsgroups in Chapter 6.

Chat

Chat, or Internet Relay Chat, allows a group of users to talk to each other, often at the same time. This method of direct, real-time exchanges permits useful conversations, but it can be an annoying and confusing way to communicate. Nonetheless, it is very popular, especially with kids. Lawyers seem more involved in mailing lists and newsgroups, because you don't have to be online all the time to participate in the discussion.

Chat is a text-oriented application, and users type in their remarks, which are shown to everyone in a chat room or channel. New, more graphical Chat programs are beginning to emerge.

Before the World Wide Web became a dominant application, there were several other programs that performed useful functions for Internet users. These programs are still in use, but are quickly being replaced by the Web and its software:

FTP

FTP is an acronym for File Transfer Protocol. An FTP archive is a set of files made available on a server for other users on the Net to download. FTP is also a program used to send or retrieve files from an archive. You can now use a Web browser to get files from an FTP archive.

Gopher

Gopher is an information server that organizes online information in easy-to-navigate hierarchical menus—which was handy before graphic browsers came along. Although still available, Gopher is no longer widely used as a means of serving information now that the Web has overtaken its functions. But you may run into a Gopher server now and then, especially on some government sites.

Telnet

Telnet is a program that allows you to log in to another computer on the Internet and have a terminal session, if you have an account on the remote computer.

Real time

Synchronous communication. For example, talking to someone on the phone is in real time whereas listening to a message someone left on your answering machine is not (asynchronous communication).

Server

A computer that runs software that allows it to offer a service to another computer.

Web browsers and email software are the most widely used Net tools. Since you'll probably spend most of your online time exchanging email messages and using the Web to access information and create your own Web pages, this tutorial concentrates on describing how to use these two tools.

NUTS AND BOLTS OF EMAIL

We briefly talked earlier about using email as an essential Internet communication tool. In addition to simple text notes, you can also use email to send large documents, pictures, sounds, and programs as attachments. Virtually anything that's been reduced to digital data can be attached to an email. When creating the message, you use the "Attach" function to select the file you wish to send. The user who receives the message must have the program required to read or view the file once it is detached from the email message.

TIP

Check to make sure that the person receiving your attached message has compatible software to read what you send. Also, some commercial services don't allow you to attach files and send them to people outside of their service, and some limit the size of the email and its attachments. You can still exchange messages with people using a commercial service; you just may not be able to attach documents.

BASICS OF EMAIL ADDRESSING

Your email message needs an address for the person you're trying to reach and a return address to show who sent it. A typical address consists of two parts separated by the @ symbol: the user's name and the domain where the user is known:

username@domain name

The domain name usually identifies the hostname of an organization, which could be a commercial business, a network provider, or an educational or governmental institution.

My address is:

jacobsen@brainerd.net

jacobsen is the username and *brainerd.net* is the domain name of my Internet Service Provider.

Most hostnames end in a three-letter identifier. These three letters indicate the type of entity they are. For example, *netscape.com* is a commercial entity, while *abanet.org* is the domain name of the American Bar Association.

.edu	education
.gov	government
.mil	military
.net	network resource
.org	other non-profit organizations
.com	commercial organizations

TIP

An address must have all of its parts spelled correctly for it to reach the right person (except for the letter's case—COM and com mean the same thing in an email address). An improperly addressed message will bounce back to you. When possible, cut and paste email addresses to avoid misspellings.

Bounce

A bounced message means that it is returned to your email address and does not reach the addressee. Bounced messages contain information about why the message did not reach its destination.

The users on your local network share the same domain, so you don't have to use the domain name with local email.

THAT EMAIL LOOK

The email arriving in your box looks strange at first. There is a lot of verbiage at the top before you get to the meat of the message. These lines are called message headers, and most email programs give you the option of seeing the full header or just the important sender and subject information.

A barebones header looks like the one shown in Figure 3-1.

When you create a new message, you must supply the "To" field and, optionally, the "Subject" field and the "CC" field. The mail program will automatically supply the "From" and "Date" fields when you

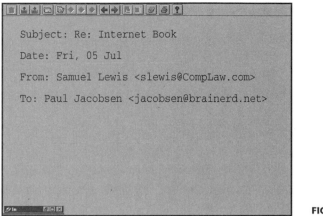

Subject: Re: Internet Book

Date: Fri, 05 Jul

From: Samuel Lewis <slewis@CompLaw.com>

To: Paul Jacobsen <jacobsen@brainerd.net>

FIGURE 3-1

send the message. There are often more than five fields in a message header, but those are the most useful ones.

A full header can be a truly impressive block of text because it includes all the routing sites the message hit before arriving. Since the Net routes with no regard to distance, an email message sent from your neighbor across the street may get routed through three servers thousands of miles away, and each will be listed in the full header. And the message probably will go through different routes every time you send it.

The header includes information about who the message is from, when it was sent, the subject of the message, to whom it was intended, and where the sender wants you to reply to the message. Sometimes you might send email from your home Internet account but want the recipient to reply to your office email account. So occasionally the sender address and reply address will be different.

After the header comes the body of the message:

I'm attaching PGP3.WPD, a WordPerfect 5.1 format
document (same as the others). This is an article
discussing PGP which relates to your project.

If you have any questions or comments, or want me to
write up some more, please let me know.

Thanks,

—Sam

Following the text of the message is the attachment box, which looks as follows:

```
Attachment 2  Name: Pgp3.wpd

       Type: application/octet-stream

 Encoding: base64
```

With a mouse click on "Attachment 2", a dialog box pops up on my computer, asking me where I want to put Sam's article on my computer hard disk.

And finally, the user's designated signature file tags the message:

```
Samuel Lewis, Attorney-at-Law :
http://www.CompLaw.com/~slewis
slewis@CompLaw.com : phone: 954-922-4656
```

Email signatures are used to state phone numbers, postal addresses, Web site addresses and whatever else may be important for others to know. Most email programs provide a way to create a signature so that it's automatically inserted at the end of every message.

HANDING OUT YOUR BUSINESS CARD

The email signature is also a way to make sure people get essential information about you in every email message you send. It's like giving the reader your business card every time they read your mail. Some signatures are more lengthy, but several lines is typical:

```
Jeffrey R. Kuester, Esq.
Patent, Copyright, & Trademark Law
6445 Powers Ferry Road, Suite 230
Atlanta, Georgia 30339
Ph (770) 951-2623 Fax (770) 612-9713
E-mail: kuester@kuesterlaw.com
WWW: http://www.KUESTERLAW.com (The Technology Law
Resource)
```

You can raise or lower the aggressiveness of your signature's tone, but as you will discover, the signature block is a widely used email device to make sure people remember you and can respond to you without having to search around for numbers and addresses.

Some consider it poor netiquette to have an email signature more than a few lines long. This was a bigger concern when modems were slow and long signatures only slowed down your connection. But there's still no reason to have a long signature that only risks the ire of other readers. For example, I've seen signatures that contain keyboard-drawn pictures of dogs and cartoon characters. Although "cute," such signatures are unlikely to do much for your law practice.

Netiquette
Polite and considerate Internet communication; following the generally accepted guidelines for Internet use.

JOINING MAILING LISTS AND LISTSERVS

One way to demonstrate your legal knowledge and stay up with the latest legal changes is to join law-related mailing lists, also known as listservs. I'll briefly discuss the basics of mailing lists below, and in Chapter 6 we'll look at how lawyers use them.

An email list doesn't appear out of nowhere. An organization or individual has to create it. The process involves contracting with an Internet Service Provider to handle the technical aspects of list maintenance, leaving the substantive work of managing the list to its sponsor.

There are three widely used list-management software packages—*listserv, listproc,* and *majordomo*—but the basic principle of each of them is the same. Once the software adds a subscriber to the list address, any message sent to that address will be forwarded to subscribers within a matter of minutes.

Mailing list
A conference/discussion group on a specific topic where all messages are sent to one email address and then redistributed to the email boxes of the list's subscribers. If the list is moderated, someone will review the messages before redistributing them. Mailing lists are commonly called "listservs" after one type of mailing list software.

The creator of a list also determines its structure. These take one of three forms:

- **Open.** This a list where subscription requests are approved automatically and where participants post messages without anyone screening them in advance.

- **Approved.** This is a list where the manager receives all subscription requests for approval. Once approved, list members can post messages without interference, as with an open list. The catch is that the list manager can "unsubscribe" people without their consent and refuse to approve their return if they begin to cause problems.

- **Moderated.** This is a list where the manager not only approves subscriptions, but screens every message before the group receives it.

Once you join a mailing list, you can throw in your two bits on a subject or "lurk" in the background until you feel compelled to contribute. Sometimes you find endless (and ultimately useless) discussions about whether WordPerfect or Word is the best program for law offices, while other times you hear about an important court decision that was just released that morning. Generally, like all human interchange, these lists are a mixed bag. With some messages you'll read a few words and hit the DELETE key as you get the sense that the subject is of no interest. Others you'll save to read later, and some you'll read carefully and answer immediately. Generally, however, if you're careful about which mailing lists you join, you can minimize the garbage that you receive.

The Net has spawned thousands of email-connected mailing lists and newsgroups on any subject imaginable. (To find a listserv or mailing list you might be interested in subscribing to, check out *http://www. liszt.com/* for a current list.) These groups are quickly replacing the old computer bulletin board (BBS) groups that became a mainstay of veteran online lawyers and other legal professionals. Monitored lists like Net-Lawyers, maintained by attorney Lewis Rose, tend to be ones that draw participants willing to stick to serious subjects; there are many others with specific subject matters ranging across the legal spectrum.

Whatever kind of group you decide to join, a word to the wise: learn how to unsubscribe at the same time you first follow the instructions for subscribing to the list. Since email distribution of these lists is automated, getting stuck on a list you decide you hate can develop into a real pain. Even if you like the water you get from a particular mailing list, there are times when you want to turn it off or suspend it (when you go on vacation, for instance). Usually, when you join a list you automatically receive instructions for unsubscribing or suspending your mail. Print a copy of this list and then, because paper has a way of getting lost, make a copy and keep it on your computer in a file where you'll (hopefully) know where to look for it later.

LURK FIRST, THEN JUMP IN

The netiquette for participating in Internet forums says you should stand quietly in the background to get the flow of things before expressing your views. If you come upon a technical interchange between veterans, it doesn't make sense to write back, "Hi, people, what are you talking about?" It'd be the same as walking into the middle of a CLE seminar and asking the speakers to summarize, just for you, where they're at in the program.

If the mailing list is active, it won't take you long to get the feel of the group. You'll see what type of comments draws heated discussion, what type draws ire, and what type is ignored. Wait until you have something worthwhile to add, and you won't be embarrassed. Besides, since you're not standing up in front of anyone, it's easier to add your two cents' worth in a discussion group than it would be in a crowded room of lawyers. Even if you never say a word, chances are you'll learn from the exchange of others.

TIP

Any good email program allows you to compose whole messages offline before connecting to the Internet. You can save these messages and send them later when you are online. This feature can save you time and money by limiting the time you spend online.

NEWSGROUPS

Newsgroups (also referred to as Usenet news) are like mailing lists in that they make it possible to send a message many people can read and respond to. But unlike mailing lists, newsgroups rely on newsgroup software, and not your email program. With newsgroups, you use a newsreader program to read messages sent to the newsgroup. Newsgroups resemble large bulletin boards that address specific areas of interest.

You can read and respond to these messages on the Internet. Most newsreader programs will "thread" newsgroup messages; that is, group responses to a single posting so you read back through the "thread" of the conversation. When you reply to a newsgroup message, you have the option of replying to the entire newsgroup by selecting the Post Reply button, or you can send a private email to the person who posted the message.

HOW CAN NEWSGROUPS HELP ME?

Many of the same reasons you would want to use mailing lists apply to why you would use newsgroups. Lawyers use them for everything from seeking information about a new statute to asking for advice on how to create a good law firm Web page.

Which to choose: a newsgroup or a mailing list?	Some people prefer newsgroups, some like mailing lists, and some use both for slightly different purposes. Here are a few tips to help you decide which might be best for you.

- If you don't like dealing with a lot of mail, use newsgroups.
- If you want to make sure others know you have posted a message, use mailing lists.
- If you want to see what others have had to say about a topic recently, use newsgroups.
- If you want more control over which messages you choose to read, use newsgroups.
- If you want to follow a discussion without having to go looking for relevant messages, use mailing lists.
- If you can't find a mailing list of interest, look for a newsgroup, and vice versa.

To read and respond to newsgroup messages, you must have a newsreader. As with email programs and Web browsers, the type of Internet connection you have determines what kind of newsreader software you may use. You may have a newsreader built into your Web browser; look for a toolbar or menu option that says News (for example, Netscape has newsreader software incorporated in its browser). If you don't have a built-in newsreader, there are several free or commercial products available. To find one, try Stroud's list for Windows applications (*http://cws.wilmington.net/news.html*) or the Macintosh Orchard (*http://www.spectra.net/~dsaur/usenet.html*).

TIP

Lyonette Louis-Jacques at the University of Chicago maintains a comprehensive list of law-related discussion groups at *http://www.lib.uchicago.edu/~llou/lawlists/info.html*. Because her list includes a short description of what the group covers, it's a good place to go when you're ready to join a mailing list or find newsgroups.

FINDING NEWSGROUPS

Instead of going to the University of Chicago's Law List, you can find newsgroups on your own. It's easier than finding mailing lists because newsgroups are organized according to a hierarchical structure. For example, the *comp.* newsgroups discuss computer science and related topics; the *rec.* newsgroups discuss hobbies, recreational activities, and the arts; and the *alt.* newsgroups (probably the largest subset) discuss a truly mind-boggling variety of topics from aromatherapy (*alt.aromatherapy*) to law-related issues (*alt.lawyers.sue. sue.sue*) to Zen (*alt.zen*).

To see all the newsgroups available to you, you have to tell your newsreader program to show you this entire list. Look for a menu option such as Groups/Show All Groups, Options/Show All Newsgroups, or News/Get List of Active Newsgroups. The first time you request the entire list, it will take several minutes to download, so be patient.

Once the entire list is visible, you can scan it to find groups of interest. The list will not contain all the newsgroups available in the world; rather, you will see only the ones your Internet provider gives you access to. Your Internet provider determines which groups you can access, like a local cable company chooses which channels to carry. If your Internet provider does not carry a newsgroup you would like, ask your provider to subscribe to it. (The organization that offers news to you may have policies about which newsgroups it is willing to host.)

Once you find a newsgroup of interest, tell your newsreader to add it to your active list of newsgroups. A menu option of Add Newsgroup or something similar should be available so you don't have to download the entire list each time. If you later decide you don't want to continue reading the messages in this group, just remove it from your active list.

READING NEWS

As mentioned above, newsgroup messages are organized in *threads*. This means that a message and all its replies are linked together in a way that makes it easy to follow an entire discussion. This threading is visible in Figure 3-2, which shows a typical newsreader program screen. All the groups subscribed to are shown on the left, the *headers* of messages are shown on the right, and the text of the currently highlighted message is shown at the bottom.

FIGURE 3-2
Newsreader
program screen

There is another important difference between mailing lists and newsgroups. Recent newsgroup messages are available online for anywhere from a few days to a few weeks, whereas mailing list messages are not automatically stored anywhere online (although some mailing lists maintain archives of old messages). This means you can find a newsgroup that might be of interest and immediately read recent messages posted to the group. This serves two important purposes: it tells you if the newsgroup is appropriate for your interests, and it shows whether the question you want to ask has recently been asked and answered.

TIP

If you're looking for newsgroup messages on a particular topic, Deja News (*http://www.dejanews.com/forms/dnquery.html*) lets you specify the text you want to search for, whether you are interested in recent or older messages, and so on. You can even limit your search to messages in specific groups or from a specific author.

GETTING THE FAQS

Almost all newsgroups and some mailing lists have FAQs (Frequently Asked Questions) and their answers. If you have questions about the newsgroup, such as how it works and the topic it addresses, check the FAQs before posting a message. Many newsgroups routinely post their FAQs, while others just make them available for downloading. You'll find a copy of most FAQs at *ftp://rtfm.mit.edu/pub/usenet/ news.answers/*.

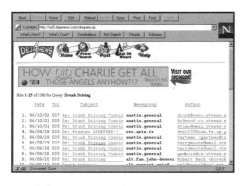

FIGURE 3-3
This DejaNews search of the term "drunk driving" found over 1500 newsgroup postings.

SOME WORDS OF CAUTION

When you hear all the hoopla about indecent material and pornography on the Net, the material in question is frequently found in newsgroups. In particular, there are a large number of *alt.sex* newsgroups that exist specifically to discuss and exchange photographs and text on adult topics. It's quite easy to avoid these groups because the name says it all. But, nevertheless, it's possible to run across foul language in almost any newsgroup.

INTERACTIVE COMMUNICATION TOOLS

You may have noticed that all the tools discussed so far allow communication between people outside of "real time." That is, the communication isn't interactive, like a phone call. While this is usually fine, there may be times when you want to communicate directly with people who are online at the same time you are. The tools generally used for this purpose are discussed briefly in this section.

CHAT (INTERACTIVE RELAY CHAT OR IRC)

Internet Relay Chat (also known as IRC, or more generally, Chat) is a multi-user, multi-channel chatting network. It allows people all over the world to talk to one another in real time. Each Chat user uses a nickname, and all communication with other users is either by nickname or by the channel that they or you are on. To use Chat, you either need to be using Internet access software with Chat capabilities built in (such as GNN), or you need a Chat program on your computer.

CU-SeeMe

CU-SeeMe is a free videoconferencing program (under copyright of Cornell University and its collaborators) available to anyone with a Macintosh or Windows and a high-speed connection to the Internet (the program is choppy over telephone line modems). By using a reflector, multiple parties at locations anywhere in the world can participate in a CU-SeeMe conference, each from an individual desktop computer.

CU-SeeMe is intended to provide useful conferencing at minimal cost. To participate as a viewer requires only the free CU-SeeMe software and an audio-capable computer with a screen that can display 16 shades of gray. To generate your own video stream requires the same, plus a camera. The cheapest camera is produced by Connectix and sells for around $90.00. Video quality is so-so, but it is free video-conferencing. Since the sound quality can be variable, many users continue to talk over the phone while they use CU-SeeMe for the video.

There are people using CU-SeeMe all over the world. You can read about some of them in an online document called "In the Eye of the Reflector" (*http://cu-seeme.cornell.edu/EyeofReflector.html*).

For more information and to download the CU-SeeMe software, go to *http://cu-seeme.cornell.edu/*. For information on enhanced, commercial versions of CU-SeeMe, go to *http://www.wpine.com/cuseeme.html*.

Internet telephones, which allow you to dial up directly from your computer keyboard, may well become a favorite tool for you, especially if you have large phone bills for calling all around the world. Check out Internet telephones at *http://www.Netspeak.com*.

FIGURE **3-4**

CU-SeeMe opens a small video screen on the user's computer screen.

USING THE WORLD WIDE WEB

The Web consists of documents containing links to other documents on the Internet. You navigate the Web by following these links, moving backward or forward from one document to another. If you don't already understand Web terminology, you should review this section before you move on to the rest of this book. But because a lot of information is introduced quickly in the chapters ahead, you may need to come back to this section from time to time.

You can also browse directories that organize Web sites, much as a card catalog system does, and keep your own list of "bookmarks" you can use to go directly to favorite sites.

BASIC WEB TERMINOLOGY

Table 3-1 defines the most common Web terms.

Browser	A user tool that displays Web documents and launches other applications
Home Page	The starting point for the set of pages available for a person, company, organization, or school; also, the first page your browser displays when you start it
HTML	HyperText Markup Language: the language in which World Wide Web documents are written
Hypertext	Documents that contain links to other documents; selecting a link automatically displays the second document
Image	A picture or graphic that appears on a Web page
Link	The text or graphic you click on to make a hypertext jump to another page
Search Directory	A Web site that indexes Web pages and allows you to search for terms you specify
Site	The location of a Web server
URL	The address that uniquely identifies a Web resource

TABLE 3-1
Web terminology

LOCATING DOCUMENTS ON THE WEB

Each document on the Web has a unique global address that allows it to be retrieved directly. This unique address is called a URL or

Uniform Resource Locator. Just as individuals have email addresses that locate a person within a specific domain, documents have addresses that locate them in a specific server domain.

A URL has three parts: the protocol identifier, the domain or hostname of the server, and the document's pathname. This follows the syntax for URLs:

protocol://domain name/pathname

On the World Wide Web, HTTP (or HyperText Transfer Protocol) is the *protocol* or language that browsers use to talk to servers. All URLs for Web sites begin with *http://* (although some Web sites are now supporting *http* and *shttp*, which incorporate encrypted files). Most Web browsers will communicate using other Internet server protocols, such as Gopher and FTP. Thus, you might see a URL that starts with *gopher://* or *ftp://*.

The next part of the URL is the *server* name. This might be as simple as the domain name, but usually it is preceded by *www*. This prefix is merely a naming convention that many follow, but it is not a requirement to be on the Web. For instance, either of the following URLs will take you to the default page for the Songline Studios Web server:

http://songline.com/

or

http://www.songline.com/

The final part of a URL is the path name. This tells the server where you want to go on the server, just like you may tell your own computer where to go to get a file. If you have the pathname for a specific document, you can supply it and go directly to that page of the Web site. Otherwise, you can begin at the default home page and navigate to the document using links.

It's often possible to guess at a URL. Almost every URL starts with *http://www*. Commercial site URLs generally end with *.com*, government sites end with *.gov*, and educational sites end with *.edu*. A law firm named Brobeck, for example, is likely to have a Web page at *http://www.brobeck.com*. Similarly, the URL for the White House (in case you want to express yourself on the tort reform bills) is *http://www.whitehouse.gov*.

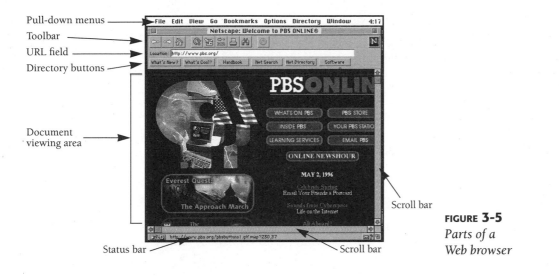

Pull-down menus

Toolbar

URL field

Directory buttons

Document
viewing area

Status bar

Scroll bar

Scroll bar

FIGURE 3-5
*Parts of a
Web browser*

A WINDOW ON THE WEB

A Web browser gives you a window to view the Web. Figure 3-5 shows a Web browser at the PBS home page. This figure indicates the parts of the browser window. The menu bar allows you to access all the functions of the browser from pull-down menus. Under the File menu, you will find Open URL, or you can use the Open Location box on the browser screen to enter a URL for a document you'd like to view. Next is the Toolbar, a set of graphic and text icons that provide easy access to most common functions, such as accessing your home page, moving back and forth from one document to another, and so on. One of the most important icons is the Stop button. This allows you to interrupt any document transfer, which is useful if you find that a document is taking too long to load.

Next, you will find the Location or URL field. It displays the URL of the current document. You can also use this field on most browsers to enter URLs directly. The URL that is displayed in this field may not always be exactly what you typed, as some Web servers translate a simple address into a more complex one.

On Netscape, there is a row of directory buttons, two of which are labeled NetSearch and NetDirectory. These buttons will take you directly to the most popular directories and search engines. I'll explain these tools in more detail later in this section and in Chapter 5.

The largest part of the browser's window is occupied by the document viewing area. This has a scrollbar which you use to view documents that are longer than what can display on the screen.

Below the viewing area is a status bar. In this area, you will see messages about the document's status, including when it has finished downloading. Also, if you move the cursor over a hypertext link, the URL will be displayed in the status bar, which is handy if you want to know where you'd be going if you click on the link.

Most browsers allow you to select which of these areas are displayed, so be sure to check the Options menu to see which areas are enabled or disabled.

TIP

Remember that Web pages are constantly changing. Several months will have passed between the time these illustrations were produced and the time you read this book. In what might be called "Web time," several months usually means a myriad of changes and improvements to a Web site.

Let's navigate through a series of Web pages to find out what bills U.S. Senator Wellstone may have introduced in the Senate during the past legislative session. Start at the Government Printing Office home page (one of many MegaSites discussed in Chapter 5):

http://www.access.gpo.gov/index.html

Enter the above URL into your browser.

Once the document begins to arrive you can click on any visible link or use the scrollbar. You don't have to wait for the entire document to download. From the menu of search instruments offered, let's click on the line for "GPO Access: On-line, On-Demand & Locator Services".

FIGURE 3-6
The GPO home page

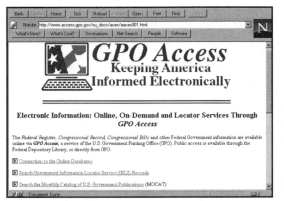

FIGURE 3-7
GPO Electronic information page (http://www.access. gpo.gov/su_docs/aces/ aaces001.html/)

From here, we select the line to connect to the Online Databases, which brings us to the page shown below. From here, we can select the database we wish to search and submit search terms into the query box. We select the database for Congressional Bills, 104th Congress, and type "Senator and Wellstone" into the query box, as shown in Figure 3-8.

Finally, our search finds 2 hits, shown in Figure 3-9.

From this page, you can link to summaries or full text of documents mentioning Senator Wellstone, including legislation he introduced. In addition, by clicking on "PDF", you can download a copy of the bill to your computer.

As you can see, you can jump from page to page in a Web site, and a link may take you from one Web server to another in your search for information.

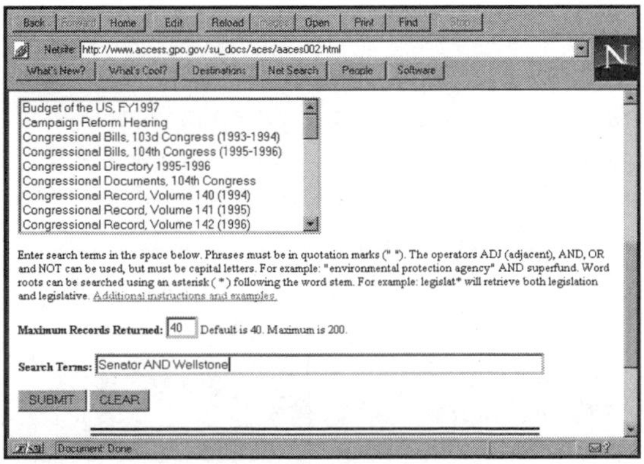

FIGURE 3-8
Connect to GPO databases (http://www. access.gpo.gov/su_docs/ aces/aaces002.html)

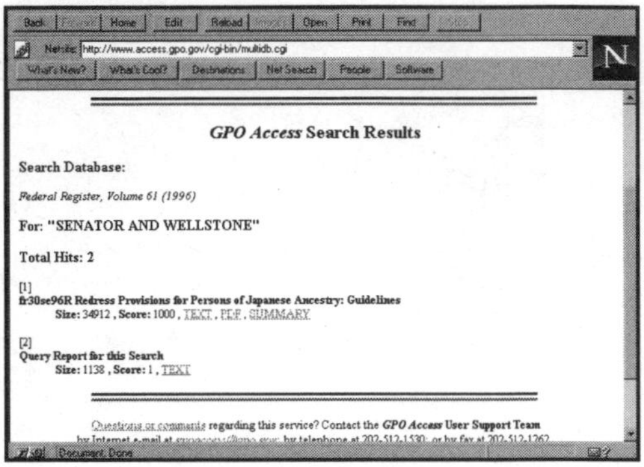

FIGURE 3-9
Search results
(http://www.access.
gpo.gov/cgi-bin/
multidb.cgi)

GOING TO A SPECIFIC PAGE

To get to a particular Web page, there are a variety of ways to enter a URL:

- Use a menu option or keyboard shortcut. Look for a menu option such as File/Open, File/Open Location, or File/Open URL. Often, there are keyboard shortcuts assigned to the options, such as CTRL-O or COMMAND-L.

- Type in the URL directly. Most browsers have an area that displays the URL of the page you are currently viewing. Type the URL of the page you want to go to and press ENTER or RETURN.

- Click on a toolbar button. Many browsers have toolbars that provide quick access to the most common browser tasks. Figure 3-10 shows a few examples of the buttons different browsers use that let you specify a URL to open.

TIP

A useful feature of Netscape is its ability to "build" a URL from partial information. For example, if you want to go to the URL *http://www.CompanyName.com,* you can type *CompanyName* as the location you want to go to. Netscape adds *http://www.* and the *.com* automatically.

FIGURE 3-10
Toolbar buttons to
go to a specified URL

TIP

An important point to remember is that URLs are case-sensitive past the domain name. For example, if you type *http://ERICIR. syr.edu/ or http://ericir.syr.edu,* you will go to the same place. But if you type *http://ericir.syr.edu/COLLECTIONS.html* instead of *http://ericir.syr.edu/collections.html,* you may receive an error message that such a page doesn't exist.

IT'S NOT WORKING!

Sometimes when you type in a URL, you'll receive an error message indicating that the server is not available. After you check the URL for accuracy, wait a few seconds and try it again, as it may now work. Another solution for a particularly long URL is to delete part of the URL and go to the next directory. For example, say the URL you have is *http://www.access.gpo.gov/su_docs/aces/aaces002.html*. If you receive an error message, try *http://www.access.gpo.gov/su_docs* or *http://www. access.gpo.gov*. This will send you to the next directory up (or page) where you can see the links available. The creators of the pages may have changed the page so that your particular link no longer works. Scrolling down on the home page *http://www.access.gpo.gov/*, you find a variety of options, including the one you tried to reach with the first URL.

DEALING WITH IMAGE FILES ON A DIAL-UP ACCOUNT

Graphics can take a long time to load through a regular telephone service Internet connection. But not all sites have a special view of their pages without the graphics. If you are tired of waiting for images to download, you can do a few things to solve the problem:

- Turn off the images in your browser menu bar. While this solves your download problem, no images will reach you, just text. Sometimes the images are important.

- As the images are downloading, you can begin reading, using the scrollbar to the right to move you down the page.

- Hit the Stop button on your browser! When you do, the images will stop downloading. This trick is especially helpful when you know the information you want resides on a different page: the link is there, but you're still waiting on the graphics. As soon as you hit Stop, the page's graphics will stop loading and the rest of the text will usually appear. If you decide you need the graphics, you can always select reload (or an "Images" button on some browsers), and the browser will request the page again from the Web site and retrieve it for your computer.

MOVING BACK AND FORTH BETWEEN PAGES

Once you've loaded the pages to your memory or hard drive (this means you've gone to the page by putting in the URL or selecting it through a hypertext link), you can navigate back and forth without waiting a long time. All browsers provide some way for you to move back and forth among the Web pages you viewed in your current session. As with opening a page, there are usually several ways to do this:

- Use a menu option or keyboard shortcut. Look for a menu option such as Navigate/Back and Navigate/Forward or Go/Back and Go/Forward.
- Click on a toolbar button. Many browsers have buttons on their toolbars that look like arrows facing left and right. The left arrow steps you back through pages you have viewed and the right arrow steps you forward.

BOOKMARKS AND HOTLISTS

If you go to a page that you want to return to, your Web browser will let you add it to a list so you don't have to remember the URL or write it down. Some common names for these lists of saved URLs are bookmarks, hotlists, favorites, and card catalogs.

Washington attorney John Maxwell, Jr., highly recommends the use of bookmarks to simplify your time on line:

Use Net browser bookmarks. Most Net browsers support the use of bookmarks. Learn to use these to save time. A bookmark allows you to save the location of a favorite site, and when you activate the bookmark you will go directly to that site instead of the long route you may have taken to find the site in the first place. Usually the bookmark feature is one of the main menu items and you just select " add bookmark" or some similar selection to add it to your list of sites. The bookmarks then are accessible as a list that you can scroll down and choose from. It's a very handy time-saving device.

No matter how your browser works, be forewarned that your URL list can easily grow so large as to be almost useless. Most browsers allow you to organize your favorite URLs into folders by subject. You can separate legal research sites from other subject sites. Also, you should go through your bookmarks from time to time and delete those URLs that once seemed important, but are now either defunct or no longer relevant to your interests.

FINDING INFORMATION ON THE WEB

What if you don't know the URL for a page you want to visit? Maybe you read about it somewhere and didn't keep the reference. Or perhaps you visited the page and want to return, but forgot to add it to your bookmarks. Or maybe you are interested in a particular topic, but don't even know if a related page exists. Search engines can help you find what you seek.

Most law professionals are familiar with the search engines used for Lexis and Westlaw. Internet search engines are similar, although they may do their work in a different fashion. Internet search engines periodically scan the contents of the Web to rebuild their massive indexes of Web pages. Some search titles or headers of documents, others search the documents themselves, and still others search other indexes or directories. When you request specific keywords, the engines search the indexes they have built for those words. Your keyword search is not a live search of the Web, but a search of that engine's index.

There are two types of ways to search the Net: Directories and Web robots. Directories (or indexes) are collections of resources that you can easily browse or search. Yahoo is one of the best known directories. People create and maintain these directories by combing other sites, organizing the information on their Web pages, and making sure the links to the other sites remain accurate. Web robots (or search engines) depend on software, rather than people, that automatically searches the Web for new material.

The distinction between directories and robots is blurring. Directories are incorporating search engines and search engines are incorporating browseable indexes. And not all search engines are created equal. That is, different engines find different pages, even when you give them the same search terms. This is because they differ in how they index and store the information in Web pages. If your first search doesn't turn up the information you're looking for, try another search engine. If none of them locates what you want, try using different search terms.

We'll discuss search engines in more detail in Chapter 5, when we explore how to do legal research on the Internet.

PUSHING THE ENVELOPE

Most of the hottest Internet development these days revolves around the Web. Audio, video, virtual reality, animation—it's almost impossible to keep up. Here are some locations for more information on some of the latest trends in Web development:

RealAudio™ *http://www.realaudio.com*	The RealAudio home page lets you listen to music, news, talk shows, and more while you are browsing the Web. If you have a 28.8 modem, you can download and use the latest release of RealAudio (which at press time was release 3.0). If your modem is slower than that you will have to use RealAudio1. But, like so much of the Net these days, support for these older "version 1" technologies is rapidly disappearing. Soon a 28.8 modem will no longer be a luxury, but a necessity.
Java™ *http://java.sun.com/*	Java is a programming language that lets Web page developers add software applications, games, animation, and other features to their Web pages.
Shockwave™ *http://www.macromedia.com/*	Found on the Macromedia home page, Shockwave enables the playback of high-impact multimedia on the Web.
The VRML Repository *http://www.sdsc.edu/vrml/*	Virtual Reality Modeling Language (VRML) is a developing standard for describing interactive three-dimensional scenes delivered across the Internet.
Web Review™ *http://webreview.com*	Songline Studios produces an online magazine, Web Review, that keeps up with Web technologies and the people who use and create for the Web. Clicking into Web Review weekly will keep you current.

WEB PUBLISHING

In Chapter 7 we'll take up the question of whether you should build your own Web site or let someone else do it for you. And in Chapter 8, we'll discuss the important aspects of building a law Web site. You may want to only skim the following section if you're not sure that you want a Web site. Then, after you've read Chapters 7 and 8, you can come back and study this section in more detail.

But you should know one thing: as you're about to see, anyone, from large corporations to young kids, can create and manage a Web site. It is this great equalizing capability of the Web that has fueled its incredible growth. The question is whether or not you can budget the time to manage a Web site properly by yourself. If not, what you learn here will help you shop wisely for a service provider to do it for you.

Here's an introduction to the basics of Web publishing, along with pointers to sites where you can learn more on the Web itself. In Chapters 7 and 8, we'll look at Web sites for lawyers in more detail.

HTML—THE LANGUAGE OF THE WEB

When Web technology was first designed, the goal was to develop a way to describe the elements of a page's structure without specifying how the page should actually be displayed. In other words, the Web page specifies *what* to display, and different browsers decide *how* to display it. For this reason, the same Web page is available to anyone on the Net, whether they're using UNIX, DOS, Windows, Mac, OS/2, or any other operating system. If there is a browser that runs on that system, users of the system can view the page.

You don't need to understand HTML to use the Web, and if you're certain you'll never code your own Web page you can skim the following section of this book. But if you may want to create your own Web page in the future, you need to first understand some basics.

Every Web page is a plain text file that contains "tags" or codes. These tags tell the browser how to display the file. The codes represent instructions written in HTML (HyperText Markup Language). You can use any text editor (such as word processing programs) to create or modify HTML documents.

TIP

You can learn how others code their Web pages. In Netscape, once you have a page up on your screen, select "View Source" from Netscape's View menu. That will show you a text version of the page, including all the HTML codes. This is a great way to learn how to get your page to look like one you admire.

HTML codes specify heading levels (as in an outline), paragraph styles, inclusion of images and sound, addresses of pages to link to, and anything else the browser needs to know. For example, Figure 3-8 shows how a browser displays a Web page (in this case, the home page for the Library of Congress at *http://lcweb.loc.gov/*).

Figure 3-11 shows the text and HTML codes that make up the first part of the page.

I won't go into detail explaining all the codes. Here are just a few that this page uses:

- `<html>` specifies the beginning of the document.
- `<img src=` specifies a graphic to display, along with text ("alt") that should be displayed if the browser can't display graphics.
- `<p>` specifies a new paragraph.
- `<a href=` specifies that the text from here to `</a>` is a hypertext link to the Web page in quotes. The Web page between the code can be a document you've created or a link to a URL on someone else's computer.

At first, HTML authoring was similar to the state of word processing about 15 years ago—you inserted codes into your document to indicate formatting styles and didn't know what the finished document would look like until you printed it out. Today, just about every word processor prides itself on being WYSIWYG (What You See Is What You Get). The latest generation of HTML editors emulates a WYSIWYG environment for HTML authoring.

These "structured editing" products let you create Web pages without having to insert the HTML codes manually. Some of these tools are free. Most of the ones that require payment have demo versions available that you can download (copy to your hard disk) and try. Then, if you like it, you buy it. Also, some are add-ons to word processors such as Microsoft Word, letting you author HTML from within the word processor.

```
<!doctype html public "-//W30/DTD WWW HTML 2.0/EN">

<html>
<head>
<title>Library of Congress World Wide Web (LC Web) Home Page</title>
<base href="http://lcweb.loc.gov/homepage/lchp.html">
</head>

<body bgcolor="#ffffff">

<a href="http://lcweb.loc.gov/homepage/lchp_txt.html">[text-only]</a>

<!-begin imagemap for head->
<p align=center>
<a href="http://lcweb.loc.gov/homepage/lchp.html">
<img src="/homepage/images/homehead.gif"
border="0" alt="[Library of Congress World Wide Web
LC Web) Home Page - Header]"></a><br>
<!-end imagemap->

<!-begin imagemap for bar->
<a href="http://lcweb.loc.gov/cgi-bin/imagemap/homepage/homebar.map">
<img src="/homepage/images/homebar.gif" border="0"
alt="[Library of Congress World Wide Web (LC Web)
Home Page - Button Bar]" ISMAP></a><br>
<!-end imagemap->

<!-begin imagemap for body->
<a href="http://lcweb.loc.gov/cgi-bin/imagemap/homepage/homebod3.map">
<img src="/homepage/images/homebod3.gif"
border="0" alt="[Library of Congress World Wide Web
(LC Web) Home Page - Main Body Image]" ISMAP></a>
</p>
<!-end imagemap->

<p>
```

FIGURE 3-11
HTML coding for a home page

The following sites contain pointers to reviews of a number of HTML editing tools:

The Stroud List
http://cws.wilmington.net/ or http:// www.cwsapps. com

One of the Internet's most popular and respected sites for reviews of, and links to, Windows 95 and Windows 3.x Internet programs of all kinds. Choose HTML Editors from the main menu.

YAHOO's Macintosh HTML Editor List
http://www.yahoo.com/ Computers_and_Internet/ Software/Internet/ World_Wide_Web/ HTML_Editors/Macintosh/

List of links to a variety of HTML editors for the Macintosh.

At the following sites, you can obtain HTML editing software. Note that some of the software is only for particular operating systems:

GNNPress™
http://www.tools.gnn. com/press

One of the first WYSIWYG editors to be widely available, GNNPress provides a robust set of tools for authoring and managing Web sites. They also provide a server where you can temporarily store your pages for free while you are testing and developing them, as well as a permanent storage location if you need one. GNNPress is available at no cost to GNN subscribers.

Adobe PageMill™
http://www.adobe.com/ proindex/PageMill/

Adobe PageMill Web page authoring software provides an integrated authoring tool and preview browser.

Netscape Navigator Gold™
http://www.netscape.com/

Netscape Navigator Gold integrates the features of Netscape Navigator with Internet publishing capabilities, making it easy for you to see exactly how your page will look in Netscape while you are editing it. Netscape also provides storage locations for your pages.

Bare Bones Software BBEdit™
http://www.barebones. com/bbedit.html

One of the most popular text editors for HTML authors working on a Macintosh. Extensive HTML tools and extensions are available for BBEdit.

HotDog WebEditor from Sausage Software
http://www.sausage.com

Developed by an Australian, this URL will bring you to their site, where you can buy the popular Web editor. It's a simple-to-use-and-learn HTML editor that sells for just under $50.

FrontPage from Microsoft *http://www.microsoft. com/frontpage/*	Since it's from Microsoft, it's compatible with Microsoft Office and has their "wizards" to help you with any problems. The product is designed for the nonprogrammer and has WYSIWYG editing.
Home Page from Claris *http://www.claris.com/*	You can download trial software from this site and, if you want, buy it retail for under $100. They have versions for both the Mac and Windows..

MAKING YOUR PAGES AVAILABLE ON THE NET

Once you write your page, you have to put it on a Web server where the world can access it. If you want, you can have your own computer server connected to the Internet, but this can be costly and involves technical issues that only the computer-savvy should attempt. The simplest is to store your pages on someone else's Internet server (usually on your Internet provider's computer) in a particular directory. The document can then be referenced by a URL unique to your site.

Using Email in Your Law Practice

4

Electronic mail (email) is probably the most common use of the Internet today. In fact, in a small survey of lawyers conducted in the Fall of 1995, Lex Mundi's Steve McGarry found that email was lawyers' *primary* use of the Internet.

The level of email use puts McDonald's "Hamburgers Sold" to shame. Estimates are that over 1 billion email messages are sent *every month*, up from less than a quarter of that three years earlier.

By the year 2000, 60 billion email messages are predicted to be sent every year. It is no surprise, then, that Kansas lawyer Bruce Ward believes that "someday soon lawyers will be communicating with one another and with our clients primarily through email."

▶ Why Are Lawyers Using Email?

▶ When in Rome...

▶ Email Language—Acronyms, Emoticons, and Other Good Stuff

PERSONAL ACCOUNT

David P. Berten

Bartlit Beck Herman
Palencher & Scott
*David.Berten@bartlit-beck.
com*

WHY ARE LAWYERS USING EMAIL?

Why do so many lawyers already use email? Email combines some of the best attributes of regular mail, the phone, and the fax. Lawyer David Berten, a partner with Chicago's Bartlit Beck Herman Palencher & Scott, in an article in *U.S. Business Litigation*, admitted his "love" of email:

> *When it comes to computers, there is a tendency to oooh and aaah at the latest and greatest technological development, and for good reason. Butter-fly keyboards, CD-ROMs, and lithium-ion batteries not only deliver improved performance, they sound sophisticated and hip. But of all the technological advances of the last 10 years, I am most impressed with what many would consider the most mundane technology around. I am nutty about email.*

> *My enthusiasm about email comes from experience and a sincere belief that it's as important to the practice of law as the telephone, photocopier, and fax machine. Skeptics will dismiss that statement as hyperbole that only a computer geek would write. Experienced email users know it is correct. Email has changed their lives.*

> *At its most basic level, email is simply a way of writing down what we would otherwise call people to tell them. "There will be a staff meeting at noon." "Please pull me a copy of* Brown v. Board of Education.*" "Do you have the* Johnson *documents?"*

> *But even at this level, email has advantages over other forms of communication. How many times have you confronted lame excuses for inactivity? "I didn't get your message," or "You never asked me for that," or "I thought you wanted the* Johnson *documents." Email exposes all interlopers.*

As David predicts, email is becoming as important to law as the phone, the copy machine, and the fax. Lawyers like things in writing. Email gets it in writing with the ease of using the phone. And with today's need for instantaneous communications, email delivers a message *now*.

And email has more important attributes than simply the instantaneous transmission of a message. Most email programs allow the user to "attach" an electronic version of a document to the message. In the time it takes the bytes to travel the phone wires, the message and the document arrive in the "inbox "of your recipient.

But the fax can do nearly the same thing, can't it? No. With the fax, you just get a picture of the document. You can't do anything with it other than read it. But with an electronic document attached to an email, you can make changes in the document and then send it back for further revision.

David Berten relates a story of how email allows a firm to continue working together, even when separated by thousands of miles:

> *A partner of mine tells the story of how he and two associates wrote a brief together. Nothing earth-shattering about it, except that the partner was in London on business, one associate was in Miami on vacation, and the other associate was at his house 30 miles away from our office. They were working over the weekend on a 30-page brief that had to be filed on Monday.*
>
> *Ten years ago, all three would have canceled their plans and worked together in the office—with a secretary—to shepherd the brief through completion. Five years ago, the two associates would have canceled their plans and faxed drafts of the brief to the partner in London. Email allowed all three people to keep their plans and work on the brief together. The mid-level associate sent the draft to the partner, who polished it, and to the associate, who researched open issues that remained.*
>
> *Thanks to email, all three lawyers could spend more time with their families, and the secretary's weekend wasn't affected at all.*

And David Berten's law firm isn't alone. Hundreds of thousands of lawyers regularly use email to save time and money in their law practices. Personally, I've had situations where, without email, I couldn't have done my work.

For example, among other things, I do work on a contract basis for other law firms. At 10:00 one night I got a call from a lawyer (who practiced in a city 150 miles from me) asking for a brief to be prepared for a temporary restraining order. The brief had to be filed by 1:00 the next afternoon. Since he knew the facts, he wanted me to write the argument sections only and he'd fill in the facts with his word processor.

Before I was on the Internet I would have stayed up all night to write it so that I could fax something to him when his office opened, so that his secretary could retype it. Or I could stay up all night to write it and *then* drive the 150 miles the next morning with a disk in hand. But with the Internet, I still got my sleep. After working on the brief for another hour that night, and then getting up at 7:00 the next morning, I had my portion of the brief done by 11:00. I then attached it to an email and the lawyer had a perfect electronic copy in his office in a minute. With an hour of additions by him, it was filed with the court on time. On top of it, I didn't generate a single page of paper and my out-of-pocket cost of the project was zero.

My story, and others like it, demonstrate that email can bind lawyers together when they don't practice in the same office. Parry Aftab is a New Jersey lawyer who has created the Virtual Law Firm Network, an informal group of 17 lawyers who regularly trade referrals and co-counsel with each other. With email, it's easy for lawyers with a mutual client to keep each other up-to-date. Of course, other ways to communicate are used to keep lawyers informed. But the ease of email makes it more likely to happen.

For lawyers not bound together by a law firm, email is their brick and mortar. Short of building a dedicated electronic network, email over the Internet is the only practical way to join lawyers together. And email is not just used to bind lawyers together who are building virtual law firms. It is also used to create temporary alliances.

David Berten writes about his young firm's first big case and the critical role email played in the way his firm handled it:

> The case is a representation of a Fortune 50 company in a major antitrust lawsuit, and email is critical to it. Approximately 10 lawyers from my firm work with lawyers from several other firms, several in-house counsel, and a series of consulting experts. The entire group, as many as 50 people, is held together through email. With quadruple-tracked depositions scattered across the country, there literally is no other way for information to move from the people who know it to the people who need to know it, right now.

> One of the lawyers working on that case is our managing partner. In addition to the 100 or so substantive emails he gets, he has to address at least 100 more on everything from where we are going to put another copier to how we should structure an alternative fee deal with a client. He'd be the first to admit that he could not do his job without email. He is kept abreast of even minor developments in the major case and he doesn't need to schedule a meeting to resolve the copier issue. Email lets him run the firm with a bare minimum of bureaucracy. No other form of communication comes close.

With email, you can keep a hundred people informed just as easily as you can one person. There is no need to distribute a hundred photocopies of a memo, or mail a hundred letters, or have the fax dial a hundred phone numbers. Instead, with certain options in more powerful email programs, those hundred people can get the same message with very little additional effort.

But, as with anything so powerful, there is also a dangerous side. Because it is *so* easy to send an email, mistakes are made. Murphy loves email. The ease of making a mistake on email is demonstrated by a recent event on a mailing list. A subscriber to the list, after receiving what he thought was a spam (advertising) message, hastily pushed the reply button to the message and typed "Do not ever email me again." Instead of telling one person that he didn't want to receive their solicitations anymore, he sent his gruff message to every single subscriber of the mailing list—nearly 2,400 other lawyers (so much for his networking efforts!). Needless to say, the sender received a torrent of nasty return mail, ranging from "what the hell are you talking about?" to things much less printable. Knowing a powder keg when he saw one, the list moderator immediately removed the disgruntled lawyer from the mailing list.

The sender remained unaware of his error until he began receiving the nasty replies, which confused him. Then it dawned on him that he had been careless and didn't realize the offending message was a posting on the mailing list. With his tail between his legs, he apologized for his hastiness and pleaded to be reinstated to the list.

Carelessness with email can have even more disastrous consequences. Email, because of its instantaneous nature, can have some of the same dangers as using the fax. For example, I'm aware of a situation where a large law firm was defending a case with a service list of more than seventy other law firms. There were two fax service lists—one that included all lawyers, including plaintiff's counsel, and one that only included the other defense counsel. Certain confidential communications were only to be distributed among defense counsel.

Well, you guessed it. A secretary inadvertently used the wrong fax list for a message, and plaintiff's counsel was faxed a confidential defense message. The plaintiffs were thrilled to receive it, and were reluctant to give it up when the secretary (pleading for her life) begged them to return it (which they did). And the same thing can—and probably has—happened with email. Like any tool, you must be careful when you use it.

Email is powerful and is changing the way the legal profession practices law. But with anything so new and useful, lawyers will spot the problems. When cellular phones first became popular, their risks were generally unknown. Soon, all lawyers became aware that cell phones were not secure, as others could listen in on the conversation. State bars began to rule that confidential communications should not take place over cell phones.

Like the cell phone, email has its own list of security concerns that have yet to be resolved. In the next section, some of these issues will be raised.

IS EMAIL SECURE?

Because it's a new technology, Net lawyers have heavily debated the security of email and questioned its appropriateness for the law practice. In the end, we'll see that email holds promise as one of the most secure forms of communication, but there are potential bumps along the way.

Before we get into the specific security issues facing email, let's generalize about the security concerns of *all* forms of communication. Those are:

- *Confidentiality*—keeping a message private and secret from others
- *Authentication*—verifying the identity of both the sender and receiver
- *Integrity*—ensuring that the message wasn't altered in transit
- *Non-repudiation*—preventing persons from denying they sent or received information
- *Authorization*—restricting access to information

Each of these concerns is present with all forms of communication, including letters sent through the U.S. mail. With letters, for example, there is the risk of *confidentiality*, which is protected by sealed envelopes and federal laws restricting the opening of the mails. A handwritten signature seeks to provide *authentication* and *non-repudiation*.

Because the mails have been in use for hundreds of years, these issues are of little concern today. But Internet email, still in its infancy, has the legal profession concerned about some of these issues. This especially becomes a concern if email is going to be used in electronic commerce.

Just what are the risks of email? Well, for example, some contracts with Internet Service Providers allow the ISP to read all of your email messages, if they so desire. And there's "sniffer" software that can look for certain messages on the Internet. Because Internet transmissions go across the Net in packets, sniffer software has its limitations. In addition, using it is probably a federal offense, but these limitations don't mean you shouldn't be aware of the problem.

None of these concerns are completely unique to email. Your overnight-mail service may reserve the right to look at your letters, and phones do get tapped. But we're generally aware of these concerns and have learned to deal with them or accept the risks as minimal. Email is different because it's new; as a result, the legislature and the courts haven't kept up with the technology, and we don't know exactly what they'll do when they get there.

But that hasn't stopped lawyers from trying to figure out the answers. Some attorneys contend that email sent across the Internet should be viewed the same as a postcard—it's there for anyone along the way to read. But this grossly overstates the risk, because most email messages are not complete while in transmission, being sent in "packets" of data over varying routes. Someone would have to make a very concerted effort to read an email message as it flew by at the speed of light.

Others compare using the Net to a cellular or cordless phone. Many state ethics boards have ruled that lawyers have no expectation of privacy for communications over such phones. But email, again, is different. Email is not broadcast, like a cellular or cordless phone, but is usually sent over the (presumably secure) phone lines.

So, is it just like a phone conversation, which is expected to be confidential? Well, again, not really. Email messages, because they are written, are recorded (generally for very short periods of time) on various Net computers, and thus can be intercepted for a longer period of time than a phone call.

There simply isn't any perfect analogy, which is what causes the uncertainty and risks. But the risks are not insurmountable or particularly difficult—just unique. And there is an irony in all of this discussion about security. As is, the Internet *may* be less secure than normal paper routes of transmission. Yet, with the advent of new technology, email can be more secure than *any* other common form of communication.

WHAT'S THE SOLUTION?

The legal profession generally views various forms of encryption soft-ware as providing the solution. If "encryption" sounds high-tech, it is. If it sounds like something for spies rather than lawyers, it isn't. The legal profession is regularly using encryption technology today. In a few years, it will become as common as cell phones.

First, a little primer on cryptography. The most common existing type of cryptography in use is "single key." The single key can be used to encrypt a message from plain text into ciphertext, which can only be read by someone with the same key. For example, if your key is that each letter of the alphabet is matched with its correlating place in the alphabet (A=1, B=2, etc.), then a message written with the numbers 1–26 can be easily decrypted. The first problem with single key cryptography is that both the sender and the recipient need to share the same key. Both must trust each other not to compromise the secret. In some circumstances, this may be fine, but it doesn't ad-dress the problem of communications with those whom you cannot completely trust.

The second problem is that you must securely transmit the key itself. Unless you can have a face-to-face meeting with the other person (in the middle of an open field at midnight, where you speak in hushed tones), there is no secure method to transmit the key. The answer to this dilemma is split-key cryptography. It uses a pair of keys—one public and one private. Each key is a very long string of numbers and letters. The public key is freely distributed, including over the Inter-net. For mathematical reasons involving extremely long prime num-bers (which are beyond my understanding) the private key cannot be derived from the public key, yet the two keys are mathematically linked to one another. Both are needed to read an encrypted mes-sage. Since a person keeps his private key confidential (never having to share it with anyone), there is no risk of disclosure like you have with single-key cryptography. Already, lawyers are using split-key cryptography, and an increasing number of attorneys' Web sites have a link to get the lawyer's public key.

The armor of split-key cryptography is not without its chinks. There is the risk that someone will substitute a different public key, thus making any messages encrypted with that public key readable by the impostor who holds the private key for the substituted public key. The solution is to have trusted third parties become repositories for public keys, who will certify that the public key is only from the rep-resented person.

PERSONAL ACCOUNT
Samuel Lewis
Romanik Lavin Huss & Paoli
http://Complaw.com
email: slewis@
CompLaw.com

The most-common form of split-key cryptography on the Internet is pretty good privacy, or PGP. Samuel Lewis, a lawyer with the law firm of Romanik, Lavin, Huss & Paoli in Hollywood, Florida, and a member of the Florida Bar's Computer Law Committee, has started the PGP Awareness Project. Sam demonstrates and explains the use of PGP:

——-BEGIN PGP MESSAGE——-
Version: 4.0 Business Edition

hIwC4/J8glukrDUBA/9AaUIn3gJqi2ibrAIUwvUTLSLv2ohppJSN
I8dN3wawEqPkYx/EQfnNCcqXygmFojGiuccj2037gbl84ci0jGH
RmS9LYOBxxAIEBka01/SqXrW1oqR00jGda6Cv7BQIWcbmEL
0BsapS39CeiT/AR+J6UE/a8Q7ymToXEiy7SQz5sYSMAmut/K
4DTRgVAQQAuG3aBGfF8TY/9gNriDZI0iY+E+uMyJ7+FPpcyL
uxKIhLDPxPz4eZeble7C7pnuHRYZOzfJicwCccLY8ktINsS1eZt
kkxNI5dpgNvwFE2/rOBMk6C/ojQ4dMJUzXCJNRgo6Lf6S48O
E1vc0qhohBgL5NzZWCAjLHbo48ms4opGRmmAAAAtDh1mS
uZEVqgQy4AIWgs9yJX3kECU9vEAdAcff+kIKHwvU8WW83C
N6m1o02NsvFLqzdxDmMk/3tPatISIk45IoR2N4Eaw8qfQSZB/5
LzJ62QJ9YIo/BHMmYqrUNYhM6KTpp0PmrLSGVLjUXahO9P
Fw2P3bj4MttJGPUn/aWhnGRb+Hjv/Y57Gkq7jZvKuL1hwjt0TO
sSyIR9/MiX6B/MDk2HeI3fqNJg8C5/SqGyQAihyFCR5w==
=3Pz8
——-END PGP MESSAGE——-

Can't make heads or tails out of it, can you? Here's a hint—never in his wildest dreams would William Shakespeare have imagined that any of his plays would end up encrypted by a split-key encryption scheme. Sure, encryption—the process of turning a message into a code which nobody but another person who knows the code can read—has been around for centuries. Caesar sent encrypted orders to his field generals. If you're having trouble making out the above message, it's because you're not one of the two intended recipients. If this all seems confusing, then read on, because there is little doubt that this is going to impact your practice in the years to come.

The encrypted text above was created using a program called PGP. PGP, which stands for "Pretty Good Privacy," is encryption software created by Phil Zimmermann, and is distributed free at MIT's Web site for noncommercial purposes. There are other products on the market which do essentially the same thing as PGP, but since PGP is freely available, it is used by many for encrypting email on the Internet.

This software employs a split-key encryption system. Simply put, split-key encryption is a scheme that requires two different keys to unlock a message. One key is kept secret (the private key), while the other key is freely distributed to the rest of the world (the public key). When someone wants to send a locked message to you, they encrypt it with your public key. This key "talks" to your private key, which is the only key that can unlock the message.

The message above was encrypted with two public keys because it was sent to two different people, each of whom had their own PGP public key. Only the recipients' private keys can unlock the message. In this case, the message reads as follows:

To be, or not to be, that is the question.
Whether 'tis nobler in the mind to suffer
The slings and arrows of outrageous fortune,
Or to take arms against a sea of troubles,
And by opposing end them?

Clearly, there's nothing about this message that needed protection. Anyone could have gone to the library and looked up Hamlet in a copy of Shakespeare's complete works. Still, it does give you an idea of what encryption is all about. In short, an encrypted messages looks like garbage to anyone who doesn't have the key to unlock the message.

PGP, due to its unique encrypting power, has an interesting history. It's such a powerful encryption tool that it may actually be illegal to export it. Its developer, Philip Zimmermann, spent years under DOJ (Department of Justice) investigation when PGP was suddenly placed on the worldwide Internet for free downloading. It seems the 1954

FIGURE 4-1

If you want more information about Sam's PGP Awareness Project, check out the Web site at http://www.complaw. com/pgp.html.

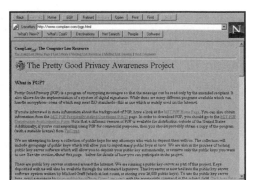

Munitions Control Act included encryption devices among the list of munitions that cannot be exported without government approval. Of course, the irony is that PGP is available on the Internet, which, of course, goes everywhere. In early 1996, the DOJ dropped its investigation when it determined that Zimmermann wasn't responsible for putting PGP on the Net and because, frankly, the cat was already out of the bag anyway. But the concern over PGP expressed by the National Security Agency and FBI is testament to its power and security. If the world's master code breakers, the NSA, can't break PGP-encoded messages, there is little danger your encoded email is going to get read by anyone but those for whom it is intended. At least for the foreseeable future, a PGP-encrypted message cannot be decrypted by anyone but the intended recipient.

You can download a free copy of PGP at MIT's Web site (*http://web. mit.edu/pgp*) and learn more about it at PGP's Web site (*http:// www.pgp.com*). PGP is so popular that nearly 1,000 people each day download the software from the MIT site alone. If you begin using PGP but need more help than is provided in the PGP manual, you may want to check out a Web site for PGP users at *http://www. rivertown.net/~pgp*. If the site doesn't answer your questions, you can join a PGP users mailing list (from the site) and post your question on the list.

PGP and other encryption software is not only good for the *confidentiality* concern, it also is very effective in addressing *authentication*. A sender can use her private key to digitally "sign" a message. Then the recipient can use the sender's public key (which is mathematically linked to the private key) to confirm that the sender is really who she says she is. In addition to authentication, it also serves as a means of *non-repudiation*. Since only the sender (presumably) has that private key, the sender must have sent it, and she cannot repudiate it.

Samuel Lewis discusses the use of PGP for digital signatures:

> *Encryption is but one aspect of PGP. PGP also incorporates a system of digital signatures. Similar to the way that PGP can protect a message, it can create a digital signature that can be matched to your public key to ensure that you sent the message, verify the time the message was signed, and that the message was not altered after it was sent. While the signature is certainly not as flashy as your typical "John Hancock," digital signatures enjoy a benefit over their ink-based counterparts in that it is much easier to*

*determine if the digital signature is authentic. A typical digital signature ap-
pearing at the end of a message might look something like this:*

```
——-BEGIN PGP SIGNATURE——-
iQCVAgUBMcMUHWut/K4DTRgVAQFYUwQAuiLm7kXcYWb
W4sczAH4AO9d1+Q5LnqmyWdV+RDaD0uNX6SVvGcUoEN
TZFhvotFNC6lTc+swRkW8dlO8+R0Viy3FBGvg43LmpUdgcX
PYMlaLMLfaIpZDSddrvfzJfHkELGH9BcB9esxmYjOmGHEp
UCod9IkAz70MH      mLmhd/agydE==0F16
——-END PGP SIGNATURE——-
```

*Florida recently passed digital signature legislation which allows documents
digitally signed—and not necessarily with a scheme like this, but just plac-
ing your name at the end of the message might be sufficient—to be legally
binding. Utah and California have also passed laws relating to digital signatures.*

It looks like PGP can take care of all of our problems. So why don't
lawyers just encrypt everything and be done with the issue? Samuel
Lewis gives a quick answer:

*PGP is not the easiest program to use, especially by itself. The version dis-
tributed by MIT is a DOS-based program, and you will have to learn many
different commands to make the program useful. In other words, for all of
the other software you could get for your computer, PGP is probably the
least user-friendly and most complicated to use. On the other hand, there
are many different programs that you can use in addition to PGP which will
make using PGP as easy as a few mouse clicks. The company producing the
commercial version of PGP has a Windows version, which is one of the easiest ways to use PGP. It only requires that you highlight the text to be encrypted or signed, and then cut and paste. It's only a matter of time before
some encryption method is built into your typical email program.*

In addition to the ease of use problem, there are other reasons
lawyers don't encrypt every message. For universal use of split-key
encryption, everyone must have his own private key and everyone
must have the public key of everyone else. And as you saw above,
we're not talking about something short like a name, but instead a
long string of characters. I have enough trouble keeping track of post
office addresses, let alone email addresses. Keeping track of everyone's public key adds to the confusion, although there are places on
the Internet where you can get the public key for those who have
registered their keys at that site.

But as Sam mentioned, at some point encryption software will be incorporated seamlessly into email programs. Like address books in

today's email programs, public keys will be easy to keep and organize as part of the program's internal address book. At this time, you can buy several Windows applications for PGP that make it easier to use. And by the time this book hits the shelves, a company called FTP Software, Inc., under license from Philip Zimmermann's company, should have a commercial email product that will offer encryption and decryption with the ease of a mouse click on an icon. You can watch their Web site at *http://www.ftp.com* for availability.

But if you don't want to buy the software, or if no one else has a PGP key, what do you do?

The first question: is encryption *really* necessary?

The issue is two-fold. First, just how confidential is your message? And, second, if you don't encrypt it, are you waiving the attorney-client privilege or breaching a duty to keep a message confidential?

Some lawyers say it's better to be safe than sorry, and suggest that for client communications, encryption should be used for all but the most routine of messages. For others, they see this as unnecessary because it could create the standard of care for lawyers. In other words, a court could hold that an unencrypted email message has no expectation of privacy and is the same as talking over a cellular phone.

Although opinions are not uniform, the growing consensus is that encryption is necessary for only the most confidential of messages. And if you're worried about malpractice issues, you may take comfort in knowing that at least one insurance company has decided that encryption is not necessary for every message. Attorneys' Liability Assurance Society (ALAS) has said that it is unnecessary to encrypt most communications on the Internet, except for matters so important that any risk of interception must be avoided. However, ALAS warns that attorneys must be careful and watch the issue, because courts and state bars may fail to do a careful analysis and disagree with their opinion.

Washington attorney John Maxwell, Jr., explains why he doesn't think encryption is generally necessary:

> *I have heard some concerns raised about the confidentiality of email. Frankly, I see little cause for alarm. The volume of email traffic, coupled with the inability to determine the exact nature of a data transfer at any point of the Net, makes the idea of someone intercepting your mail a remote concept. You would have better luck pouring a glass of water in a river and*

PERSONAL ACCOUNT

John Maxwell, Jr.
Meyer, Fluegge &
Tenney, P.S.
*http://www.wolfenet.
com/~maxjd/genmft.html*
maxjd@wolfenet.com

then trying to identify that same water a mile downstream from the rest of the water in the river. If there are truly sensitive matters to be discussed one could always encrypt the email, but unencrypted email is still more secure than the telephone—with one exception. If you do not want to put it in writing, then you should use the phone because email will generate a written file at the transmitting end and receiving end, and that file will remain on the computer until deleted.

PERSONAL ACCOUNT

Peter Krakaur

Internet Legal Services

http://www.legalethics.com

ils@legalethics.com

Peter Krakaur also questions the attention lawyers have given to the issue of whether encryption is necessary for email. He urges the legal profession to not lose the forest for the trees:

I question the need for PGP as an appropriate mechanism to adopt universally to "protect" attorney email. It is illegal for someone to intercept email and it is illegal to intercept a telephone call. Given a core understanding of the technology, one can intercept email. It is equally true that given a core understanding of telephones, one can intercept a regular telephone call. Why the fuss with email alone?

I fear the day that a court will say "you waived the privileges that attached to this communication because you did not encrypt it." Encouraging attorneys to use PGP without further clarification seems to me to lead us on a path that would establish an encryption standard.

So what should attorneys do? Several articles and discussions have made the analogy between email use and cellular phones. On the technology side, the analogy is poor. Email does not flow over the airwaves where one does not have a "reasonable expectation of privacy" (to use the language of some of the opinions). Rather, email seems to be more akin to regular telephone use. Information flows via telephone lines and can be intercepted by system personnel along the way, whether it be a systems administrator at an ISP, a telephone repairman or telephone systems administrator. On the ethics side, however, the analogy may prove useful. The ethics opinions dealing with cellular phones (some of them issued before interception of those communications was made illegal) is that there is a risk of interception, and that the attorney should advise the client of the risk of interception and seek a waiver from the client. (Mass. #94-5, NYC #1994-11, NH #1991-92/6, Iowa #90-44, Wash. State #91-1 [addressing cordless phones]; Ill. #90-7) A South Carolina ethics opinion used the cellular analogy to suggest the same rule for electronic communications (SC #94-27). In short, a good practice when communicating with clients is to inform them of the risk of interception and get a waiver. Attorneys who want to learn more should take a look at the 1996 ALAS Loss Prevention Manual, Tab IIIC.

The concern behind my comments is a fear of singling out email as a "prob-lem." There is a risk of interception with any medium: mail, telephone, email, whatever. To focus exclusively on a relatively new medium, email, does it a disservice. Before the profession jumps to encrypt email as a practice (or encourage the use of encryption, which could lead to a stan-dard) I suggest the profession evaluate other security risks associated with the practice. What are the agreements attorneys have with all third parties associated with their practice (copy centers, system maintenance compa-nies, telephone repair persons, florists, etc.)? More importantly, what are the security measures attorneys have in place for their computer networks, lap-tops, and home computers? On a practical level, these pose far greater security concerns. The idea of addressing them separately has appeal, but realistically I think that people will focus on email only, that restrictions on its use will be put in place, and that people will simply ignore the other is-sues because they are not new or novel. In short, if we want to place height-ened security measures on email, let's do it across the board for all communications. I trust that if we think of the idea of scrambling regular telephone calls, we will pause to think about what is really a "problem" and what is an appropriate "solution."

Taken in context of other security concerns, Peter Krakaur's point is that email is only a small part of a much bigger problem that lawyers have with security. But Peter, who runs the *legalethics.com* Web site, also realizes that the ethics issue may be separately addressed by some states. For example, at the time of this writing only a few states have addressed the issue. Iowa says that attorneys must encrypt "sen-sitive material" before sending it via email or obtain the client's writ-ten acknowledgment of a risk of disclosure. (See *Iowa Ethics Opinions 95-30* [rescinded] and *96-1*.) Arizona has issued an informal, non-binding statement that "confidential material" sent in an email should be encrypted to protect the confidentiality duty. A South Car-olina advisory opinion suggests that sending unencrypted email raises confidentiality issues without an express client waiver. By the time you read this, other states may have addressed the issue, and even these states may have revised their rulings. The opinions, how-ever, fail to bring the issue down to earth.

Samuel Lewis, who is very familiar with the technology, only encrypts a very small portion of his email. His experience gives guidance:

I cannot stress enough that unless you are sending sensitive client communi-cations, there's no need to encrypt your messages. Thus, it is critical to understand what is safe and what needs protection, and then it is important to know how to protect the message.

Even if what you're sending might be considered sensitive, you don't necessarily need to encrypt it. I know some attorneys who don't lose any sleep over the fact that they send messages to clients via email without encrypting even the more sensitive messages. On the other hand, I know many more attorneys who use email for all but the sensitive messages. Given the need, especially the ethical requirement, to protect client confidentiality, it would seem that some form of encryption is warranted for sensitive client communications.

While you might be able to avoid the entire dilemma by refraining from sending any sensitive client communications through email, such abstention is a more drastic and unwarranted approach. One of the goals of the PGP Awareness Project is to teach attorneys that while it is safe to send less sensitive messages without encryption, sensitive messages sent with encryption are equally safe. In fact, an encrypted email is a more secure way of transmitting a sensitive client communication than the fax or the telephone. Perhaps the only form of communication more secure would be to whisper the message into the client's ear behind closed doors. Thus, you could use email for all client communications without ever concerning yourself about subjects like inadvertent disclosure so long as you use encryption for sensitive messages.

Perhaps my own case will give you a better idea of how often you're likely to need to use PGP. On an average day, I typically receive 50 messages, of which more than half require a response. It is rare that any of the messages or my responses are so sensitive as to warrant encryption. In the last three months, I have received a total of two encrypted messages, five signed messages, and have sent a total of four encrypted messages. The messages I sent were so sensitive that I might not have felt entirely comfortable conveying the same message over the telephone, much less via a fax or cellular phone. Keep in mind that four messages over three months, when considering that an average of 75 messages are coming or going each day, is a minute portion of all email sent. On the other hand, this should demonstrate that email with encryption can provide a means for transmitting sensitive client communications without fear of disclosure.

Where do these various opinions get us? Until encryption is universal and easy, it's clear lawyers won't be encrypting every message. But ethically, lawyers may have a duty to inform a client about the disclosure risks of email, especially if the lawyer knows more about the risks than the client.

Many lawyers now use disclaimers in their email messages to warn of the risks—and some are not getting signed releases from their clients. It's not because the problem is unique with email, but only because it's novel. Disclaimers may be just as important for messages sent through the mails or communicated over the telephone, but everyone is generally aware of their risks. But because email is new, lawyers may have an obligation to educate clients about its particular risks.

The best way to find out what other lawyers are doing is to watch their email and surf their sites on the Net. To save you a little time, I'll reprint draft disclaimers that Peter Krakaur presented in May of 1996 at The Second Annual Statewide Ethics Symposium in California for discussion purposes only. Because the law is changing quickly and the rules of every jurisdiction vary, you should check with your state bar for guidance and not rely on these draft disclaimers to meet your jurisdiction's rules.

For example, when communicating with a client, some lawyers may include one or both of the following messages at the end of the email message.

```
Email communication on the Internet may NOT be
secure. There is a risk that this confidential
communication may be intercepted illegally. There
may also be a risk of waiving attorney-client
and/or work-product privileges that may attach to
this communication. DO NOT forward this message to
any third party. If you have any questions
regarding this notice, please contact the sender.
```

```
DO NOT read, copy or disseminate this communication
unless you are the intended addressee. This email
communication contains confidential and/or
privileged information intended only for the
addressee. If you have received this communication
in error, please call us (collect) immediately at
(123) 123-4567 and ask to speak to the sender of
the communication. Also, please notify the sender
immediately via email that you have received the
communication in error.
```

Before you blindly include disclaimers on all client communications, however, you should question their need at all. For example, some lawyers believe that a disclaimer is unnecessary given that email is private and confidential by federal law. Also, a disclaimer may be used to demonstrate that you *knew* you were using an insecure form of communication and, instead of using something effective like encryption, chose something ineffective like a disclaimer.

However, if the risk of interception is by another lawyer, the use of a disclaimer at least announces that you *expect* your message to be confidential and *expect* only the intended recipient to read the message.

There is another cloud over email security. National security agencies such as the NSA, CIA and FBI are pushing hard for a law that would require those who use dual-key encryption such as PGP to file their private key with a federally appointed escrow agent. The reasoning is that unless these agencies have access to private keys they will not be able to monitor terrorists and organized criminals whom they now wiretap. Privacy groups are opposing the law. In any event, even if such a law is passed, email communications will be no less secure for attorneys than telephone calls, since a court order would be required before the escrow agent could release your private key to authorities.

Hopefully, the issue of email confidentiality will become a non-issue in the near future, either by easy-to-use encryption software or definitive court rulings. And confidentiality isn't the only issue to worry about, as the problems of authentication, non-repudiation, and integrity still lurk. However, for these problems, businesses are already stepping up to the plate to offer services that may solve them.

For example, it was reported in the summer of 1996 that the United States Postal Service was launching a pilot project to test the electronic postmarking of documents sent over the Internet. Supposedly, the USPS's electronic postmark will carry with it the same weight and authority as standard mail, including the Service's authority to investigate tampering of the mails. Some lawyers see this as an Orwellian threat to privacy (all stamped email would have to pass through the Service's computers), while others see it as a great opportunity to bring certainty to electronic commerce. The USPS intends to make its postmarking software available to email software designers so that it can be incorporated into email programs. Each use of the postmark would cause the sender to incur a charge, such as 10 cents. (So much for email rendering the USPS obsolete!)

In addition to electronic postmarking, the USPS intends to offer a certificate-authority service to register a public encryption key. For a small fee, you could register your key with the USPS, which would provide certainty to third parties that the key was, in fact, your key.

Until all of the security issues with email are solved, lawyers will simply have to use common sense when sending confidential messages by email.

If you want to read further about this issue, there are many online resources. Check out any of the following:

- Charles R. Merrill, "A Cryptography Primer for Business Lawyers," at *http://www.ljextra.com/forumpages/merrill.html*
- Robert L. Jones, "Client Confidentiality: A Lawyer's Duties with Regard to Internet E-Mail," at *http://www.legalethics.com/articles.htm*
- Arthur L. Smith, "E-Mail and the Attorney-Client Privilege," at *http://www.legalethics.com/articles.htm*
- Joan C. Rogers, "Malpractice Concerns Cloud Email, On-line Advice," at *http://www.legalethics.com/articles.htm*

For more about PGP and its colorful history, read Simson Garfinkel's *PGP: Pretty Good Privacy,* published by O'Reilly & Associates, Inc.

WHEN IN ROME...

The Internet is as much a *place* as it is a thing. Like a foreign country, the Net has developed a culture all its own. And like visiting another country, it's wise to be aware of the local culture, especially if you want to be successful in it.

Two fundamentals of Net-culture are a strong attachment to freedom of speech and an equally strong anti-commercialism. As the world gets on the Net, however, expect each of these to become of lesser importance, to the chagrin of old-time Net-users. Nevertheless, when using email, it's vital to be aware of email netiquette. Not only for when you're the sender, but when you're the recipient—you may not even be able to *understand* some email messages unless you're familiar with the traditions.

But let's first look at one of the things you never want to do with email.

SPAMMING

In short, a "spam" is an unsolicited commercial email message. Spamming involves sending the same message to huge numbers of

Snail mail
Mail sent through the
postal service

Flames
A virulent and (often)
personal attack against the
author of a Usenet or
mailing list posting. People
who frequently write flames
are called (among other
names) "flamers."

email recipients, usually through the convenient process of posting on newsgroups or mailing lists. It's the Internet equivalent of junk mail. But at least with junk snail mail, it costs the sender something to send it, thereby (in theory) discouraging its overuse. It's not the same with spamming—a spammer can send out thousands of email messages with no more cost than computer time. It is the ultimate junk mail. And Net users are afraid that without controls, our email inboxes will become useless repositories of Net-commercials. Then no one would bother looking at their email. Email would die in its infancy.

But like the old American West, vigilante justice roams the Net. A true spam message will generate flames in response. A spam message also risks revenge—instead of a single flame, a spammer may be sent a message that it designed to repeat itself indefinitely, causing the spammer's email inbox to overload (and also causing the ISP to cancel the spammer's account). Or a spammer may be sent a huge file that will tie up his computer for hours or even days. I know there are much more creative responses to spammers, but I'm sure you get the idea.

And how did the name "spam" come about? Spamming reportedly is in honor of a Monty Python sketch from the 1970s. In the sketch, waitress Terry Jones (in Python's famous drag) recited the dinner menu of "egg and bacon; egg sausage and bacon; egg and Spam; egg bacon and Spam; egg bacon sausage and Spam; Spam bacon sausage and Spam; Spam egg Spam Spam bacon and Spam; Spam sausage Spam Spam bacon Spam tomato and Spam; Spam Spam Spam egg and Spam; Spam Spam Spam Spam Spam Spam baked beans Spam Spam Spam; etc."

I think you get the point.

A handful of lawyers, unfortunately, have been at the forefront of Net spamming. A husband and wife team of Arizona lawyers have become *the* case study of how *not* to use the Internet for marketing, with their efforts becoming known as simply the "Green Card Incident." The firm reportedly spammed members of nearly 6,000 newsgroups (which means hundreds of thousands, maybe millions, of people) in less than 90 minutes through a local Internet provider. The spam ad was for the United States "Green Card" lottery. So many email complaints resulted from the spam that their Internet Service Provider reportedly crashed 15 times trying to handle the email overload. The "Green Card" lawyers, as they have become known, were not apologetic about their efforts, even writing a book on how to market on the Net (needless to say, I'd recommend other books on Net-marketing). Because they continued their spamming efforts, some recipients designed "trip guns," which automatically mailed "flames" (or worse) to the lawyers whenever a message was received.

This speaks to the practical danger of spamming, aside from what it may do to your reputation on the Net. Currently on the Net, it is considered in bad taste to send unsolicited marketing email. People generally tolerate junk mail in their snail mail boxes more than they tolerate it in their email boxes. Simply stated, unsolicited commercial email violates netiquette. Its only proven effect is to offend. As it is now illegal to send unsolicited faxes, look for future legislation addressing the same issue with email.

Having said that, it doesn't mean that you can't use email for marketing on the Net—far from it. But the marketing efforts have to be more subtle and usually tied in with providing information and/or services to others. For example, during a mailing list discussion, a person could (softly) plug their product or service, *if* it is offered in response to a need posted by another member. Or even more subtle (and more effective) is to be active on a mailing list or newsgroup and show the members your knowledge about a subject by sharing information and informed opinions. And there are newsgroups and mailing lists just for new announcements, where readers *expect* to see commercial plugs.

Lawyer Peter W. Martin believes the Net's culture isn't really inhospitable to lawyer marketing any more than any other culture. In his article "Five Reasons for Lawyers and Law Firms to Be on the Internet," he says:

> *Let's return to the Internet as large city metaphor. Like any city, this one has long-term residents living in comfortable neighborhoods where the old ways, old laws, and established mores are held dear. As newcomers barge in, bringing new activities and, often, insensitivity to the existing culture, clashes are inevitable.*

> *Lawyers making their way onto the Net are not immune. I trust many have heard of the lawyer who sent an unsolicited ad for his immigration legal services to several thousand Internet Usenet groups and received 30,000 replies, the bulk of them "flames" from persons who objected to this use of the Usenet neighborhood for unsolicited direct mail.*

> *The case does not prove that the Net is inhospitable to lawyers, any more than one should conclude that lawyers don't belong in country clubs from the outrage that would be harvested by a lawyer in business attire making*

his way around the course on a full day, stopping players mid-swing to hand out his business card.

Lawyers belong on the Internet. They are on the Internet. And once there, no great surprise, some of them will act like fools.

And remember, a short but informative signature line or lines tagged on to the end of your email messages is never considered out of place.

If you follow a few basics of Netiquette, you can avoid acting like a fool.

EMAIL LANGUAGE— ACRONYMS, EMOTICONS, AND OTHER GOOD STUFF

Some of what we're going to talk about in this section seems pretty silly in the context of formal lawyer talk. On the Net, you'll see "emoticons" (emotions + icons). For example, :-) expresses a grin (to see it, point your left ear to the ground). Since typed messages are so sterile, people sometimes use emoticons to relay more meaning to a message. (More emoticons are in this book's glossary). And you'll also see acronyms commonly used in email—some you already know (ASAP), but others may be foreign (IMHO).

You may ask, why should lawyers worry about this trivial stuff? Even if you never use them, you should at least understand what they mean. Not all of our clients are as boring and stodgy as lawyers. And remember, you're in another culture. When visiting Norway, you may not want to eat lutefisk (does anyone?), but you should at least know what it is.

Gabriel Wachob discussed why lawyers have to be aware of Net-culture:

For many lawyers, using the Internet, especially for communicating with colleagues and clients, is something very new and different. They are not used to the subtleties and customs of the seasoned Net users. As an example, look at the use of common acronyms to shorten communications. Lawyers may view this as informal, perhaps even sloppy, compared to the rather strict confines of legal writing.

On the Net, however, if you want to project an image of being knowledge-able and part of the community, you have to at least be familiar and versed in the customs and practices of the locals (what an irony: there are "Net lo-cals" spread around the world). I think that most here would agree with me that image is very important for lawyers, be it in Networld or the real world. Imagine, for example, if you didn't know about contractions, and you simply never used them in normal conversation (like the android Data on "Star Trek: the Next Generation"). Those you communicated with would have a negative (most likely) reaction to your speech. I think the same thing happens (to a lesser extent, to be sure) when newbies communicate with seasoned Net people. (I just realized..."newbies" is a Net term.)

What follows is a list of some Net acronyms. There are many more, but here are some of the more common ones you may see:

- IMHO = in my humble opinion
- BTW = by the way
- OTOH = on the other hand
- FWIW = for what it's worth
- RSN = real soon now
- WYSIWYG = what you see is what you get
- ASAP = as soon as possible
- PDQ = pretty damn quick
- TIA = thanks in advance
- CU = see you

In addition to acronyms and emoticons, you'll see other writing conventions broken with impunity. Not uncommonly, people will write a message with no capital letters. It's probably pure laziness, but for informal Net-communication it's acceptable practice. Other conventions are more practical, because email typically doesn't support the use of special fonts, such as bold or italics. Thus, to emphasize a word, a person will frame a word in "*" or "_", as in "I *know* we'll win the case" or "I _know_ we'll win the case." If you want to be read as shouting, put it in capital letters: "DO NOT accept service!" (but don't write an entire message in all capital letters, unless you really want to shout out the *whole* thing).

Although the Net has developed its own email culture, writing messages isn't really that much different from regular mail correspondence. You'll see that email correspondence is more informal, but many of the common sense rules that you've learned during your professional life also apply to email.

But to make sure that common sense prevails, attorney and Webpage consultant Bruce Hake has put together a list of email tips. I've

CONTACT

Bruce Hake
President, Hake Internet
Projects, LLC
http://www.ilw.com/
bruce@hake.com

quoted several below, but you can see his entire list of 12 rules at the Immigration Lawyers on the Web Online Web Site Owner's Manual at *http://ilw.com/om.htm*.

- Reply promptly. This is the cardinal rule. Never let more than 24 hours go by without replying—and whenever possible you should reply much sooner than that. Most people who come to Immigration Lawyers on the Web looking for a lawyer contact several lawyers there, and they have probably contacted other lawyers on the newsgroups or in other ways. The early bird gets the worm.

- A summary reply is OK. Although you absolutely must reply quickly, you don't always have time for a careful response. It is good practice in such situations to send a short acknowledgment email saying, "Thank you for your query. I will send you a careful reply as soon as I can." People appreciate this kind of courtesy very much.

- Get help, but not too much. Some organizations have several full-time employees to manage a Web site. If at all possible, you should designate someone in your office to monitor email from your Web site on at least a daily basis. Ideally, the person would check email several times a day. But don't rely on this person to answer all your email for you! A client-lawyer relationship is a personal relationship. Assistants can handle much of the ongoing client contact responsibilities in active cases, of course. But prospective clients need the personal attention of the lawyer, just as much in email as if they had walked in the door.

- You don't have to type. Some lawyers have someone in the office print out emails to which they dictate responses. This is cumbersome but can be very effective.

- Protect yourself. Be aware of the risk that an email correspondent may assume you are acting as his or her lawyer and will rely on anything you say. The formation of a client-lawyer relationship does not require an express contract for it to be upheld by a court or bar authority: if the person reasonably believed you were acting as legal counsel, you're on the hook. Therefore, you should routinely include a disclaimer somewhere on most or all emails to non-clients (and in postings to public newsgroups) expressing two concepts: (1) a client-lawyer relationship has not been formed; and (2) what you say should not be relied upon as legal advice without advice of counsel. Good practice is to set up your email and browser

programs so that a "signature file" is attached to the bottom of all
your emails and newsgroup postings. Here is an example:

> John Lawyer
> Smith & Jones, P.C.
> Chicago, Illinois
> *john@smithjones.com*
> *http://ilw.com/lawyer/*
> Information herein is generalized and should not be relied
> upon without advice of a lawyer. This communication does
> not create a client-lawyer relationship.

- Don't mindlessly requote everything. Most email readers' automatic quotation feature is a blessing and a curse. If both correspondents mindlessly quote everything back and forth, the emails can quickly grow to ridiculous, mind-numbing length. Quote selectively. Chop away material you do not need to respond to. Get to the point.

- Keep good records. You can get incredibly confused incredibly quickly if you don't keep good records of all email contacts. I recommend using a generic "prospective clients" folder in your email program to store all emails back and forth with prospective clients. Once a prospective client becomes a real client, the emails should be moved to a new folder. In addition, hard-copy printouts should be made of all the correspondence for the case file. Also, be sure your electronic email records are backed up! Hard drives fail. You don't want to have to reconstruct your life if your hard drive fails and you lose all records of 20 pending and potential matters.

- Use the telephone. Email is so easy to use that it can seduce you into a false sense of friendship and understanding. In fact, however, email communications are potentially misleading and incapable of supporting by themselves a complex relationship such as a client-lawyer relationship, because so much of human communication requires nuances of tone that are entirely missing in email. Therefore, while email is useful for initial contacts and for ongoing communications, it is extremely important to arrange telephone or in-person contact as soon as possible. I think it is good policy to charge a consultation fee for a telephone contact, if the person is too far away to come in to your office.

- Warmth counts. Email is a cool medium. Moreover, it is very easy to brush people off in email with perfunctory responses. If you're going to do email, you need to do it right. That requires some real warmth and imagination. You have to make an active leap of the imagination to distill the human reality of the situation presented out of a cool and cursory communication. Then you have to project some genuine warmth and empathy in responding. Some lawyers who are masters of in-person or telephone interactions turn into robots when they try to use email. Don't let that happen to you. Don't let the "virtual" nature of the communication obscure the fact that the people writing you are real.

With these tips in mind, start using that email! Once you begin, you'll realize it's one of the greatest advances in communication that you've seen in your lifetime (assuming you aren't a contemporary of Mr. Bell!).

Research on the Net 5

It should come as no surprise that research is the advantage most often cited by lawyers already on the Net. Simply put, the Internet is the largest library in the world, and it's gaining volumes of information every second.

But the quantity of information comes at a cost. When on the Net, it's easy to reach information overload and end up more confused than informed. I've heard it said many times that the Net is like a library with no card file and its books scattered aimlessly across the floor. It's an apt analogy that is, fortunately, becoming less true every month. Sure, the books are still on the floor because the resources are spread around the world on different computer servers. But with the magic of hyperlinks, the books are organized into virtual bookshelves of information. Later in this chapter we'll see how MegaSites and search engines (the automated card files of the Internet library) have helped organize these bookshelves.

Most lawyers using the Internet discovered quickly that it's a uniquely useful research tool. In a small survey of lawyers conducted in the fall of 1995, Lex Mundi's Steve McGarry found that 23 percent of lawyers use the Internet primarily for research. Considering how much email is used, that's a lot of attorneys using the Net mostly for research.

- ▶ An Ocean of Information
- ▶ An Overview of What's on the Net
- ▶ How to Make Sense of the Chaos—MegaSites
- ▶ Using Search Engines and Directories
- ▶ The Devil Is in the Details—Citing Internet Resources

AN OCEAN OF INFORMATION

In my mind, three words describing the Net could also describe some oceans of the world: Free, Diverse, and sometimes Shallow. Once you're on the Net, the resources are nearly always free. The types of resources are diverse. But the depth of certain legal sources can be pretty shallow since anyone, qualified or otherwise, can post material on the Net. It's up to the information consumer to sort out the accurate and useful from the bogus. Thus, the Internet is like a vast ocean with deep holes and shallow flats.

FREE

For some types of research, the Internet is an affordable alternative to the expensive commercial databases such as Lexis and Westlaw. And in some cases the Internet beats them because it gets the information out quicker. The Internet can also be the only source for some rarely used legal resources that don't have a large enough constituency to support input into a commercial database. For example, some foreign law materials are not available on the commercial databases, but are on the Internet.

Despite its limitations, the best thing about the Internet is its cost—it's virtually free. Except for the hourly costs you pay for your connection (which could be only pennies an hour), almost everything on the Internet is free for the finding.

PERSONAL ACCOUNT

Pat Northey
New Zealand attorney
pat@iprolink.co.nz

Pat Northey, a lawyer in New Zealand, told me an example of how he saved money using the Internet for legal research:

> In New Zealand it can cost up to NZ$250 to obtain a "recent" U.S. Supreme Court decision for our lawyers. With the Internet we can get the decision from the Cornell site for a matter of cents. You can imagine how that can assist a client matter. Lexis is too expensive for some client matters. The Internet gives all clients a different opportunity if the material is relevant to the issue.
>
> I think the guys like to make the analogy "evens the playing field."

Although Pat's New Zealand residence makes the example an extreme one, it demonstrates the growing usefulness of the Net for worldwide access to free information.

American lawyers are also saving hundreds of dollars every day using the Internet for legal research. Bruce Hake, a lawyer and Internet consultant, extols the virtues of using the Internet for research in his immigration law practice:

PERSONAL ACCOUNT

Bruce Hake
President, Hake Internet Projects, LLC
http://ilw.com
bruce@hake.com

> *The Internet has also become my primary, free research resource for major portions of my practice. On my Web site—Immigration Lawyers on the Web—I have a resources page (http://ilw.com/resources.htm) where I've collected starting points for immigration law related resources on the Internet. One area has been a particular time and cost saver: human rights information. That kind of information, especially background information on foreign countries, is vital for many kinds of immigration cases. I used to routinely spend hundreds of dollars and much time per case for expensive Nexis online research, clippings services, and trips to the library. Now, I can do perhaps 95 percent of that research—and get better quality information—for free in much less time just from that Web page. I designed that page to be useful in my practice, and it really works!*

Although the vast majority of resources on the Net are free, there are attempts—struggling so far—to charge for some of the information. Some material will always be free, such as government documents, caselaw, and the like. But when the provider begins adding significant value to the information, that's when the free ride ends.

For example, Westlaw adds value to its cases by adding headnotes and organizing the caselaw into a systems of reporters. Thus, you pay for that added value. Also, when you get on Westlaw or Lexis, you can be confident that the database is complete. On the Internet, there is no guarantee that the free data is complete.

Despite these limitations, the Internet is especially useful when you know specifically what you're looking for. But if you're trying to do a comprehensive search, you can't (at this time, at least) count on the Internet unless you're paying for the information. This limitation of the Net may not last too long. Lex Mundi's Steve McGarry has started Project Argonaut, which seeks to create a coalition of governments, law schools, bar associations, and members of the private sector to create a uniform legal database. If successful, the project will permit searches across jurisdictions and databases.

DIVERSE

This is the best part of the Internet, in my opinion. When lawyers need to do research, we go to a law library. There, we find the familiar reports and treatises and annotated statutes. But if we want to learn something outside the narrow confines of "the law," we're out of luck. Now we must make a trip to the public library. There, I get lost. I admit it, the Dewey Decimal system still doesn't make any sense to me, despite the valiant attempts of my third-grade teacher. I wander around for hours finding everything but the subject I'm researching until a librarian takes pity and leads me to the right section.

PERSONAL ACCOUNT

Peter Krakaur

Internet Legal Services
http://www.legalethics.com
ils@legalethics.com

The Internet is an easy cure for the legal myopia bred into lawyers. It is a virtual smorgasbord of information that goes well beyond the law and contains information on subjects which may have extraordinary use in our practices. Peter Krakaur tells how the Internet would have saved him a great deal of time if it were available for him when he started practicing law:

> One of the first projects assigned to me as a first-year associate was to determine what was a reasonable sale of cattle under the UCC. Having grown up in New York City, I was not an expert on how to raise cattle. Indeed, I was admittedly ignorant of what the difference was between a bull and a heifer.

> Like many legal issues facing attorneys, that project required that I understand the law and the facts. That is, I had to research not only the relevant legal precedents, but also the relevant facts—I had to become an expert (more or less) on cattle raising.

> At the time (before the Internet was a practical research tool), I acquired this expertise by going to the library and conducting research in cattle journals and magazines on cattle raising. I then flew to the client's cattle ranch and met with our expert—the cattle rancher—who "schooled" me on cattle raising. I also researched caselaw in the UCC reporter to determine what the courts held were the relevant issues in the determination of a "reasonable" sale. Given that the answer to my research project required I understand both the law and the facts, my caselaw research was in two stages. That is, initially I looked at some caselaw to get an idea of the issues. I followed this up with research on the facts to see what went into a cattle sale. Armed with that knowledge, I returned to the caselaw to complete the analysis.

If I were given the same assignment today, I could access caselaw from a variety of jurisdictions to see what factors were deemed relevant by the courts for a sale of cattle. While these cases would not provide me with the complete legal answer, I could get a basic understanding in about 20 minutes of what courts in a variety of jurisdictions hold go into the determination of a "reasonable" sale of cattle. Of course, my research would be free.

Using the same Web browser that I use for finding the caselaw, I could in about half an hour learn the basic (or more advanced) facts of cattle raising. For example, I could go to the Internet and search livestock databases (e.g., http://www.crimson.com/livestock/srchgnrl.html), review cattle breeds at the Cattle Pages (http://earth.cy-net.net/cattle/), review USDA Economics Data (http://usda.mannlib.cornell.edu:70/1/data-sets/livestock/ 93105), visit Cattlemen on the Web (http://www.ncanet.org/ cattlemen.html), read Beef Today (http://www.beeftoday.com), or review several of MONE's Bovine Links (http://www.ionet.net/~mone/ bovine.html) to help point me to cattle information. In short, I would have had at my fingertips one huge library of information on cattle to find spot prices, learn about breeds, brucellosis, or a variety of factors that might affect a cattle sale.

I do not claim that the Internet can make me or you an instant expert on cattle (or any other topic for that matter). What it will do is provide you with a great deal of information that you can use to increase your core competency in any particular subject matter. Had I had the Internet for the cattle project assigned to me as a young associate, on my first visit to the cattle rancher I could have answered his questions and avoided confirming his suspicions that I was just a "city boy."

The broad content of the Internet is its greatest asset. It is so easy to publish a Web page that someone, somewhere, has probably put any information you seek on the Net. For example, soon after I had connected to the Internet I needed information about the timing and location of the Nobel Peace Prize ceremony. Although I had my Internet connection, I had barely learned how to use email, let alone the search engines. So I drove to the local library, where I fruitlessly wasted an hour looking through stacks of books on everything from Norway to dynamite.

So I decided I'd have to learn how to use that (now archaic) browser supplied by my ISP and the one search engine it linked to. I punched in the words "Nobel Prize." To my shock (and dismay) I got thousands of hits. But near the top of the list was the Nobel home page in Sweden. With a mouse click, I was in virtual Sweden, reading pages of the precise information I needed. Not only did I get the dates I wanted, but I saw a picture of the awards ceremony being held in the Norwegian Storting (their Parliament). In ten minutes—less time than I spent driving to the library one-way—my research was complete.

THE SHALLOWS

Despite the broad content of the Internet, the depth of some legal resources on the Net is limited. It wasn't long ago that few of us had heard of "electronic publishing" or could explain what it meant. Not until the advent of PCs did it really make much sense to the average lawyer. So it's not surprising that the amount of authoritive legal materials in electronic form is limited. For a world that has been hooked on paper-based information for half a millennium, the transition may take a while to complete. But each day the pace of that transition increases exponentially.

Once the information is in electronic form, it's a breeze to make it available on the Internet. But if the information doesn't exist in electronic form, it has to be converted—either by scanning it or by someone typing into a word processor. Certainly, this is what Westlaw and Lexis had to do when they created their first databases, and that's why you pay so much for their services. And since the Internet generally provides its stuff for free, it is only elementary logic that information usually won't be on the Net unless its prior life was in electronic form.

Caselaw provides the best example, because only recently has it been provided by the government in electronic form. For example, very few states provide caselaw earlier than 1991 on the Internet. Lawyer Peter Krakaur relays the most common question he gets from other lawyers:

> More often than not, the first question attorneys ask in relation to legal research on the Internet is, "Can I get caselaw?" The short answer is "Yes." The Internet serves as a cost-effective way to search, read, and monitor caselaw in many jurisdictions. At present, however, the Internet does not offer the same scope of caselaw that is available on the shelf or in fee-based computer research services.

Not only is the caselaw just the recent decisions, it will be in its raw form. No headnotes and no star pagination to West's proprietary system (this will become less of a problem in the future; see the section that follows regarding legal citation of Internet materials).

Of course, lawyers use more than just caselaw in their practices. The lack of older materials on the Net is not a problem for some resources. For example, rarely do you need to see the 1964 version of the United States Code. It's not on the Net, but you *will* find the most recent version. And that's all you usually want. So, except for caselaw, the Net's shallow nature may not be too limiting.

But for now, the Internet won't replace much of your legal library or even those overpriced CD-ROMs. Maybe in a few years most lawyers will forsake these resources. For the present, however, the Internet must be integrated with your other research tools and it would not be responsible for you to believe that you can do comprehensive legal research on the Net (unless you're accessing Westlaw through the Net, which you can do if you have a Westlaw account). Too many resources are not yet available on the Internet.

Joseph Hodges, Jr., a solo probate lawyer in Colorado, discussed how he integrates his current legal resources with the Internet to create a harmonious whole:

PERSONAL ACCOUNT

Joseph Hodges, Jr.
Solo practitioner
jghodges@usa.net

Another example involves legal research. The worldly content of the Lexis and Westlaw databases is not accessible from the Internet yet (although you now can access these two services from the Internet using your account ID with them if you have one), but a great deal of it is there now, and more and more of it is coming online, for free, every day. Thus, for example, let's say I have a Colorado legal question that is governed by Colorado statutory law as interpreted by the Colorado courts. While I am at the office (I am in an office suite that has a Colorado casebook Westlaw library), I can search through the books all I want. However, I often need to work on such matters at home, and I certainly cannot take that library home with me. To the rescue comes CD-ROM technology combined with the Internet. Using a portable CD-ROM drive, I can take all of my legal research CDs home with me and use them there. With a subscription to the Colorado cases and statutes on disk from Lois, Miche, or Westlaw, I can have that entire office library available to me both at home and wherever else I might be when I am not in the office. For current updates, I have access to all the recent U.S. Supreme Court and 10th Circuit cases from the Internet. Colorado case law is not online yet, but it is just a matter of time.

In the meantime, if I care to find out what my fellow Colorado attorneys think about the legal issues involved, I can post an email to the colo-law listserv. In addition, the entire Colorado Revised Statutes are available on the Internet now, both in plain and annotated versions, and both fully searchable online and for free. I can think of no other way to duplicate this sort of easy and affordable access to such legal resources.

The Internet is a vast ocean of resources that may have exactly what you need for your next research project. Before we discuss how to find its main resources, I'll give you a brief overview so that you won't be fishing with your eyes closed.

AN OVERVIEW OF WHAT'S ON THE NET

Trying to describe what's on the Net is like trying to describe a Brazilian rain forest by studying a leaf. You can only look at one Internet site at a time, and with information being added at the rate of a *million pages* every month, there is no possible way to describe the Netforest. In fact, there may be thirty million pages of information by the time this book is published. The Internet is simply growing too fast. It's already too big to see in anyone's lifetime.

With fear and trepidation, I'll *try* to give an overview of *some* of the things *most likely* to be used by *most* lawyers on the Internet (is that enough qualifiers?). By the time you read this book, what is written here may no longer be accurate (especially the URLs, which have a terrible habit of changing). And by no means do I suggest that my listing is complete—I'll leave that to those who have virtually dedicated their lives to that mission (take a look at some of the MegaSites listed later in this chapter). Yet this overview should prove useful for its stated purpose: to give the legal researcher an idea of what's out there in the cyber-ocean.

FEDERAL CASELAW

Although the depth is shallow, the caselaw on the Net opens a new world for many practitioners unwilling to pay the costs of Lexis or Westlaw. And there are times when the Internet is more timely, because you often can go directly to the source without having to go through a commercial intermediary.

PERSONAL ACCOUNT
John Maxwell, Jr.
Meyer, Fluegge, &
Tenney, P.S.
http://www.wolfenet.com/~
maxjd/genmft.html
maxjd@wolfenet.com

For example, Washington lawyer John Maxwell, Jr., wrote me about how he won a motion and impressed his client by getting a newly issued case directly from the Internet:

> *The best thing that has happened on the Net for me is the LLI BULLETIN for the U.S. Supreme Court, where I receive by email a digest of new cases as soon as they are issued. Also the State of Washington, where I practice, has just made available the latest State Supreme Court and Court of Appeals cases decided in the last ninety days. The ability to use these cases has made a great difference for several recent clients of mine.*

> *For example, in a recent divorce case there was a jurisdictional battle in which my client had filed in one county and his wife in another county. The clear answer to this dispute was on the Net in the form of a recently decided State Supreme Court case concerning the attempt by the Seattle Seahawks to leave Seattle. While I was aware the case had just been decided based on the printed media, the Net allowed me to attach a copy of the decision to my brief within minutes of reading about the case. That really impressed the client, who was actually more impressed about that than winning the motion.*

Although most courts don't go back too far, you can still get an awful lot of caselaw from the Internet, especially federal. Thanks to recent additions, you can now get many of the U.S. Supreme Court cases dating back to 1937. For cases later than 1990, you should visit Cornell's site at *http://www.law.cornell.edu/supct.table.html*. In addition, at *http://www.law.cornell.edu/supct/cases/historic.htm* are selected historic decisions of the U.S. Supreme Court pre-dating 1990, such as *Roe v. Wade*, *Griswold v. Connecticut* and *Brown v. Board of Education*. Recently added to the Net were all of the U.S. Supreme Court cases from 1937 to 1975, which were previously organized by the Air Force for their FLITE database of legal information. You can access these cases at *http://www.fedworld.gov/supcourt/index.htm*. The cases can be searched by keyword or case name.

The Cornell site indexes the cases by topic and allows you to bolean search the cases. According to the site, the search engine views the syllabi of the Supreme Court for your keywords. You can also search party names, which is a useful tool when you know the name of the case but can't remember its citation.

In addition to recent Supreme Court cases, you can find recent cases from every federal circuit. Instead of listing the URLs for each of these sites, I suggest you simply open up one of the MegaSites listed later, most of which have hyperlinks to cases for each circuit.

OTHER FEDERAL MATERIALS

There is a wealth of other federal material on the Web. Most of the MegaSites include links to the material available. But as an overview, you can search the entire U.S. Code and the entire Code of Federal Regulations at some of the sites. At another site, you can look at the Congressional Record and see what your favorite politician is doing (or not doing). And, when it's 11:30 P.M. next April 15, you can access the IRS's site and get that form you need and avoid a late penalty.

PERSONAL ACCOUNT

Lawrence S. Goldberg
Schulte Roth & Zabel
http://www.legalethics.com
goldberg@srz.com

Lawrence S. Goldberg, partner at the New York City law firm of Schulte Roth & Zabel, relates how the Internet provided him with a copy of new federal regulations:

> *On a Sunday in March of this year, I was preparing for a seminar I was to conduct on the Bank Secrecy Act. The seminar was to be presented for a foreign bank the following week. From my home I checked the Government Printing Office's Web site, to determine the status of new regulations addressing the completion of suspicious transaction reports. Sure enough, just two or three days before, new regulations had been published in the Federal Register. I downloaded the new regulations, and was able to integrate the new regulations into my outline easily (without having to retype them). All from home, without expensive research time and with perfect integration of the regulations into my outline.*

Although federal materials were the first to make it on the Net, states are now catching up.

STATE LAW MATERIALS

As of 1996, most states have put their appellate court opinions online, but only the more recent decisions. The oldest state cases online date back to around 1991, which means that you can't use the Internet as a comprehensive source for researching state court opinions at this time. But as older cases are put online, the Internet should become a more comprehensive resource for researching state caselaw.

In addition to caselaw, many states have other legal materials online. For example, several states provide access to electronic versions of their rules, and numerous states have sites for their revenue departments where you can download tax forms. (Funny, isn't it, how tax forms were some of the first government data to go online?) Since each of the states vary, and more and more material is coming online every day, the easiest way to keep track of what your state offers is through a MegaSite. Since it's hard for any one site to keep up with fifty jurisdictions, I'd suggest that you monitor more than one Mega-Site to make sure that you hear of your state's offerings as soon as they come online.

FORMS ON THE NET

When law firms first began to computerize, the biggest advantage I saw was that secretaries no longer had to retype an entire document to make changes. Now, of course, this trait seems mundane, but it wasn't so a mere decade ago. This is also where the Internet shines, because all of its data is inherently in electronic form.

Grabbing an electronic version of a case off the Internet may not offer any particular advantage to reading the hardcopy version on a West reporter (unless you quote a significant portion of the opinion). But downloading a legal form from the Net makes using a hardcopy formbook seem downright Neanderthal. Once the form is on your hard drive, it's so easy to modify it.

Even if you don't modify an electronic form on your computer, the online availability of government forms can save you an awful lot of time. Colorado attorney Joseph Hodges, Jr., a solo probate practitioner, tells this story of how a form off the Internet saved the day:

> The other day one of my charity clients needed to register a trade name with the Colorado Secretary of State. Similarly, another charity client wanted to register as a foreign nonprofit corporation authorized to do business in Colorado. I thought I had a supply of the required forms for this on hand, but I didn't. Due to the urgency of these two matters, this meant that I would have to drive all the way downtown to pick up these forms and again later to file the completed forms. Then I remembered seeing a Web site for the Colorado Secretary of State's office off one of the HTML links that are on the Colorado Bar Association Web site at http://www.usa. net/cobar/index.htm.
>
> Sure enough, that link led me to another link for access to the forms online. This latter link allowed me to pick both the forms I wanted and the word processing format I wanted for an automatic download, which I did. I then opened up my word processor, loaded in the forms and printed them out. The end result was forms that in format and appearance looked exactly like the printed forms. I then had my secretary finish off the forms with a typewriter, had the clients come in to sign, and then messengered them to the Secretary of State's office for filing, all on the same day. This experience

alone justified the cost of my having access to the Internet, and by value billing for the work at a reasonable rate, I feel confident that I can recover for the rush nature of these two projects and still come out ahead. The only thing I did not try to do, for fear it might mess up the pre-formatted text of the forms, was to finish them off by using my word processor to fill in all of the blanks before I printed the forms—next time.

Not only is the government providing its forms online, but many legal forms are becoming available. The 'Lectric Law Library has an extensive form file, although it is limited to the more basic types of forms you may need (e.g., partnership agreements and the like). But even if you need something more esoteric, you are likely to find it online with a little searching.

For example, I recently needed to see some software licensing agreements to find sample language for several particular provisions. The 'Lectric Law Library didn't have what I needed, so I tried an "advanced" Alta Vista search. After sorting through some chaff, I found the wheat—an extensive treatise on software agreements, with sample language for virtually every provision imaginable! Within half an hour, I had drafted the language. In my earlier days when I practiced at a large law firm I would have accomplished the same by walking door-to-door, asking other lawyers if they had something I could use. I probably would have found the same material, but it may have taken longer. And it probably wouldn't have been in electronic form, meaning my secretary would spend an hour retyping it. So the Internet can give small firm practitioners some of the same advantages available to their big-firm brothers and sisters—a free form file with virtually unlimited forms.

WIDESPREAD PUBLIC LEGAL INFORMATION

Legal information is certainly available to the public today, but in massive law libraries intimidating to even the most sophisticated layperson. In public law libraries in my state, I've repeatedly seen members of the public struggle to even find the statute books, let alone figure out how to find anything in them.

The Internet won't suddenly make long-winded statutes comprehensible to the average Joe or Jane, but it will make the law more accessible and approachable. In the article "Digital Law: Some Speculations on the Future of Legal Information Technology" (found at *http://www.law.cornell.edu/papers/fut95fnl.htm*) lawyer Peter Martin predicts that "the exploding reach of the Internet promises to bring an enormous collection of legal materials into small offices and schools and homes in very remote settings." Now legal materials are only accessible by lawyers familiar with arcane citations and organizations dictated more by custom than logic. But, says Peter Martin, in "a point-and-click networked environment, a high school student or professional in some field other than law can retrieve particular decisions by a Supreme Court justice or follow a precise statutory reference without knowing 'legal citation.'"

For example, if a layperson wants to find out what federal laws govern wetland development, that person would have to first *know* to look in the U.S. Code and the Code of Federal Regulations, among other sources. Then, the person would have to know where these sources are found. Once the person had reached a legal library, he or she would have to get a reference librarian to find the books and their indexes. Although this process may be obvious to you and me, remember—we went to school to learn this stuff.

On the Internet, it's much easier. From a MegaSite, that same person can use search engines to find relevant statutes, or search out treatises or law reviews discussing wetlands. It won't replace the legal training of lawyers, but it *will* be more efficient and easier to use than what's currently available.

California attorney Richard Alexander believes that the Internet takes public legal education a giant step forward. Not only will it increase the legal information available to the public, it will also make it easier for legal consumers to find the *right* lawyer:

> The World Wide Web is providing lawyers and the profession with the means to do what we do best—educate. And it can be done at a fraction of the cost of traditional mass media.

> The central strength of the Net is that it allows lawyers as information professionals to provide knowledge that the public can use on demand. The Web is not the place to publish a firm brochure that nobody will look at more than once, but rather a medium for you to share your expertise in specific areas of the law and to give the public the information that it cannot get from any other place.

> For example, for twenty years I wrote law reviews, journal articles, and newspaper editorials that were published and promptly buried in libraries where only the most stalwart could find them. Today I publish those same

PERSONAL ACCOUNT

Richard Alexander
The Alexander Law Firm
http://www.alexanderlaw. com

ra@alexanderlaw.com

articles on my Web site that is fully indexed by fifty search engines, open 24 hours a day and instantly available to anyone.

The World Wide Web allows you to serve the public's need for information and to provide the detailed information that sophisticated purchasers of legal services want. In doing so it helps the public better understand how to select the right professional for a given problem.

From my years on the Board of Governors of the State Bar of California I know the great difficulty that the public has in finding the right lawyer. I attended many public hearings concerning the need to improve our system of discipline and although I heard many people complain about their lawyer, I never heard one person ever admit that they had selected the wrong lawyer in the first place, which was often the case.

The public does not choose lawyers with the dedication they bring to buying a car, and most have no idea what the average corporate general counsel does to find the right lawyer in a given locality for a special case or assignment.

When consumers can find the "right" lawyer who is experienced and knowledgeable, many complaints about lawyers will come to an end. But finding the "right" lawyer is difficult, even for attorneys, and it takes a substantial amount of time, effort, and sophistication. For non-lawyers it is a daunting task. The Web makes the process easy for the average person.

For example, my Web site is filled with substantive information about my practice and it is easy to use. If a visitor has a specific problem they would like us to consider, they can open "How to Become a Client" and provide me with a thumbnail sketch of the case. For those we cannot help, we provide a list of lawyers in their home state and recommend they read my article "How to Hire the Right Lawyer."

The Internet is a gigantic step forward in public information, and with its exponential growth I am hopeful that an increasingly sophisticated public will use the Internet to make better decisions about selecting lawyers.

With the explosive potential of the Internet in its infancy we are at the threshold of a new beginning in sharing information that will eclipse the printing press. I am thrilled to be a part of it and I want you to join me.

A rising tide raises all ships. Share yourself with the public and you raise not only your practice, but everyone's. Provide free information and helpful advice. It is a win-win situation. Thousands of people will find out who you are and what you do, and what is more, by providing needed information you can help people solve problems.

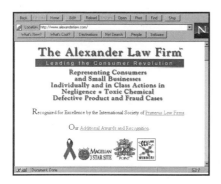

Dick Alexander's enthusiasm for the Internet is obvious. And he makes a point that is consistent with Internet culture: give stuff away for free and you will be repaid many-fold. For Dick, giving away free legal information on his Web site brings business to his firm. People go to his site because they can find information about consumer law. And if they happen to need legal help, who do you think they'll contact first?

In the future, then, the Internet will play a big part in making law available to the public. Fortunately, this doesn't mean that lawyers will be unnecessary. In fact, the public may have an even greater appetite for legal services once they're educated about the law. And if you're on the Net, you'll be able to feed that appetite.

LAWYERS

The Internet may also soon become the favored means of finding a lawyer. Today, people find lawyers through word-of-mouth, yellow pages ads, TV commercials and print ads. Although word-of-mouth may always be the most effective, the Internet beats it for raw, objective information. A Web page combined with the information in the directories provides a legal consumer with more information than can be provided in any other medium.

The Internet is quickly becoming the best resource for finding comprehensive lists of lawyers—not only in the United States, but throughout the world. Most of the MegaSites have extensive links to lawyers and law firms. A few of the sites have tried to generate revenue from this venture, charging lawyers to be listed at their site (e.g., LawInfo's site charges $180 yearly for a listing). But the trend is for MegaSites to list lawyers without charge, simply for the pride of publishing a comprehensive legal site.

The types of lists on the Internet vary greatly. For example, at Washburn Law School's site, the listing is organized by each state. Within each state you are provided with a list of lawyer Web sites, with hyperlinks to those sites. On the other hand, at the Web site for Martindale-Hubbell's Law Directory (*http://www.martindale.com*), you can search for lawyers listed in their publication, garnering about the same information you would from the hardcopy version of their publication. At West Publishing's Legal Directory (*http://www.wld.com*), you can search for names of lawyers, structuring your search by geography and practice area if you wish. And, with West's site, a basic listing is free (you can pay for a more extensive description), which means that West's site promises to become more comprehensive as time goes on.

Although many lawyers may remain skeptical about the Internet as a way for consumers to find them, attorney and Internet consultant Bruce Hake has an example of how it works:

> *A lawyer in Boston (Roy Watson) ordered a Web site from my company in March, but has not yet built it. However, we included him in our online index of immigration lawyers (http://ilw.com/ilwlist/). He was delighted to report to us in late June that he's already gotten a good client from that listing. The story of how that came about is an excellent illustration of how lawyer listings on the Internet can work. Some prospective clients seek lawyers on the basis of substantive expertise. But many also have a specific geographical target. This was a good example of both. The client was a computer professional in Switzerland who'd gotten a job offer in Boston. He went out on the Internet for the specific purpose of finding an immigration lawyer in Boston. He went to one of the big search engines and found Immigration Lawyers on the Web; went to the ILW "Firms" page; searched in the index for "Boston"; found Roy Watson's listing and hired him.*

In Chapter 7 of this book, we discuss in greater detail how a Web site can bring legal business to your electronic doorway. But it's even easier to get yourself listed in lawyer directories than creating a Web site. Once you're online, sign on to other legal directories and punch in your name. Remember, if you can't be found, you won't be hired!

LAW JOURNALS, PERIODICALS, AND LEGAL MEMORANDA

There are numerous law journals online—some contain full, searchable text of articles and others only include the table of contents and subscription information so that you can order a copy from them. For example, Washburn Law School's site (*http://lawlib.wuacc.edu/*

washlaw/lawjournal/lawjournal.html) contains a searchable listing of well over 100 journals. Their list shows which journals include the text of the articles and which only have a table of contents. Indiana Law School also has numerous law journals online at *http://www.law. indiana.edu/law/v-lib/journals.html*.

In addition to law journals, you can search more than 17,000 periodicals through a service known as Uncover (*http://www.carl.org/ uncover/*). Searching their database is free, and once you find the article you want you can get it free from your library, do a search on the Internet for it (try Alta Vista's advanced search engine), or order a copy from Uncover for a fee.

In addition to published material, more and more law firms' Web sites contain memos with substantive legal information. Most material online is newsletter-type articles or law review type material, not argumentative memos or briefs. But whatever the form, if the article is on the subject you need, it can be of great use. And because some of the sites have full-text searching capabilities, it shouldn't take long to find out if the site has a memo on the subject you need.

DICTIONARIES

Even before I started law school, I went out and bought the latest edition *of Black's Legal Dictionary*. I was entering a strange new world, and I wanted to understand the local dialect. Today, you can find much of this information online. I'm aware of at least one site with a legal dictionary, and I'm sure there are many more (check *http://www.lectlaw.com/ref.html*).

But sometimes lawyers need more than a legal dictionary to do the job, and this is where the Internet shines. Most lawyers may have copies of Black's and Webster's on their shelves, but they won't have much else.

R. Scott Carpenter, a public defender in Knoxville, Tennessee, told me how he used the Internet to help represent some of his clients:

PERSONAL ACCOUNT
R. Scott Carpenter
Assistant Public Defender
rscarp@usit.net

> *In discovery, the prosecutor of an alleged drug offense often produces an audiotape of the undercover agent talking among several persons. Words and phrases heard on such tapes are often unfamiliar to me. Street language and drug slang is common to many such cases and isn't ordinarily found in Webster's Dictionary. Two Web sites got me over the language barrier and increased my understanding of what was actually said on the audiotape. One*

site is called "Drug Related Street Terms/Slang Words." The other useful resource for me is a searchable index of definitions called "The RapDict: A Rap Dictionary."

Scott probably didn't have the "RapDict" at home, and probably never will. With the Internet, he was able to use these books without leaving his chair.

LOCATING PEOPLE

Because of a computer's ability to store and retrieve massive amounts of data, one of the best uses of the Internet is providing worldwide access to directories of people. Of course, those afraid of Orwellian consequences bemoan that it is becoming increasingly difficult to remain anonymous in this society. If you're one of them, you won't be happy to learn that your phone number and address may now be available to the world.

There are several "white pages" services on the Internet. Four 11 Corporation claims over 5.5 million listings (*http://www.four11.com*). Switchboard (*http://www.switchboard.com*) spins dirt in their face, claiming over *90 million names* with phone numbers and some email addresses. Using either of these sites is simple, requiring you to type in the information you know, even if it's only a first and last name. Be warned, however: unless the name is unusual, and unless you know a state and preferably a city, you will probably get so many hits that the results will be of little value.

For lawyers, of course, these services can be a godsend in locating witnesses, missing defendants, judgment debtors and the like. For example, in a recent case I worked on I needed to locate American witnesses who had recently left their jobs at a Russian hotel. Most had moved back to the States, but I didn't know where they had moved. With unusual names, I was often able to find the person without knowing where they lived in the United States. For more common names, if I knew the state they'd moved to, I could often narrow the list down to a few individuals. This type of searching would have either been impossible without the Internet, or I would have had to hire a private investigator. And best of all, it took only *minutes* and it was *free*.

PREPARING FOR ORAL ARGUMENTS

With its multimedia capabilities, the Internet can also deliver information that you can't get anywhere else. If you're privileged enough to have a case pending before the Supreme Court, you can hear what it's like to be questioned by the Justices. Go to the Oyez Web site (*http://oyez.at.nwu.edu/oyez.html*) and you can hear oral arguments from selected cases going back to 1961.

But the Internet has more mundane uses when preparing an oral argument. Public defender R. Scott Carpenter tells of how he used the Internet to prepare for a murder trial:

> *Preparing for the murder trial of a man who bludgeoned his wife, I found myself unable to conjure the words that best expressed to the jury the defendant's rage, which evolved during the mutually abusive relationship and ultimately resulted in the deadly assault. Using search tools called Alta Vista and Deja News, I searched both the Web and Usenet (newsgroups). I found a goldmine of language in the vein I could not articulate from my own experience. In online discussion groups, men talked about the emotion generated by psychological abuse. Such finds yielded concise explanations of why rage erupts, like "the hope instilled by expressions of love intensifies the sense of betrayal and confusion." At sites where psychologists write about the couples they counsel, I read their descriptions of "people who engage in a mutual dance of destruction."*

Like the Rap dictionary, these types of books are not the type Scott typically keeps on his shelf at home. But when he needs the resources, they are there at his fingertips, through the Internet. And, no printed source can duplicate the first-hand accounts that he found in the Internet discussion groups.

But how do you find all of this stuff? There are two primary methods: MegaSites and search engines.

HOW TO MAKE SENSE OF THE CHAOS—MEGASITES

I really don't know what to call this type of Web site. They are the best starting points for beginning your legal research. But to me, the prefix "mega" sounds *big*, and the content linked to these sites is *big*. So, at least in this book, they'll be referred to as "MegaSites."

PERSONAL ACCOUNT

Jeremy March
Deputy Legal Counsel for
the Southern California
Association of Governments
march@scag.ca.gov

California attorney Jeremy March gives you an idea of how using MegaSites has saved him time and money:

I have discovered a number of useful Web sites which contain word-searchable versions of the California and U.S. Codes and at least some of the materials which I could previously examine only at the County Law Library. My basic Internet law library now consists of the following Web sites:

1. *An up-to-date, word-searchable version of the California Codes, which is maintained online by the State Legislative Counsel at http://www. leginfo.ca.gov. This site is so easy to use that it should serve as a model for any other state (or administrative agency) seeking to put its laws or regulations online.*

2. *A searchable but somewhat less up-to-date version of the United States Code at http://www.thomas.loc.gov. This site also has word-searchable versions of bills being heard by the United States Congress.*

These two Web sites have virtually eliminated my need to pay for Lexis and Westlaw searches.

3. *The GPO (Government Printing Office) Gate site maintained by the University of San Diego at http://ssdc.ucsd.edu/gpo. Among other things, this site has word-searchable versions of all issues of the Federal Register (a daily regulatory bulletin published by the U.S. government) for the last three years, and a searchable version of the Congressional Record. This site has enabled me to cancel my subscription to the Federal Register.*

4. *Various other legal resources (such as law review articles) can be found on the USC Law Index site maintained by the University of Southern California (http://www.usc.edu/dept/law-lib/index.html), the 'Lectric Law Library site (http://www.lectlaw.com) and the Electronic Library (http://www.elibrary.com). The Electronic Library, which is a pay service (but offers a free trial), also has a wealth of books, magazine and newspaper articles, photographs, and other documents online dealing with a great many non-legal subjects.*

5. *The Alta Vista search engine (http://www.altavista.digital.com), which is used to conduct word searches through the entire World Wide Web, sometimes leads me to a Web site containing or discussing a specific legal source (such as a section of the Code of Federal Regulations) which I may need.*

FIGURE 5-2
http://law.house.gov/

Jeremy's list of MegaSites is decidedly weighted toward California law, which makes sense for his position as Deputy Legal Counsel for the Southern California Association of Governments. Once you start researching on the Web, you'll develop your favorite MegaSite and use it for most of your research.

Following I'll list some of my favorite legal MegaSites. You will find others once you start surfing the Net. But these sites will get you going and give you a quick idea of what's available for the Net researcher.

Before we go to the list, let's take a brief look at a couple of MegaSites to give you an idea of what they look like. First, we'll look at the home page for the House of Representatives Internet Law Library (see Figure 5-2).

With this government-funded site, you don't get blown away by a slew of pretty graphics, which sends the clear message that the site is all business.

Let's say you want to search the Code of Federal Regulations. With a mouse click on "U.S. Federal Laws," you reach the page shown in Figure 5-3.

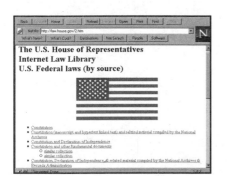

FIGURE 5-3
http://law.house.
gov/2.htm

Scrolling down, you find the Code of Federal Regulations. With another mouse click, you reach another page, and with one more link, you reach this page that allows you to search the CFR:

Now you can search the entire CFR from your desktop. Unless you keep a wall of CFRs in your office, or have paid (handsomely) for a CD-ROM containing the CFR, there simply is no quicker way to do this kind of research.

Let's assume you don't need to find something in CFR; instead, you want to check out your opposition in a new case you recently filed in Minneapolis claiming design defects in a locally manufactured concrete product. You don't know if the lawyer is fresh out of law school or a 70-year-old curmudgeon. And what is his specialty? Does he know anything about construction law, or are you going to be able to bowl him over when you start talking about the inherent defects in his client's pretensioned concrete beams?

One quick way to get your answers is to go to the Web. A good site for this task is the Web site for Washburn University's School of Law. WashLaw's home page looks like the page shown in Figure 5-4.

With a click on the "Law Firms" button, you reach the page shown in Figure 5-5.

Another click, and you get a listing of the lawyers in Minnesota with Web sites. The first page is shown in Figure 5-6.

Once you find the name of the lawyer's law firm, a hyperlink will instantly connect you to his Web site. At that Web site, you'll probably find a picture of him, learn his age, find out where he went to school and if he graduated with honors, and whether he practices construction law. In a couple of minutes, you know a lot about your opposition.

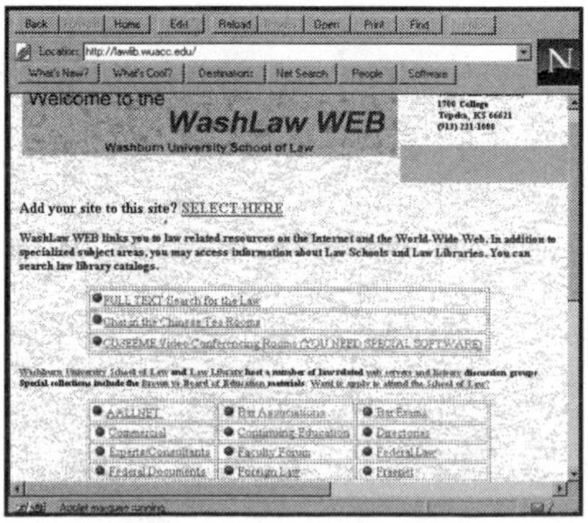

FIGURE 5-4
http://lawlib.wuacc.edu/

FIGURE 5-5
http://lawlib.wuacc.edu/
washlaw/lawfirms.html

Now that you have a taste of how you can find information with a MegaSite, I'll list a dozen or so of them that have become bookmarks in my browser. Because there are so many, I've arbitrarily separated them into the categories of Government, School, and Private MegaSites.

U.S. GOVERNMENT RESOURCES

The House of Representatives
http://law.house.gov/

The U.S. House of Representatives Internet Law Library is rightfully known as one of the most comprehensive legal sites on the Internet. There is a refreshing lack of graphics so your old modem won't be clogged by useless information. Its extensive collection ranges from international law to legal profession directories. And not only does it reference federal laws, but it also connects to the laws of all states and some territories. Federal laws are arranged by both published source and by agency, so you should be able to find your way around the site. The site, which claims 1,600 links to law resources on the Internet, is one of the best sites for the legal researcher.

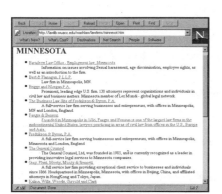

FIGURE 5-6
http://lawlib.wuacc.edu/washlaw/
lawfirms/minnesot.htm

**Government
Printing Office**
*http://www.access.gpo.
gov/index.html*

An excellent resource for information from the executive and legislative branches of the government. You can full-text search a long list of documents churned out by federal agencies, such as the Federal Register and Comptroller General Decisions. If you're looking for federal documents, this may be your best shot. If you know what you want, you can go directly to the Superintendent of Document's home page at *http://www.access.gpo.gov/su_docs.*

The Library of Congress
http://lcweb.loc.gov/

The Library of Congress Web site is not to be confused with the House's site. And one look will make sure the confusion doesn't last: although the site duplicates some of the services of the House site, it has just as many graphics as most commercial sites, making it slower to load if your modem is "speed-challenged." It also doesn't have the House's extensive library, making it not as useful for the legal researcher. But one of its interesting features is the ability to see the text of bills and other legislative materials, sometimes within hours of their release in Washington.

United States Congress
http://thomas.loc.gov

This site is actually a link to the Library of Congress home page, but, is also a standalone site. The site is maintained by the U.S. Congress, and is an excellent resource for legislative activities. You can find the Congressional Record, Committee Information, and copies of historical documents. You can even access an article about how sausage (I mean, law) is made.

LAW SCHOOLS

**Washburn University
Law School**
http://lawlib.wuacc.edu/

"WashLaw" is one of my favorite sites because it is so comprehensive. It has links to about anything you'd want, including experts, federal resources, bar associations, law journals, and a comprehensive, state-by-state list of law firms and lawyers which are hyperlinked to their Web sites. In addition to its comprehensive group of links, it now has chat rooms about numerous legal subjects. Showing that it is keeping ahead of the curve, the site also has conference rooms for the video conferencing technology CU-SeeMe (the site has links for downloading the necessary software, although you'll still need the right hardware).

**Cornell University
Law School**
http://www.law.cornell.edu/

This site is also known as the Legal Information Institute, or LII, at Cornell. Like WashLaw, it's one of the most comprehensive legal sites on the Internet and includes links to many other MegaSites as well. It also has a hypertext version of the U.S. Code, which can be very useful for quickly digesting complicated statutes. The material is organized by either legal topic or by source.

Indiana University Law School

http://www.law.indiana. edu/law/v-lib/lawindex. html

The Indiana Law School site maintains what is called the World Wide Web Virtual Law Library. Like other similar sites, information is organized by either "Legal Information by Topic" (e.g., administrative law) or "Legal Information by Organization Type" (e.g., law journals). The site is down-to-business and light on graphics, but heavy on substance.

Villanova Center for Information Law and Policy.

http://www.law.vill.edu/

This Web site, sponsored by the Villanova University School of Law, is another comprehensive site with the standard links of a MegaSite. Even if it doesn't become your primary MegaSite, it has some unique connections that make it worthy of a bookmark.

Emory University Law School

http://www.law.emory. edu/

This site is home of the "Emory Law Finder." Being heavy on the graphics, you may need to avoid the site unless you have a fast modem or tell your browser to turn off the graphics. It has many of the same resources as the other sites, but unless you know exactly where you're going, you may have to go through several pages to get there.

University of Chicago Law School

http://www-law.lib. uchicago.edu/lib/

This is a more limited site than the others, but has enough to keep you busy. It also has some useful tools that I haven't seen on other sites, so it may be worth visiting if you can't find it elsewhere. For example, it has a section of links to citation guides—both for the Internet and traditional legal sources, including a copy of the Bluebook. Also, it's the home of Lyonette Louis-Jacques' Law List, a comprehensive list of legal mailing lists on the Net.

PRIVATE SECTOR

Heiros Gamos

http://www.hg.org/

What I like about this site is that it knows the practice of law is more than legal issues, although it's not the best site for traditional legal research. Its home page claims that it is "the largest and only comprehensive legal site with over 12,000 original pages and more than 10,000 links." HG also has unique user-modifiable databases for meetings, publications, employment, law firms, experts, court reporters, ADR professionals, private investigators, and process servers. The references will be kept up-to-date by software that automatically and regularly emails the listed entity to confirm the listing. The site is sponsored by Lex Mundi, a worldwide association of law firms.

FindLaw

http://www.findlaw.com

FindLaw's site is recognized as one of the best overall research sites on the Internet. Its main feature is a set of extensive links to other Net resources, which can be searched by topic or keyword. You can also access its law-limited search engine, LawCrawler.

LegalEthics
*http://www.legalethics.
com/pa/main.html*

If you're looking for information on legal ethics, this is one of the best places to go. In addition, the site has the Practicing Attorney's Home Page, which has links to just about everything. It divides Internet legal resources into fifteen primary categories.

**Law Links From
Counsel Connect**
*http://www.counsel.com/
lawlinks/lawlinks.html*

This site is sponsored by Counsel Connect, a private network of lawyers. Under their legal button there is a nice subject-matter index that provides links to other sites. Links to caselaw and statutes are found under the "Government" button, while the "Library" button will get you to other MegaSites.

'Lectric Law Library
http://www.lectlaw.com/.

You'll either love or hate this site. The 'Lectric Law Library takes an irreverent approach to providing you with legal information, far from the "just the facts, ma'am" approach of some of the university sites. To use the site, you have to take a tour with "Ralf, the Library's Head Librarian as well as its renowned Legal Scholar in Residence." If you want a large resource where you can quickly get your work done, this is not your site. But if you occasionally want a little fun doing your research, you *may* enjoy Ralf's humor.

LawInfo
http://www.lawinfo.com

The stated purpose of the site is "To provide the public free access to quality legal representation, services and information," and to "provide attorneys, legal industry suppliers and consultants a high-tech medium to increase and improve their client base." It has a CLE service that can be accessed through free audio software linked to the site. Its attorney referral service is a work-in-progress, and its listings are slim outside of California. The reason may be that it costs to have a reference at their site. With free law firm listings at sites

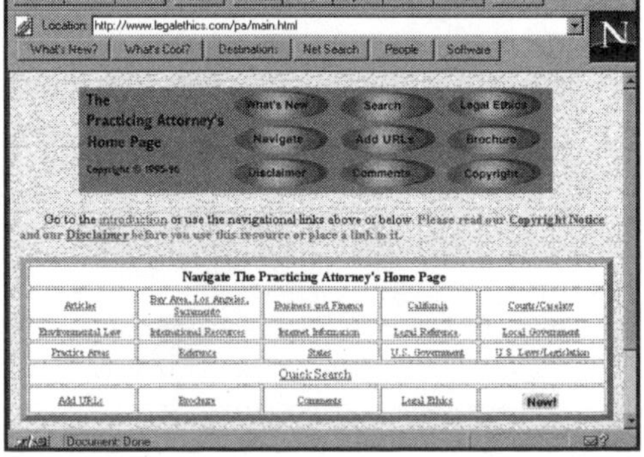

FIGURE 5-7
*The 'Lectric Law
Library site...an
irreverent approach—
http://www.lectlaw.com/*

FIGURE 5-8
Surfing Lawyer Website (http://www. netlegal.com)

like WashLaw and Heiros Gamos, it remains to be seen if lawyers will pay for Internet listings. More unique to its site are the attorney job listings and a place to post your own résumé if you're in the market for a new legal job.

Law Journal EXTRA!
http://www.ljx.com

The site is recognized as one of the best legal news sites on the Web, which is understandable because it's published by the publisher of the National Law Journal. In addition to legal news, it has a wide collection of federal and state law resources for lawyers. It even has a database of reported verdicts and settlements. Its simple and low-tech home page belies that it is a very diverse site.

LawMarks
http://www.cclabs.missouri. edu/~tbrown/lawmarks

This is a comprehensive legal-link site, but it can be slow loading because of the graphics. In its "Court Opinions" page, it has search engines, including one for natural language searches. It's generally a well-organized site.

Surfing Lawyer Website
http://www.netlegal.com

For Canadian lawyers, this may be your favorite Web site. Recently launched, the site claims to be Canada's most comprehensive legal site, featuring links to sites of interest for Canadian lawyers and the general public.

USING SEARCH ENGINES AND DIRECTORIES

Anyone who has used Westlaw or Lexis is familiar with search engines and how they work. But we all know that even with these commercial resources, you can get a lot of garbage in a search. On the Internet, it can be even worse because there is so much useless information available. In a small survey of lawyers conducted in the fall of 1995, Lex Mundi's Steve McGarry asked for the ways lawyers would improve the information on the Internet. The top suggestion was improving the Net's search capabilities.

I have a feeling that since the fall of 1995 things have improved somewhat and are continuing to improve every year and every month. For example, more and more search engines and directories can limit their search to legal sites on the Net. But it still takes practice to get good results with a Net search.

Even though the search engines aren't perfect tools (and never will be), you'll miss a lot of information on the Net without using them. Lawyer John A. Maxwell, Jr., who practices in Yakima, Washington, urges all lawyers to learn to use the search engines:

> Learn to use the search engines on the Net to find things. There is too much data to rely on hierarchical directories. As a result you need to be able to use the tools to find Web pages containing the specific information you seek. Enter: the search engine. This is a robot program that goes out 24 hours a day on the Web and reads the content of Web sites, digests it, and indexes and stores the indexed information on the search engine's database. When you go to the Web page for the search engine and type your search terms, it spits out lists of Web sites that contain the terms for which you are searching. There are a large number of search engines; some are better than others and all use different search patterns and criteria. You should find and use the search engine that works best for you, and this process takes some time.

As we discussed in Chapter 3, there is a distinction between search engines and directories (or Web robots). But the distinction between the two is blurring as they each incorporate aspects of the other. For simplicity, I'll call them all search engines, as their purpose is to find information. The key is experimenting with the various types offered to find the one you like the best.

The practical uses of search engines are great, and go beyond getting the things you could find at a legal MegaSite. For example, Knoxville public defender R. Scott Carpenter found just what he needed with a search engine to prepare the defense of one of his clients:

> In a case where my client, a juvenile African-American male who grew up in and around the projects, had a defense of self-defense, I was searching for ways to demonstrate the heightened sense of danger with which persons like my client live. In my jurisdiction, middle-class whites invariably make up

the majority of one's jury. Prosecutors always argue that carrying a gun proves premeditation to kill the deceased. How could I most corroborate my young defendant who would testify he carried a gun for protection? He could name over a dozen of his contemporaries who were dead from gunfights. I went to the National Archive of Criminal Justice Data site, and ran a search of the database using the words "urban," "homicide," "African-American."

Jackpot! I found the Bureau of Justice Statistics' study from December 1994 entitled "Young Black Male Victims" which found that black males ages 12 to 24 were almost 14 times as likely to be homicide victims as were members of the general population. This documentary proof solidified the defendant's testimonial claims that he experienced a heightened and reasonable fear that he was in danger.

Whenever I do a Net search, one thing that always amazes me is the amount of information out there in cyberspace. This hard-to-conceive gob of information demonstrates why it is so important to frame a good search. For example, let's say you're giving a speech to a group of business people next week. All of them have worked with lawyers, and so they appreciate a good lawyer joke, especially from a lawyer. You remember parts of one joke about a lawyer at the gates of hell, but you can't remember the rest of it.

So it's time for a search. At the Alta Vista Advanced Search page:

- You type in the word "lawyers." In seconds, Alta Vista has "about 20,000" sites for you to look at. I think you'd better try again.

- Now you search for "lawyers near jokes." A few seconds later, you have links to 121 hits. Still too many. So try: "lawyers near jokes and devil." Bingo. Four hits. A little reading and you find the joke you wanted at the second site.

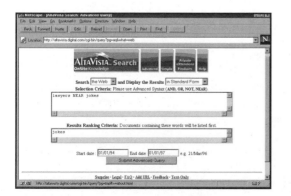

FIGURE 5-9

http://altavista. digital.com/cgi-bin/query?pg= aq&what=web

PERSONAL ACCOUNT

Ian Dearden
Australian defense attorney
idearden@gil.ipswichcity.
qld.gov.au

Of course, searches can deliver information more useful than tired lawyer jokes. In fact, the search engines can save the day. Ian Dearden, an Australian defense lawyer and the President of the Queensland Council for Civil Liberties (modeled on the ACLU), wrote me with the following story about how Net search engines delivered the information he needed faster than any other resource:

> For some three or four years we have had an ongoing scandal in Queensland about the treatment of prisoners in watch-houses. These are police cells designed for overnight stays, but because of enormous pressures on prison beds numbers in recent years, they have been used as quasi-prisons, for which they are not equipped.
>
> At 10 P.M. one evening, I sat down to write a speech that I had to deliver the next morning at an important public seminar looking at this problem. I was aware that the conditions in these watch-houses breached international agreements on prisoners' rights, but where could I find the exact details? What were the instruments? What did they say? And how was I going to do this with no time to research (as usual)?!!
>
> Into Netscape I delved, onto Netseek (or some similar such search engine), in with the words "prisoners" and "rights," and although it was not easy, and I followed many links before I got there, I did eventually end up (after an hour) at the University of Minnesota Human Rights Library, and there I found all the United Nations documents on the rights of prisoners, setting out chapter and verse. A few clicks, the relevant parts were inserted in the speech, the full texts were included as supporting material, and the document eagerly perused by the participants in the seminar. The speech was a success, and I actually sounded like I knew what I was talking about.
>
> Once again, the Internet comes up trumps. All for the price of a phone call, and $Aus1.00 per hour. I wouldn't be without it for quids!!!

Ian searched for Web sites and found the exact one he needed for his speech. But sometimes you don't want to find information about some*thing*, but you want to find information about some*one*.

This is where the Internet glows (and may scare those of you afraid of Big Brother). With search engines, you can find virtually everything that anyone has said publicly on the Internet. Note, I said "publicly," and not what you've said in private emails.

For example, let's say that your opposition in a litigated case has hired a little-known professor from a West Coast university to be its expert witness. You can't find anything she has written in the printed media. Several search engines, including Alta Vista, will look through the postings of mailing lists and newsgroups for any name that you give it. Run the searches, and you'll find out what this expert has said. It may be garbage, but if she has said anything relevant, it may do wonders for your cross-examination of that expert. Today, this tool is very useful for finding information about experts in technical fields who are more likely to be on the Internet. And as more and more people join mailing lists, it will have even greater effectiveness in finding out what experts *really* believe.

Search engines can similarly be used to find out what a witness, juror, or another lawyer has said before. A juror's postings in a gardening mailing list may not say much directly about how they'll vote in your case, but it may be very important in deciding whether that person fits the juror profile you want for your case.

You may think this type of searching is a little too personal and may be an invasion of privacy. But people on the Net *should* understand that what they say is public information. And you can bet the other side is looking for the same information. (It's a warning to be careful about what *you* say in any mailing list or newsgroup).

I'll now list a few of the popular search engines. You don't really need the list if you use one of the more popular browsers. For instance, Netscape Navigator has a "Search" button that automatically links you to a number of search engines. That's the easiest way to become familiar with the various search engines available on the Net. And once you try a few, you'll quickly find your favorites and create a bookmark for a direct connection to them.

Here now is a quick overview of some of the search engines most useful for the legal professional:

Lycos
http://www.lycos.com/
or http://lycos.cs.cmu.edu

Lycos, named after a spider, is a popular search engine based at Carnegie Mellon University. It has an index with a search engine which crawls through the Web looking for documents to add to its index. It searches document titles, headings, links, and keywords, and returns the first 50 words of each page it indexes for your search.

Alta Vista
http://altavista.digital.com

Alta Vista creates a searchable database and has several different versions available at its home site. One of my favorite search engines is the Alta Vista "Advanced Search," which allows a more sophisticated boolean search than its regular search engine cousin.

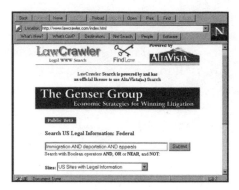

FIGURE **5-10**

Yahoo
http://www.yahoo.com/

Yahoo features a hierarchically organized subject tree of information resources and is very popular. You can narrow the search by looking only for law resources at *http://www.yahoo.com/Government/Law/* or for government resources at *http://www.yahoo.com/Government/*.

Law Crawler
http://www.findlaw.com/search/lawcrawler.html or *http://www.lawcrawler.com*

Law Crawler limits your search to sites that contain legal information. You can also limit the search to specific servers, such as those located in certain countries or operated by certain government agencies. You can search just law reviews at the Law Review Search page *(http://www.findlaw.com/lawreviews/)*.

DejaNews
http://www.dejanews.com/

DejaNews is a keyword-searchable Web archive of Usenet newsgroup messages which is useful to see if a witness, juror, or expert has said anything in a Usenet newsgroup.

Excite
http://www.excite.com

Excite currently contains searches of 1.5 million Web pages and two weeks of Usenet news articles and classified ads, as well as links to current news, weather, and more. It presents results with a detailed summary to provide you with an annotated selection.

Liszt
http://www.liszt.com

Liszt claims to search the world's largest directory of mailing lists (54,704 lists from 1,812 sites).

There are many other search engines on the Net. If you want to see the various search engines available, visit Search.Com (*http://www.search.com*), where you can conduct a search with any of ten different search engines or narrow your search to a certain subject matter. Or at All in One (*http://www.albany.net/allinone/all1www.html#WWW*), you can access more than fifty different search engines on one page. With MetaCrawler (*http://www.metacrawler.com*) you can simultaneously use nine leading engines with search-combined results ranked by their perceived usefulness. And more specific to federal legal resources, you can go to the "Meta-Index for Legal Research" (*http://gsulaw.gsu.adv/metaindex*) where you can search a number of databases containing federal circuit judicial opinions, federal legislation, federal regulations, and other legal resources.

OTHER USEFUL SITES

The following two sites aren't really MegaSites, but deserve a mention because of their content and usefulness to practicing attorneys.

Law Lists
http://www.lib.uchicago. edu/~llou/lawlists/info. html

This site is maintained and updated by Lyonette Louis-Jacques at the University of Chicago. It is recognized as *the* comprehensive list of law-related discussion groups. For most lists there is a short description of what the group covers, so it's a good place to go when you're ready to join some discussion groups. And it beats any printed list of discussion groups, because the Internet version is the most up-to-date that you'll find.

The Legal List
http://www.lcp.com/

This famous list was created and maintained by Erik Heels. It aims to list every law-related Internet resource there is. When the project was started, it probably wasn't that formidable of a task, but by now it's an overwhelming project. The future of the list, however, is in doubt. In June of 1996, Heels announced that he would be making no more additions to the list because of a change in employment. But because of its popularity, I hope someone continues to carry the torch.

Well, there you have a list of sites that will get you going in your research. Over time, you'll become familiar with a few sites that will become your favorites for legal research.

Now that you've found what you're looking for, how to use it?

THE DEVIL IS IN THE DETAILS—CITING INTERNET SOURCES

Although so many resources are on the Internet, how are you going to cite them in your legal briefs? This is particularly a problem for citing caselaw, since West Publishing aggressively protects its copyrighted page numbering system used by most citation formats.

Attorney John Maxwell, Jr., explains this problem with Internet research:

Currently one of the biggest problems with doing caselaw research on the Net is the citation system. The legal publisher West owns the West Citation System. That means that for most cases you still have to go to the library and write down the citation. In the rare instance where you are citing to a case fresh off the press and use the actual docket number, this is not a problem because West hasn't assigned a volume and page for the citation either.

The solution to this problem is a uniform system of citations. The easiest beginning step in this process is for a judge writing an opinion to sequentially number all paragraphs of the opinion. The parties to the case can sufficiently distinguish the case from other cases cited by referring to: (1) the case name, (2) the original docket number, and (3) the paragraph of the case to which you are referring.

John Maxwell isn't the only attorney concerned with the new world order of electronic research. In August of 1995, the American Bar Association appointed a committee to study the issue. The committee issued its report in May, and in August of 1996 the ABA endorsed the report. Canada has already adopted a system similar to that recommended by the ABA committee.

In summary, the ABA recommended that the American courts adopt a court citation system that is equally applicable to print or electronic media. The ABA's committee, known as the ABA Special Committee on Citation Issues, in its May 23, 1996, report stated at paragraph 17:

It is clear that citation methods which are satisfactory for printed reports are not well suited to electronic databases and reporters. The volume and page numbers which describe very naturally where material can be located in printed reports are not meaningful or convenient to apply to computer files, which are far more easily indexed sequentially as they are released. In addition, requiring electronic reports to use the page numbers from printed reports is impractical since those page numbers are not available until quite some time after the electronic report is published. The adoption of a new citation method is essential to allow electronic publication of case reports to reach its full potential.

The recommended new citation system first states the following: the name of the case, the year, a unique court designator, the sequential number of the case for that year (assigned by the court), all ending with the paragraph number of the specific reference in the case. For example, the committee gave the example of a Fifth Circuit case that would be cited as follows:

Smith v. Jones, 1996 5Cir 15, ¶ 18

Or a case from the U.S. District Court for the Southern District of New York would look like:

Smith v. Jones, 1996 SDNY 15, ¶ 18

The only thing needed to make this system work is for the courts to assign paragraph numbers to each paragraph of their opinions. Once this is done for new cases, then the citation to a case will look the same, whether it came off the Internet or from a West Reporter.

But this does not mean the end of printed case reports—at least not yet. The biggest battle was whether the existing citation system would be required as a parallel citation. The ABA Committee recommended that the existing citation system be *encouraged* as a parallel citation, but that it not be mandatory. Others argued strenuously for *mandatory* parallel citation. However, even if the parallel citation is mandatory, there will be no need to reference any page other than the first page in the printed reporter, as the paragraph system will work for both electronic and paper forms of the case.

Because the ABA's action is only a recommendation, the federal court system and each state's court system must adopt the new citation format before it can be used. Hopefully, the courts will act quickly to implement the recommendations.

Because things are rapidly changing, if you need the latest information about the status of citing Net resources you may want to monitor a few pages that address the issue. For example, the site *http://law.wuacc.edu/aallnet/aall.citation.html* contains links to proposals of the American Association of Law Libraries and the ABA, along with a User Guide to the AALL proposal. A very good explanation of suggested citation format for online law journals can be found at *http://www.urich.edu/~jolt/e-journals/citation_proposal.html*. For citation formats for non-legal sources, check out *http://www.pitsco.com/pitsco/cite.html* and *http://www.cas.usf.edu/english/walker/mla.html*. Finally, Professor Lyonette Louis-Jacques of the University of Chicago Law School has written a nice summary of legal research on the Internet, which can be found online at *http://www.lib.uchicago.edu/~llou/mpoctalk.html*.

Using the Internet in Your Law Practice

6

When most lawyers first learn about the Net, they think of two things: legal research and email. But the Internet has more to offer the legal professional. In this chapter, we'll explore places on the Net where professionals and the public gather, go to school, and exchange ideas.

▶ Discussion Groups—Luncheons Without the Calories

▶ Online CLE Courses (Bring Your Own Stale Donuts)

▶ (Informal) Discovery

▶ Getting That New Job

DISCUSSION GROUPS— LUNCHEONS WITHOUT THE CALORIES

In towns and cities across the country, lawyers get together over lunch for informal talk about their cases and new legal developments. Networking and legal discussion occur at these meetings, but fewer and fewer lawyers can take two hours out of their workday to sit around and chat with their colleagues.

Although not as personal, the Internet allows the same discussions to take place at your convenience. And in these group discussions, the participants aren't limited to those within driving distance of the restaurant. Instead, they're populated by people from around the world, often resulting in sophisticated discussions among the top lawyers in a particular area of law. Today, in this time-pressed world, the Internet is becoming the place where lawyers network, debate legal issues, and share ideas.

As we discussed in Chapter 3, the discussion groups cover subject matter from aromatherapy to bizarre sexual topics. Lawyers (supposedly) will be more interested in more mundane groups covering subjects ranging from administrative Law to Wyoming attorneys.

It is in these discussion groups that the free sharing of ideas reaches its pinnacle. Judge Dalzell, in holding the Communications Decency Act unconstitutional, said that "the Internet may fairly be regarded as a never-ending worldwide conversation. The government may not, through the CDA, interrupt that conversation. As the most participatory form of mass speech yet developed, the Internet deserves the highest protection from governmental intrusion."

As we discussed earlier, on the Internet this "most participatory form of mass speech yet developed" comes in several basic flavors: mailing lists, newsgroups, and real-time communications. In this chapter, we'll learn more about each of them and see how legal professionals use them in their law practices.

MAILING LISTS

Mailing lists, also commonly called "listservs," are nothing more than a formalized group mailing of email messages. Once you subscribe to a group, everything you send to a common email address is routed to everyone else on the list, and you get postings from everyone else.

FIGURE **6-1**
*The CompLaw site is a
good source for internet
and intellectual property
links*
http://complaw.con/

Florida intellectual property attorney Samuel Lewis, who runs a mailing list about computer law, explains what they are and the various forms they take:

> *To begin with, it should be explained that "listserv" is really not the correct name for what we're talking about. More appropriately, it is a distribution list or mailing list (since it redistributes email to every address on a list). Listserv is the name of mailing list server software created by L-Soft. In reality, there are many different list manager programs, with names like Listserv, Listproc, Majordomo, Almanac, and SmartList. While these programs have their differences, they all do essentially the same things: they allow users to join or remove themselves from lists, and they redistribute mail to everyone who subscribes to a particular list.*

PERSONAL ACCOUNT
Samuel Lewis
Romanik Lavin Huss & Paoli
http://Complaw.com
slewis@CompLaw.com

Thus, an email posted to a mailing list will be seen by everyone else subscribed to that list, whether it be ten people or ten thousand. Typically, a comment posted by one subscriber will snowball into a full-scale debate, or a question will prompt a dozen answers. Samuel Lewis explains the advantages of a mailing list compared to a Web site:

> *While Web sites can provide information, they generally tend to be static. They are great for providing information, but very poor when it comes to the sharing of ideas. This is where mailing lists shine. A person can express a particular point of view, and as soon as someone subscribed to the mailing list receives it, he or she can reply. Thus what you end up with is something similar to a party line, except that all of the comments end up in your email inbox. An unimaginable number of debates have taken place through email over the Internet.*

Joining a mailing list is the epitome of convenience. Simply send an email with the required keywords (usually "subscribe" or "unsubscribe") to a certain address, and your request is automatically handled by the software. For most mailing lists, you can receive the postings as separate email messages or in digest form, where an entire day's (or week's) worth of postings are combined into one email. Some lists also let you "suspend" your subscription while you're away on vacation and pick up your messages when you return.

Despite all this, lawyers seem to be slow in discovering the usefulness of mailing lists. In a survey of lawyers conducted in the fall of 1995, Lex Mundi's Steve McGarry found that fewer than 7 percent of lawyers use the Internet *primarily* for discussion groups. Maybe this isn't surprising, given the high degree to which lawyers use the Net for email and research. But because mailing lists are a great way to keep up on the law and to network with other lawyers, I'd expect to see more lawyers on mailing lists.

.PERSONAL ACCOUNT
Bob Cumbow
Perkins Coie
http://www.perkinscoie.com/
cumbr@perkinscoie.com

Bob Cumbow is on several lists and finds them especially useful in his law practice, which includes legal issues pertaining to the Internet:

> *There isn't a day that passes in which I don't get a piece of some lively discussion or useful information [from a mailing list] that benefits my overall understanding of the Internet, how law applies to it, and how to advise my clients. In addition, I am always the first to know when a major, long-awaited, or controversial decision is handed down.*

PERSONAL ACCOUNT
M. Sean Fosmire
Andrews, Fosmire, Solka & Stenton, P.C.
http://www.afss.com
fosmire@up.net

And the lists aren't just for the passive consumption of information. If you want to find something quickly, post a question to the appropriate list and you may have an answer in minutes. M. Sean Fosmire, of Michigan's Andrews, Fosmire, Solka & Stenton, P.C., relays this experience:

> *While writing an article on a federal statute in the health care area, I came across a reference to regulations which had been published for comment in 1994, and which had experienced some delay in being finally enacted. The article needed to include the updated information about the status of these regulations. I posted a message to a health law list (one of several excellent lists managed by the Washburn University Law School of Topeka, Kansas), and within thirty minutes I had a response informing me that the regulations had finally been effective on the previous September 29, and even providing a citation to the page in the Federal Register where that had been announced. Finding this information on my own would have taken at least a few hours of research.*

And because of their immediacy, Internet mailing lists are a great way to keep up on the status of pending legislation. Instead of relying on the normal channels for (stale) information, Colorado lawyer Joseph Hodges, Jr., finds up-to-date information on mailing lists:

PERSONAL ACCOUNT
Joseph Hodges, Jr.
Solo practitioner
jghodges@usa.net

Another recent experience involves some pending legislation in Congress. There are three bills currently pending that would exempt charitable gift annuities from the federal antitrust and securities laws. These bills are of vital interest to all of our charitable and donor clients, and a massive letter-writing and emailing campaign in support of the same is currently underway. Were it not for my ability to tap into various listservs so I can receive copies of all the emails that are circulating around the Internet about the progress of these bills, and where and to whom we should write about the same, let alone the various Web sites where I have been able to look up the phone, fax, and email addresses of our elected representatives, I would be either totally in the dark or at the mercy of the information my clients are receiving about all of this. Instead, thanks to the Internet, I am able to stay so up to date on all of this that my existing clients are even encouring other potential clients to contact me for the latest on this subject. Also, not only can I bill my clients for this work, but I can leverage the same work among several clients and, thereby, bill each client a bargain price for essentially the same information without doing serious damage to my overall net revenue line.

Mailing lists can also give you access to the nation's experts in a particular field of law. This is especially useful when you need help with a difficult legal issue. Even a large law firm of hundreds of lawyers probably only has, at most, a dozen lawyers in each legal specialty. A particularly thorny legal problem may not have been faced by any of them, leaving you to figure it out on your own. But on a mailing list, you may have hundreds—or even thousands—of lawyers in your specialty, all waiting to show their expertise. Joseph G. Hodges, Jr., extols the virtues of mailing lists for second opinions in his solo practice:

Another good example takes place every day of the week. I subscribe to several listservs that carry email content that is relevant to my primary practice areas, which are probate and estate planning. Often in these fields of the practice you have a problem to solve for which there is no set answer or recent legislation that has not been interpreted yet. Were I in a big firm, I could just go down the hall and find someone else to discuss my ideas with. But, as a solo practitioner, I do not have such a resource available to me. However, what I do have is even better. By tapping into these listservs with

a posted email about my questions, I can solicit, and quickly receive, the col-
lective judgment of ten-fold the number of lawyers I would have available to
me in a large firm. Not only that, but this advice is available to me virtually
any time of the night or day, and it can even be obtained in the background
while I am busy working on other billable client matters.

Of course, you're not going to post questions exposing your client's
confidences or your work product. But often, all you need is someone out there who has faced your particular problem before and who
can save you hours of wheel-spinning by pointing you in the right direction. At worst, you won't get an answer to your posting, and then
at least you'll know that you're not the *only* lawyer who doesn't know
the answer to your question.

In addition to sharing knowledge, there is the *potential* for generating
business. I say potential, because the conventional wisdom is that
you don't get immediate business from joining a mailing list. But the
same can be said of any networking opportunity; the point is to get
your name out in front of other lawyers to get referrals in the future.

Lawyer Calvin House received a referral from a foreign firm based on his
participation in a discussion group:

One day I found a message from a British firm asking for help in checking
the status of a lawsuit. The firm accepted our offer to do it for the cost of
having our attorney service check the court file. We made no money, but de-
veloped a contact that may lead to business.

It didn't immediately help Calvin's bottom line, but it may have an effect in the future. His experience isn't any different than any other
networking opportunity that may take years to pay off.

And for those of you who simply can't fit any more commitments
into your busy calendar, joining a mailing list is perfect. It's not like
joining Rotary, where you must be at lunch every Tuesday or you're
taken off their membership list. Joining—and unjoining—a list can
be done in a matter of *seconds*.

So, how do you join a list? Begin by reading instructions. Don't worry,
they're short and sweet, but important. For example, when I joined
the popular mailing list *net-lawyers*, I sent only the following message:

```
To: listproc@lawlib.wuacc.edu
Subject: mailing list
From: jacobsen@brainerd.net

subscribe net-lawyers Paul Jacobsen.
```

And with a click of the mouse, I joined. Within a minute, a computer-generated reply message was in my mailbox, confirming my subscription and giving me details about the list. If I decide to quit the list, it's just as easy: I would send a message of "unsubscribe net-lawyers" to the same address. Note that both of these messages were sent to "listproc," which is really computer software at Washburn University, programmed to process requests. Humans are involved in the discussion, but they don't get involved in the subscription process unless there's a problem.

TIP

File these instructions away in a safe place. I have subscribed to listservs and ignored the instructions on how to unsubscribe. Weeks later I decided I really didn't want 40 pieces of email a day from this group and tried to unsubscribe, but because I was sending my request to the wrong address I couldn't get off the list. The only way to get rid of the unwanted messages was to tell my email program to filter them out and discard them automatically. This not an efficient way to deal with a problem that can be solved easily by following the simple instructions that come with the product.

Which list to join? Fortunately for lawyers, someone has created a list of lists. Professor Lyonette Louis-Jacques of the University of Chicago maintains a comprehensive list of mailing lists and newsgroups. And, of course, the list is available on the Net: *http://www.lib.uchicago.edu/~llou/lawlists/info.html* (browsable text) or *http://www.lib.uchicago.edu/cgi-bin/law-lists* (keyword search feature).

At these sites, you'll find how to join lists such as *net-lawyers* (Lawyers and the Internet), *int-law* (Foreign, Comparative, and International Law Librarians), *and new-list* (New Lists announcement list), in addition to hundreds of other law-related lists.

And if you don't want your email inbox cluttered with messages from people you don't know, you have another choice. You can check out "Big Ear" (*http://barratry.law.cornell.edu:5123/notify/buzz.html*), which listens to a variety of law-related listservs and newsgroups, and constructs a weekly cumulative listing of what is being discussed. Or you can search the archives of various mailing lists, which give you complete access to the ongoing debate over a course of months or years.

Cornell Law School's Legal Information Institute maintains an archive of law-related mailing lists in hypertext format at *http://www.law.cornell.edu/listservs*. If you're looking for a particular subject or what a particular person may have said in a mailing list, do an Advanced Alta Vista search for some keywords or the person's name.

If you join a list and think they're the best thing to hit the legal profession since the Law in a Nutshell book series, you might consider running a mailing list. If so, don't get dollar signs in your eyes over the possibilities—altruism is a better motivation. Samuel Lewis discusses why he's running a mailing list, how it's done, and why to do it (and not do it):

> You don't run a mailing list to make a profit; you run a mailing list because you want to provide a place for people to discuss and share ideas. Your reward is the satisfaction of seeing people use the list. If this isn't enough, then don't consider doing it; running a list is too difficult and too much work.

> If you can get past the notion that you're going to do a fair amount of work without ever seeing a dime, then you can consider the other, more technical problems related to running a mailing list. Once you've made the decision to run a mailing list, how do you get people to subscribe? Well, as much as it may violate netiquette, one way to let people know about your list is to advertise it on other mailing lists. This is a practice to be discouraged, and many people will likely flame you for doing this. There is a newsgroup dedicated to announcing new mailing lists; if you're going to advertise, this is perhaps the best place. When starting a list, it is always helpful if you have a handful of people who really want the list. You'd be amazed at how quickly word spreads if there is a mailing list dedicated to something obscure that people have been wanting to talk about (the subject matter could range from anagrams to rollerblades to classical music collections and anything in between).

> If you're really crazy, not only will you run a list, but you'll moderate it. The role of moderator varies from list to list. In some lists, the moderator reads all messages before they are approved for distribution to the list. Others do little more than help people unsubscribe when they can't remember how to get off the list. Most are somewhere in between. In many cases, it comes down to your own personality. While too much moderating may reduce the enthusiasm of the people participating in the discussion, too little can allow the debate to get out of hand, often reducing itself to base personal attacks. Or worse, with too little moderation, the list can become a tool for the spammers or for people who want to talk about things that have nothing to do with the purpose of your list.

While running a mailing list won't help your firm, joining or moderating can help make you a better lawyer. In the area of computer/Internet/intellectual property law (you could fill in any new or frequently changing area of law), it is extremely difficult to keep up with the latest opinions. With the mailing list, someone subscribed to the list is bound to announce that Georgia has a new Internet police law, or that the ProCD case was reversed on appeal. Simply by participating, you can get a real feel for trends and happenings in the law. And, of course, you'll have an opportunity to stand on the soapbox yourself, and try out your own arguments. Needless to say, someone will find the weakness in your argument, and without question, your arguments will be better for it.

I've run the CompLaw Mailing List (subscription address CompLaw-request@CompLaw.com, list address CompLaw@CompLaw.com) for a year. I've seen the list grow from eight subscribers to 45, 75, 125, and now to well over 500 subscribers. This may seem small, but for a list dealing with the limited range of subjects, it is sufficiently large for debates on many different topics (what's more, the list keeps growing).

At the very least, running a mailing list has helped me keep my finger on the pulse of an area of law which changes rapidly. Clearly, this was an extreme way to keep up with changes, and is not a way that I'd recommend to others (although merely subscribing to the list and lurking—only reading the messages rather than taking part in the debate—is a great way to keep up with the debates). Still, the satisfaction gained by knowing that I have created a small place in cyberspace where people can debate the issues relating to an area of law for which I have a passion has been reward enough to justify the work involved.

If you decide to ignore Sam's advice and think you want to run a list, you might check out a couple of books like *The Internet Unleashed* or O'Reilly & Associates' *Managing Internet Resources* for more detailed information.

NEWSGROUPS

Although similar in function to mailing lists, newsgroups (also called Usenet) work quite differently. Instead of messages emailed to every subscriber, postings are kept on a host computer. That computer distributes the postings to other computers, until thousands of computer servers contain the postings. You read the postings by accessing the server with newsreader software. Many popular browsers, like Netscape, have newsreader software built into them. All you need to do is open the software and enter the name of the newsgroup. If you don't know the name of the newsgroup you want, some newsreaders will get a list for you. But be warned: the list is *very* long, so it may take a while to download unless you've got something faster than a modem connection to the Net.

Newsgroups will have many of the same discussions found on mailing lists. And you can post to a newsgroup, just as you can post to a mailing list. But newsgroups have the reputation of being a little more wild and woolly than mailing lists—they're mailing lists with an attitude. I suspect this personality (defect?) is because no one has to "join" a newsgroup, making a visit seemingly more temporary and anonymous.

There are somewhere in excess of 16,000 newsgroups on the Internet with topics exceeding even the best (and most warped) of imaginations. Their popularity is clear; an estimated 100,000 messages are posted to newsgroups each *day*. That's a lot of people engaged in conversation through keyboards.

TIP

Okay, newsgroups are popular, but what's there for lawyers? Once again, Lyonette Louis-Jacques's Law List describes hundreds of law-related newsgroups. Check them out on the Net at *http://www.lib.uchicago.edu/~llou/lawlists/info.html* (browsable text) or *http://www.lib.uchicago.edu/cgi-bin/law-lists* (keyword search feature).

For clarification, I'd like to mention BBSs (Bulletin Board Systems) while we're talking about newsgroups. BBSs work similarly to newsgroups in that you post a message for someone else to read (that's why they're called bulletin boards). But BBSs are *not* the Internet. A particular BBS may be connected to the Net, but not necessarily. Usually, you access a BBS by instructing your modem to dial a particular phone number. The computer hosting the BBS answers your call.

BBSs are often used when greater security and more privacy is desired. But they can also be used for interactive discussions, just like a newsgroup.

Now that we have that straight, let's go to the Net stuff you see in the movies.

REAL-TIME COMMUNICATIONS

Both mailing lists and newsgroups allow you to read and post messages at your leisure. But if you like things to be even more interactive, you can engage in real-time communications on the Net. In electronic Chat rooms across the world, people can engage in printed dialog with others on the Net. Using Internet Relay Chat (IRC) two or more people can type messages to each other that almost immediately appear on the computer screens of everyone else in the Chat group (like Sandra Bullock in the movie "The Net"). It's like a telephone party line, with the conversations sometimes moderated by a human.

Washburn University School of Law sponsors a number of law-related Chat groups at *http://topeka.wuacc.edu/cgi-bin/chat* (also accessed through their home page). But the day I visited—at high noon, yet, not the middle of the night—I couldn't find a soul in any of the half-dozen groups I visited. There were a lot of day-old messages, such as, "hello, is anyone in here?" but that was about it. Maybe it's just going to take a while for the rooms to catch on, I don't know. But I suspect that most lawyers are interested in substance, not flash, and mailing lists deliver the substance just fine, thank you. (Then again, maybe it's because Washburn has called the rooms "Chinese Tea Rooms." I was reluctant to enter the Chat room at first, wondering what type of bizarre things it contained that I may not live to tell about).

Lawyers *will* be interested in the newest wave of interactive discussions on the Internet. You can now get software that allows you to engage in phone conversations over the Net. Now that doesn't seem too remarkable, until you think about the cost of connecting to a computer in Europe on the Net—*exactly* the same as it costs to connect to a computer in your own town. Thus, you can call your grandmother in Sweden for the cost of your Internet connect time, which may be only pennies an hour (instead of dollars a minute). Netscape Communications will include Cool Talk with its newest browser. Cool Talk is among a group of applications known as Internet Phones. The sound quality is not great but the cost of a long distance phone call when you use an I-phone—virtually nothing—is hard to beat.

Even more exciting is new technology that allows video conferencing over the Net. The phone companies have been promising mass-market teleconferencing for decades, but never delivered. Now the Internet is fulfilling the promise. Cornell University has developed technology known as CU-SeeMe, and sites on the Web have established video conferencing rooms to employ the technology. But for this technology, and to a lesser extent, the phone technology, you're going to need something faster than a phone-line modem connection to the Internet. As Internet access quickens and software improves, expect to see more of these technologies in use. CU-SeeMe software can be downloaded free from the Cornell site at *http://cu-seeme.cornell.edu/.*

Though CU-SeeMe software supports both voice and video, most business users shun the voice portion, using the software simply to get a video image while continuing to use the phone for voice. It's not the greatest video—a little jerky since it only sends a few frames a second. But the price is hard to beat: free.

MARKETING THROUGH DISCUSSION GROUPS

PERSONAL ACCOUNT
Bruce Hake
Immigration attorney
http://ilw.com/hake/
bruce@hake.com

Lawyers are discovering that discussion groups are an easy way to market their practices. Attorney Bruce Hake tells how he uses discussion groups as the primary means to market his immigration law practice:

> *Regarding my own practice, I've been finding clients on the Internet for about 18 months. I know one American lawyer who has generated over $500,000 in business in 18 months on the newsgroups. My own sporadic newsgroup postings always generate a significant number of inquiries, and a steady stream of good new clients. The combination of newsgroup postings plus my Web site is, I'm absolutely certain, the most cost-effective way I could possibly market my legal services. This is the only way I advertise: I'm not in the Yellow Pages, don't pay for an overpriced Martindale-Hubbell listing, and am not even in the business section of the local white pages telephone listings. All my clients come from word of mouth and from the Internet, and I have far more business than I can handle.*

PERSONAL ACCOUNT
Calvin House
Gutierrez & Preciado
http://www.gutierrez-preciado.com/index.html
crh4@primenet.com

Unless you want to be accused of spamming, don't join a mailing list in order to send around your résumé or brag about winning your last jury trial. The marketing must be *much* more subtle. Post an intelligent comment that shows you know your stuff. Or, in the best tradition of the Internet, give something away. Lawyer Calvin House explains how he used postings in discussion groups to increase visits to his Web page, which ultimately increased his legal business:

> *Earlier this year, the California Judicial Council proposed an amendment to the California rule governing media access to courtrooms. I put together a*

page about the amendment, with links to other Web resources about media access. I then announced the availability of my page to the mailing lists, newsgroups and message boards. The resulting hits on my Web site led to additional subscriptions to my newsletter. I was able to repeat the process when the Council adopted the final version of the amended rule. This generated additional hits and newsletter subscriptions.

There are also less traditional ways to use mailing lists for the practice of law. Ben Wright, whose law practice focuses exclusively on electronic commerce, is the author of a book titled *The Law of Electronic Commerce: EDI, E-mail and Internet*. He writes how he uses discussion groups to help his clients:

PERSONAL ACCOUNT

Ben Wright
Attorney and author
*73457.2362
@compuserve.com*

I use the Internet directly to advance the interests of my clients. Through the Internet I publish articles and post messages to espouse my clients' points of view. Many of my clients are vendors of products and services for EC/Internet. I go to carefully selected mailing lists and post articles about my clients' products and then respond to questions/debate. For example, one of my clients has a technology for signing electronic documents. I wrote an article on how this technology is being used by the IRS for the signing of electronic tax returns. Then I strategically posted the article on mailing lists interested in electronic commerce. The purpose was to advertise the client's product, show how it can be used, and discuss the legal concerns surrounding its use. This tactic has generated sales leads for my client.

Some of my clients are keen to see the law of EC develop in certain ways and not in others. I use Internet discussion groups to monitor which states are proposing new legislation, to express in a very public way our support or reservations about particular legislation and to debate the issues with interested parties. I can point to specific instances where my public (electronic) postings have caused lawyers in different states to call me and seek my input as they started to draft legislation.

The Internet leverages the effectiveness of my solo law practice. It allows me to very efficiently monitor and cast a voice on developments throughout the world. Without the Internet, the cost of achieving the same results would be dramatically greater. I'd need to hire employees or subcontractors, at a cost that would make my clients blanch.

Once you join a few mailing lists, you'll find they're a convenient and efficient way to take care of some of your business.

A COUPLE OF CAVEATS

Nothing good is without a bad side, and the same is true for discussion groups. Although many of the law-related groups are populated by lawyers, the subscribers aren't limited to lawyers. There is no way to know if another member of a group is a lawyer or not (the computer doesn't check attorney registration numbers!). Some of the newsgroups seem to be full of people seeking free legal advice ("I fell on my Uncle's doorstep—can I sue the old codger?").

From some of the discussion, it should be obvious if you should keep out of the fray. But you may be interested in other discussions, even though many of the participants aren't lawyers. For example, in a recent thread, group members discussed whether Web pages without text (all graphics) violated the American with Disabilities Act. I'm sure both lawyers and Web page designers were actively involved in the discussion. And I'm sure that some of the information given by the lawyers amounted to legal advice.

And therein lies the problem. If you give legal advice over the Net, can you be sued for malpractice if the advice was wrong?

Ronald D. Rotunda of the University of Illinois College of Law, who teaches professional responsibility, was quoted in an article about lawyers online: "I don't want to sound discouraging, but attorneys should be cautious about what they do online.... If it looks, tastes and smells like legal advice, then a court may decide that it's legal advice." *

PERSONAL ACCOUNT
Peter Krakaur
Internet Legal Services
http://www.legalethics.com
ils@legalethics.com

So should you avoid giving anything *resembling* legal advice over the Net? If you take this approach, you're likely to avoid joining any online discussion on the off chance that a non-lawyer would rely on your legal advice. Peter Krakaur, who sponsors the Web site *legalethics.com*, in a posting to the *net-lawyers* mailing list, discusses the problem and its solutions:

> *When you communicate via email, there is the potential that the recipient(s) of your message may view your communication as legal advice. (Of course, the same holds true for written or print communications.) Whether the recipient(s) can rely upon your message or whether they can sue you for malpractice are separate (but related) issues and fact-dependent. There are also a variety of other ethical issues, such as disclosure of client confidences, communicating with a represented party, and conflicts that can arise with email use. You might consider reading the ethics rules in your state with the*

[1] Resnick, *A Shingle in Cyberspace*, Nat'l. L.J. (9/27/93).

Internet in the back of your mind. I think you will find that many issues jump out at you with this mindset.

There are links to some of your state's rules available online and to some of your state's ethics opinions (summaries). Go to http://www.legalethics.com/ states/ks.htm for the links. I also recommend a review of the materials that were distributed at the COPRAC symposium in May of 1996: http://www.legalethics.com/issues.htm. There are two hypotheticals and associated questions that should help you get a feel for some of the issues associated with Internet use. There are also copies of some draft disclaimers I put together for discussion that relate to Web Page and email use.

Whether one views the issue in terms of complying with the ethical rules or in terms of limiting exposure to malpractice suits, the issue of disclaimers should not be taken lightly. Of course, the ultimate decision on how you meet your ethical obligations is your call. I do not mean to suggest by this post that a disclaimer is required in every situation. If someone asks a question in a discussion group, seeking legal advice, it would be appropriate to include a disclaimer IF one wanted to respond directly. Of course, I always balance this decision with a strong concern for my First Amendment right to discuss issues in an open forum.

==

```
This email communication is not intended as and should
not be interpreted as legal advice or a legal opinion.
The transmission of this email communication does not
create an attorney-client relationship between the
sender and you. Do not act or rely upon the information
in this communication without seeking the advice of an
attorney.

Peter Krakaur Internet Legal Services
ils@legalethics.com

http://www.legalethics.com
http://www.legalethics.com/pa/main.html
```

As you can see from Peter's email, he uses a disclaimer for his postings. A disclaimer may or may not be appropriate for your email, depending on your jurisdiction and what you're saying in your message.

Whether you need a disclaimer to avoid liability is a question currently without an answer. But other concerns lurk. If someone sent

FIGURE 6-2

Legalethics.com provdes timely advice and links to legal resources about the online law community http://www.legalethics. com

you an email revealing confidential information, could you be disqualified from representing an opposing interest in litigation? California attorney Mark Welch is concerned about this possibility:

PERSONAL ACCOUNT

Mark Welch

Attorney at law
http://www.ca-probate. com/
markwelch@ca-probate. com

I use a very brief disclaimer in my signature line, but whenever I am replying to email that appears to be seeking legal advice, I provide a more detailed disclaimer. I remain concerned that someday, someone will send out email over the Internet, revealing confidential information about their case, and then will seek to disqualify all attorneys who received the email on the grounds that they have a conflict of interest. (A local attorney found herself dislodged from a case because one of the attorneys from her firm had simply answered a phone call from the opposing party a year earlier and told him, "I don't handle dissolution cases." The judge decided that was enough to disqualify the attorney's partner, and although that was a bad ruling, it wasn't worth appealing. The client had to retain new counsel and all proceedings were delayed for months, and hundreds of hours of work went unpaid as a result.)

PERSONAL ACCOUNT

Michael Daymude

Attorney at law
attorney@prodigy.com

From this discussion, it's clear there are potential problems with posting to discussion groups. But don't let them paralyze you and cause you to avoid the Net altogether. The problems are the same as those you face every day, just in a different venue. Lawyers routinely give free legal advice every day at sites other than the Internet. Lawyer Michael Daymude puts the issue into perspective:

If you are an attorney on the Net and haven't given free advice at cocktail parties or over the Net, you are a strange bird indeed. Every place I go, people ask me for advice as soon as they find out I am an attorney. And, I tell you, I don't start my meter running when I am at the dry cleaners—so the advice is always free.

Most of the time, the answer is: "It depends," or "I can't really answer that question without knowing a lot more about the facts," or "Gee, I am sorry, I can't help you—I don't handle tax matters." Many times, the legal advice is: "Yes, you should see an attorney."

Of course, to make any of this advice make sense to the person asking the question you must ask them a few questions and advise them, generally, how various laws may be applied to the facts. The advice really is always that a more thorough investigation of certain legal issues and facts is required, that the person should employ counsel ASAP for specified, stated reasons, and that upon a more thorough investigation other laws and issues may be important.

Now, this is legal advice—but I fail to see how it constitutes the unauthorized practice of law in any jurisdiction or is likely to constitute "wrong" advice or unauthorized practice that will get anyone into trouble when offered by an attorney who is licensed to practice in the state where he/she is physically located.

Free, informational advice of a general nature from attorneys should be encouraged to educate people in the law. It's hard to believe that ANYONE would find fault with an attorney who gives back to the general public in this way through participation on Internet discussion groups or in any other manner.

Participating in Net discussion groups doesn't raise any particularly unique problems, just new variants of old issues lawyers learned in law school. The thing to remember is that you don't know who may read your posting in any discussion group. And because of that, you must *assume* that it will be read by non-lawyers and whatever you say is *not* confidential. Finally, it always wise to check with your local bar to see if they have any particular rules on the subject.

ONLINE CLE COURSES (BRING YOUR OWN STALE DONUTS)

I don't know about you, but attending Continuing Legal Education courses is not much fun. The coffee is weak, the donuts stale, and the speakers dull. And, worst of all, I have to attend the classes on someone else's schedule—usually the day before a major brief is due.

But I guess I want to keep my license.

The Internet promises some relief. More and more CLE providers are providing courses online. For example, the private network of Counsel Connect (*http://www.counsel.com/inside/seminars.html*) has presented more than 70 seminars online for legal credit. With Findlaw's service (*http://www.findlaw.com*), you can get credit for surfing the Net. The CLE courses are available online virtually all of the time, making them easy to fit into your schedule. You can get one hour of credit for every 10 questions answered, making it an interactive CLE experience. You may also want to check out LawInfo (*http://lawinfo.com/cgi-win/clesplash.exe*) which is seeking to expand its CLE offerings nationwide from their southern California roots.

PERSONAL ACCOUNT
Stephen McGarry
President, Lex Mundi
Heiros Gamos Web site:
http://www.hg.org
smcgarry@onramp.net

This is clearly a growing trend, as CLEs are certainly one thing that could use improvement in presentation. To find out about the latest developments in online CLEs and who is offering them, check some of the MegaSites referenced in Chapter 5 of this book. For example, Stephen McGarry, who operates the Hieros Gamos Web site (*http://www.hg.com*) suggests that anyone interested in online CLEs check his site for up-to-date information:

> *At present all CLE providers (online and offline) may list and link their courses directly on the Hieros Gamos searchable meetings calendar. A new feature of our database will permit users to list their specific CLE interests by topic. When organizations post their new CLE courses in the database, registrants for that topic will automatically be sent an email notification containing the links. This feature will not only match interested attorneys with specific courses, but also permit immediate access to the HTML brochures and registration forms linked by the organization. The same database is used for employment and publications.*

FIGURE 6-3
Increasingly professionals are finding required continuing education courses online.

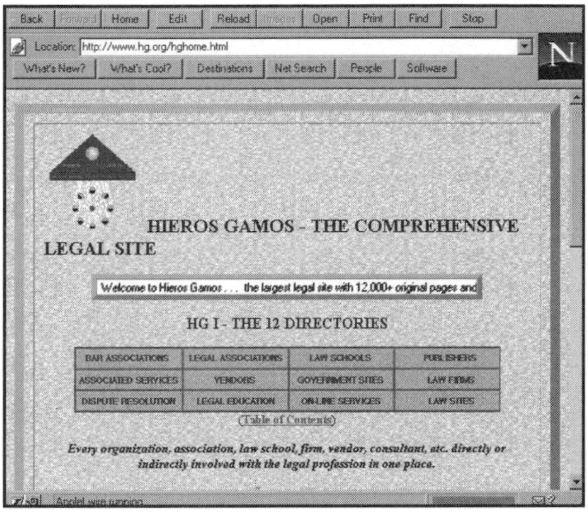

FIGURE 6-4
Steve McGarry's meg-asite offers other links to CLE sites
http//www.hg.org/
hghome.html

Once you start doing your CLEs online, what excuse are you going to use to get out of the office for a day?

(INFORMAL) DISCOVERY

Of course, as email becomes more prevalent, lawyers will use it to serve interrogatories, document requests, and other formal discovery. Even now, the Internet is being used to provide access to large databases of documents that have been produced during discovery. Standard practice in today's major litigation involves scanning all documents into a database so that they can be instantly available from any networked computer. Although not yet common, the next evolutionary step is to electronically produce the documents, too. Instead of stacking 63 bankers boxes of documents in response to your opponent's document request (in some windowless room with no access to a restroom), you can give them a couple of CD-ROMs or, better yet, let them access a dedicated server through the Internet so that the database can be continually updated.

Why in the world would you make it so easy on your opposition? Well, if they did the same for you, you'd probably do it. Clients would be the beneficiaries, saving thousands of dollars in clerk and paralegal time to view, organize, and scan the opposition's documents.

But until this becomes commonplace (*when*, not *if*), there are other more immediate ways in which the Net can be used for discovery.

Ever wondered if the other side has given you everything you've asked for in your discovery requests? As the Internet grows, it will be increasingly difficult for any information to stay hidden, making it easier to answer this question. Since the Internet creates a means of worldwide information distribution, once information is on the Internet, it is impossible to keep it a secret.

The tobacco industry recently discovered the Internet's reach. In 1994, thousands of pages of a tobacco company's documents were donated (by someone calling himself "Mr. Butts") to the University of California at San Francisco's Tobacco Control Archives. The documents consisted primarily of studies about nicotine and other health effects of tobacco smoke. UCSF made approximately 4,000 pages of the documents available through their Web site. The tobacco company fought to remove the records, claiming they were privileged and confidential, but the California courts rejected requests for injunctive relief.

Before the advent of the Net, plaintiffs' lawyers salivating at the thought of seeing these documents would fly to San Francisco and spend days in a cramped room looking at the five cubic feet of paper. Now they can get on the Net and view the documents for the cost of connect time. Better yet, the documents, since they are electronic, are organized by subject matter and searchable by keyword.

As another example, do you think your opposition has told you everything about their client? Or their expert witnesses? It'll only take you seconds to find out if something is on the Net. Using Alta Vista, try an Advanced Search with the person's name. For example, type in "John Doe" to find anything written by John Doe. Sometimes you'll come up with a blank, but other times you may be pleasantly surprised. If their expert has published anything on the Net, or even if she has posted something in a newsgroup, you can find it with the Net's search engines.

And how many times have you seen those ads in trial lawyer's magazines seeking information about a certain expert witness or information about a defective product? Using the Net (either with Web sites or discussion groups) to centralize this service is obviously more efficient than a printed magazine of limited circulation. In Chapter 9, you'll read how lawyers have used the Net to find needed information to build class action lawsuits, taking advantage of the inexpensive but massive reach of the Internet.

You can also use the Internet to find experts for your case, and see the c.v.'s of your opposition's experts. For example, at *http://seam-*

less.com/experts/, you can get lists of experts organized by expertise or jurisdiction. Finding an expert this way beats paying some service (which marks up the already exorbitant fees) to find you an expert.

Chicago lawyer Ralph D. Davis once needed a linquistics expert in several languages for a case of mistaken identity. The expert was needed to testify on how a particular and unusual surname would be transliterated across those languages. With the Internet, he not only located an expert, but a man who was also an Ivy League university professor with the exact same surname in question. Because the professor had already studied the origins of his surname, he could easily testify as a linquist on that particular name. Ralph Davis's client was impressed with his ability to quickly locate the perfect expert on the Net.

Lawrence S. Goldberg, a partner with the New York law firm of Schulte Roth & Zabel, relates how he also found key information on the Net that saved his client money:

PERSONAL ACCOUNT
Lawrence S. Goldberg
Schulte Roth & Zabel
goldberg@srz.com

> *I was representing a borrower in a large financing. I wanted to see what "market practice" was for certain terms and conditions for comparable borrowers. After obtaining a list of competitors, I was able to check their SEC filings and download the credit agreements on record. This definitely gave our client a leg up when it came time to negotiate with the agent.*

And Bob Cumbow, who practices in the area of intellectual property, sees the Net as a great tool to police his client's trademarks:

> *As search engines become more and more efficient, it becomes easier to use the Web for legal research as well as factual research. This is a revolution for trademark and copyright attorneys. In the traditional paper-print world, you can't advise your client on a matter of trademark or copyright infringement until someone brings the infringing act to the client's attention (usually a confused customer). Now you can actively go out and hunt for infringements. This is known as "policing" one's trademarks and copyrights, and it is a tremendous new capability for creative artists, businesses, and others whose livelihood depends upon protecting their intellectual property.*

I'm sure there are untold ways to innovatively use the Internet for informal discovery. And as Internet technology strengthens and the size of the Net grows, searching the Internet for information will become as common a practice as serving document requests.

GETTING THAT NEW JOB

It may sound like you're hearing a broken record, but one of the greatest strengths of the Internet is the inexpensive distribution of information to the entire world. When looking for a job, one of the biggest tasks is finding out who's hiring. So what better use of the Net?

Despite its usefulness, Internet head hunting/job hunting is in its infancy. And the Internet will never replace interviews and word-of-mouth. But where jobs are now filled through traditional advertising, the Internet will quickly become a key resource.

PERSONAL ACCOUNT

Jeffrey Kuester
Attorney with Louis T. Isaf, P.C.
http://www.kuesterlaw.com
kuester@kuesterlaw.com

In some areas of the law, the Internet is already *the* primary resource for hiring lawyers. Jeffrey Kuester, a patent, copyright and trademark lawyer from Atlanta (*http://www.kuesterlaw.com*), writes about how he used the Net for his firms' last four hires:

While I am convinced that the World Wide Web is appropriately named because of its nature as a time trap, it is nevertheless a very effective vehicle for large-scale targeted communication. Likewise, newsgroups and mailing lists provide excellent resources for communicating with large numbers of people with specifically identifiable interests. With this in mind, our law firm recently set out to use these vehicles for finding new hires, since the amount of business for our patent, copyright, and trademark law firm has exploded over the past few years.

As you might imagine, it is no simple process to find people with advanced technical degrees who are also interested in working with a bunch of lawyers, especially patent lawyers! Nonetheless, since patent agents and patent attorneys need a background in science or engineering, it was only logical to try to use the Internet to find these people, since the Internet is full of people with these types of degrees.

The methodology involved was very simple. First, we constructed a basic text file which very specifically described the type of person we were hoping to find. In our case, we were looking for electrical engineering and computer science people. Next, we sent this text file to all of the job-related newsgroups and mailing lists for engineers and programmers. We also displayed this text file as a "we are hiring" link from the Web page.

The results were simply overwhelming. Our last four hires discovered our firm from our activities on the Internet. We now employ very qualified and capable people with the exact interests and backgrounds we needed to find. For example, our last two hires are Ph.D.s in electrical engineering! We fully intend to continue using the Internet to find well-qualified individuals.

FIGURE 6-5
*Jeffrey Kuester's web site
http://www.kuesterlaw.
com*

Not everyone is going to have this success. But as the Net becomes better known as a place to find legal jobs, it will become a key hiring tool.

There are already numerous Internet sites to both look for work and post job openings. Just a few are listed below to get you started if new work is on your horizon:

- Jobs are posted at LawInfo's site at *http://www.lawinfo.com/employment/offered.html.*

- Resumes are posted at LawInfo's site at *http://www.lawinfo.com/employment/résumés.html.*

- Jobs are posted on the *lawjobs-l* listserv managed at Washburn University. To look for work, you can join the listserv by sending the message: "subscribe lawjobs-l firstname lastname" to *listserv@lawlib.wuacc.edu.* You can post job openings by emailing Mark Folmsbee at *zzfolm@acc.wuacc.edu.*

- You can look for work at *http://www.headhunt.com,* where there's a list of positions and links to other lawyer job sites.

- Paralegal job openings can be found at the National Federation of Paralegal Association's site at *http://wwwparalegals.org*

- You can check the Hieros Gamos Employment Resources page at *http://www.hg.org.*

- Check for work at the Law Mall *http://www.lawmall.com/.*

- Post your résumé at *http://seamless.com/jobs/index.html.*

Using the Net to find work goes beyond looking at classified cyber-ads. The Net can be used as a one-stop tool for getting a new job.

PERSONAL ACCOUNT
Doug Humes
Attorney at law
dhumes@voicenet.com

In the online newsletter "The Internet Lawyer" (*http://www.internet-lawyer.com*), attorney Doug Humes explains how he used the Internet as his exclusive source to find and investigate a new job opportunity:

Using the Internet as part of a job search strategy is not the sole province of the techno-geeks. Even traditionally technology-impaired groups, such as attorneys, can incorporate the resources of the Internet into their job search, if they know where to look. Here's a case study of how I made use of those resources.

Last week a friend sent me an email about an ad for a company called Shared Medical Systems. I first went to my home page collection of job resources (http://www.voicenet.com/~dhumes) and clicked my link to the Philadelphia Inquirer's classified section (http://phillynews.com/ads/). Like many other newspapers (see Careerpaths at http://www.careerpath.com for six major metros), the Inquirer has virtually its whole newspaper online, with classifieds in a searchable data base. I searched for "attorney" and quickly found the SMS ad.

To find out more about SMS, I first went to Hoover's Corporate Directory (http://www.hoovers.com/corpframe.html). Hoover's searchable directory returned four different links that would send me directly off to SMS information, including their latest stock quote, a stock chart for the last 100 days, a Web search using Infoseek, and their SEC filings. I followed each link in order. The stock quote (from http://www3.dbc.com/) returned the stock quote information that you would find in the daily newspaper. The stock chart (from http://quotes.galt.com/) showed a leap in price from 39 to 60 between December and March. The Infoseek search (http://guide-p.infoseek.com/), using "Shared Medical Systems," turned up a consultant who does business with them, but curiously (for a medical software company), no Web page for SMS.

The last source, SEC filings at Edgar (http://www.sec.gov/edgarhp.htm), is one of the best resources on the Internet for finding information about publicly-traded companies. At Edgar I found the motherlode of information for SMS, including their 10Ks and 10Qs for the last several years. The problem here is that 10Ks in particular are huge documents that take time to download. So I went back to my home page to pick up a helpful tool. At http://worthnet.com/www/seczip/index.htm, they will search Edgar for you, and then zip your selections and email them to you. I tried this out with the last 10K and all 1995 10Qs. I figured I would take a computer break and then come back in an hour and see if they arrived, but first I checked my email before logging out. Amazingly enough, the SEC documents were already in my mailbox. Once you receive them, you have to both uu-decode them and unzip them, but don't be intimidated here — this is knowledge that you are going to need to be fully functional in cyberspace anyway. (Encoding and zipping files is used to reduce their size and thereby decrease transmission time. Once they are loaded onto your hard disk you can unzip them.)

In the SEC reports, you get a great overview of the company, their financial statements, and most importantly (for me), a list of their directors and officers. I use these with my network of friends to see if they know any directors or officers, and so develop more information on the job, as well as what person at SMS is actually doing the hiring.

I next went to Catapult's Business Site's list (http://www.jobweb.org/ CATAPULT/emplyer.htm), and followed a link to Pathfinder (http:// pathfinder.com/@@S7yB3gYAM;8Is7ale/welcome/), a collection of magazines and other documents that can be searched for your target. My search for "SMS" returned 60 documents, most of them entirely off-subject, or with a small mention of SMS buried many pages down. I found an SMS user's group and went to their site, where I was educated about SMS's new Invision product, and then found the link to an SMS home page. This really should have been my first stop, as they list career opportunities, product information, and press releases among other things.

The SEC information had included SMS's general counsel, so my next stop was Westlaw's searchable database on attorneys (http://www.wld.com/id-search.htm. My search for the general counsel turned up no listing (not every lawyer is there—it's voluntary). I then did a corporate search for Shared Medical and found their corporate listing. I learned that their legal department is between two and ten lawyers, and four attorneys are listed. Each listing includes law school and graduation date, and areas of concentration. The names of the attorneys provide me with more information for networking.

My final stop for the night was my favorite of all the Net resources: Switchboard (http://www.switchboard.com/). This is all the phone books for the country wrapped in one, plus more: a searchable data base to find people and businesses. I put in the name of the general counsel of SMS and up popped her home address and phone number. She lives the next town over. I searched for the other attorneys, and found the same information for two of four. This snooping for home addresses isn't a regular feature of my search, but you never know what information might give you a networking link to something else.

So after about an hour and a half on the Saturday night that the ad first ran, I have a pretty good overview of the corporation, and I have names of the influential people in the company to use in networking. This alone will not necessarily get me an interview or a job, but I am a few steps ahead of everyone else. That's the power of the Net in this information age: it gives you access to all of this information, available in searchable form, from the privacy and comfort of your home computer. While nothing will replace your network as the best source for actually hearing about a job, the Internet gives you ready access to information that will better equip you to go after it.

As Doug said, his investigation may not get him a job. But it allowed him to thoroughly research an opportunity without leaving his chair. Or, as Ma Bell used to say, "Let your fingers do the walking."

Do You Need a Web Site?

7

Maybe the question should instead be, what will a Web site do for you? It's a fair question. Today, there are a million different demands on a lawyer's time. Attorneys must be selective before going off and embracing something new and time-consuming. What will a Web site accomplish for you? Will it bring in new clients? Good clients? *Paying* clients? Or will it just be another expensive drain on your time?

Using the Net as an information resource was easy to understand. But, being a lawyer trained to question everything, I was skeptical about the value of setting up a Web page. When Web pages first became common (in that ancient year of 1993), I envisioned something created by a socially challenged 17-year-old kid so that he could e-publish his collection of adolescent jokes.

But that former 17-year-old now owns a company that just raised $50 million in its initial public offering. Like the kid, Web pages have grown up in the past few years.

▶ The Numbers Are There—Statistics and Other Lies

▶ What About Getting Some Hefty Retainers?

▶ Another Lawyer Gave Me Your Name

▶ The Best New Client Is an Existing Client

▶ Saving Time and Other Impossible Dreams

▶ But I Still Don't See the Need

THE NUMBERS ARE THERE—
STATISTICS AND OTHER LIES

A good advocate can prove anything with statistics if they're skewed the right way. But it's difficult to view the Internet statistics in any way but one: the growth is simply staggering. Data produced by Network Wizards, an Internet consulting firm in Menlo Park, California, estimates that there were 9.5 million hosts (machine addresses) on the Internet in January 1996, up from only 1.3 million in January of 1993. Similarly, there were 240,000 domains on the Net in January of 1996, up over ten times from 21,000 in January of 1993. Not many things grow to ten times their size in three years—except for the Web portion of the Internet. If the Internet is running on premium gas, the Web is powered by high-test jet fuel. Matthew Gray of the Massachusetts Institute of Technology estimates that there were 230,000 Web sites in June of 1996, up from only 23,500 the year before and only 130 (yes, that's only three digits!) three years earlier. It's exploding!

Sure, you may say, there's a vast cyberworld out there, but who's living in it? The feds haven't cranked up the census apparatus on Net citizens yet, so no one really knows for sure. But John Naisbitt says that estimates of current users range from 10 to 50 million people, and the number is expected to hit one billion by the year 2000 by some estimates. Even if that prediction is off by a hundred million here or there, it's still a number only astronomer Carl Sagan could grasp.

And those tens of millions of residents are not just cyberpunks with a nickel in their pockets and no bank account. Demographic studies by O'Reilly & Associates show that most Internet users are 35 to 50 years old and earn $50,000 a year or more. In general, they are educated and affluent, and more likely than the rest of the population to be owning or running businesses. For many business lawyers, that describes a *good* client, which is a very good reason to pay attention to the Internet.

WHAT ABOUT GETTING
SOME HEFTY RETAINERS?

For private attorneys many decisions, of course, come down to a matter of economics in today's legal environment. Even if there are a lot of people in cyberspace, there's no business reason for you to be there unless your presence helps your legal practice in some way. Will it increase your revenues or, conversely, will it decrease your expenses? Or both? Or neither?

Earlier we talked about how the Internet (especially email and research) can make you more efficient—how it has the potential to *decrease* your expenses. Here, we'll look at the other side of the coin and see if other lawyers have increased their *revenue* with the Internet. We'll view the entire range of experiences of lawyers who have created Web pages.

There certainly isn't some Universal Truth out there concerning the results you can expect from a Web page—if there were, you wouldn't be reading this book. You'd either have a Web site or you wouldn't. Unfortunately, it's just like the advice we usually must give our clients: "*It depends ...*"

The success of a Web site depends on a number of things, not least your expectations. If there is something close to a Universal Truth for a Web site, it's that it won't suddenly create clients flocking to your electronic doorway. In fact, so that you aren't disappointed, many experienced Net lawyers suggest you create a Web site for some reason other than just getting clients. We'll talk more about how this works in the next chapter.

Michigan attorney M. Sean Fosmire has this to say about expectations from Web sites:

> *If you want to set up a Web site for your firm, do so with the idea of using it to provide information to clients and to the public, and to keep a visible profile among Net users. Consider it public relations rather than advertising. Do not expect it to generate new business, because you will wait a long time for that to happen.*

If that were the end of the story, you may conclude a Web site isn't worth the bother. But do you speak at seminars because you expect to get new business as you walk out the door? Did you write that law review article last year (during your vacation, no less) because it would immediately generate legal work?

PERSONAL ACCOUNT
Mark Welch
Attorney at law
http://www.
ca-probate.com/

markwelch@
ca-probate.com

Creating new business, as we all know, takes time. A typical experience may be similar to that of Mark Welch, an attorney in California who created a Web site focusing on Estate Planning. Mark talks about the initial results from his site:

> In late December, I received my first client inquiry from someone who told me that a friend had located my information on the Internet. In early January, a second potential client inquired after her son in another state located my Web site on the Internet and suggested she talk to me regarding poor legal advice being given to her by another attorney in a pending probate. I was retained in that case. In February, I received several calls from southern California residents I couldn't help because they were so far from my office. Also in February, a young local couple found my Web site and came in for an initial consultation, although it's unclear whether they will retain me to proceed with any estate planning work. In mid-March, another potential client who'd found my Web site called regarding a potential multi-million dollar will contest, which quickly sounded too complex for my solo practice, but which may turn out to be very lucrative for the firm I sent her to.

In other words, maybe it generates new work, and maybe it doesn't. For Mark, it certainly brought some work through the door, and as much as could be expected from any type of indirect marketing. It's not a total bust; Mark has learned that there are some clients, or at least potential clients, on the Internet.

PERSONAL ACCOUNT
Christina Johnson
Attorney at law
http://seamless.seamless.
com/cj/

cjohns08@reach.com

The experiences of other lawyers have been far less ambiguous. San Francisco attorney Christina Johnson, a solo practitioner concentrating in intellectual property, has gone well beyond just getting potential clients. Christina says she first created her Web page because she was intrigued by the idea. "On a foggy day in December," she tracked down a Web page designer working out of his studio apartment in a low-rent district of San Francisco (if there is such a thing). Soon, she had worldwide exposure on the Internet, and it brought *real* clients:

> By January of 1995, my home page was up and running. It was very simple. Just a list of representative clients and a résumé. What I did not foresee and am still amazed by is the amount of email I received from the very beginning. I have also been surprised by the number of potential clients who have contacted me solely because they have seen my home page on the Web.
>
> The first client to retain me was a law firm in Australia who required legal work in California. When I received the retainer check, I knew the Internet worked. I also realized that the Internet was the "great equalizer" because,

although I could not afford to have a branch office in another country, I could afford the $50 per month fee to have my résumé present on the Internet for the world to see.

My next client was a South African company who asked me to obtain a trademark for them in the United States. Following this client, I have performed legal work for clients (who have "seen me" on the Internet) in Ohio, New Jersey, New York, and Massachusetts. I have also been contacted by and agreed to represent Silicon Valley clients who need an attorney to help them with their intellectual property concerns.

Mark Welch and Christina Johnson's experiences are not unique. Bruce Hake, a lawyer in private practice in Takoma Park, Maryland, and president of Hake Internet Projects says:

It has been our experience that a well-designed and well-publicized Web site is a cost-effective way to attract new clients. One of our subscribers had eight new clients on retainer after only two months online. Furthermore, we believe that a Web address is rapidly becoming expected as more and more law firms launch Web sites. This rapid growth is not surprising in light of the fact that the Web allows cost-effective global communication of data of all kinds.

PERSONAL ACCOUNT
Gregory Siskind
Siskind, Susser, Haas & Chang
http://www.visalaw.com/
gsiskind@visalaw.com

But the potential of a Web site is clearly beyond that experienced by even Christina Johnson. Probably one of the most impressive experiences is that of attorney Gregory Siskind. Greg shares the dramatic results of his Web page:

I can only speak from my personal experience, but our Web site has worked out to be a phenomenal success for us. We set up our site in June 1994 and I think there were just three or four other firms with home pages at that time. Because I had just opened my own practice after working for a large firm for several years, I had a lot of time on my hands and could devote considerable efforts to learning HyperText Markup Language, and to browsing through the Internet to learn about the medium and search for ideas. After a year and a half, I have learned a number of useful lessons.

The results:

- *We get more than 40,000 hits every week on our site. Last week set a record for us: more than 73,000.*

- *Our immigration law newsletter is subscribed to by more than 6,000 people and read at our Web site by an additional 5,000 to 10,000.*

- *We have gone from an unknown little immigration firm in Tennessee to one of the best-known immigration firms in the country.*

- *And the bottom line: more than two-thirds of our business originates on the Internet.*

As the auto manufacturers say, "Your mileage may vary." It may be hard matching the results of Gregory Siskind, especially now that the Web is getting filled with more and more law sites every day (there are a few more than "three or four other firms with home pages"). But it should be clear that clients *do* find lawyers on the Web, and if you're not there, they won't find *you*.

ANOTHER LAWYER GAVE ME YOUR NAME

Some lawyers have the luxury of never worrying about new legal business because other lawyers steadily refer work to their desks. For many lawyers, this is a painless way to get new clients. Face it, some of us would rather go to lunch with another lawyer than a potential client.

PERSONAL ACCOUNT
Marshall Kragen
Internet liaison for National Coalition for Cancer Survivorship
mkragen@access.digex.net

Experiences of other lawyers suggest that referrals may be one of the Web's greatest powers. Attorney Marshall Kragen wrote the following:

It was mentioned that you might not get many clients from a Web site. This may or may not be true for the layman looking for a lawyer. But as the Web becomes more well known, this can be a good source for referrals from other attorneys to your field of expertise. Nothing could show his expertise in advertising law more than to look at Lew Rose's home page. This is an important area, and in fact when transportation law was in its bloom, over 50 percent of my work came from general practitioners or lawyers in other fields who needed a transportation expert.

I'd have to agree with Marshall that referrals may be one of the Web's greatest strengths. Using a common situation as an example, let's say you practice law in New York, and a good client of yours has been sued in California for allegedly infringing a copyright. No one from your firm is licensed in that state, so you need local counsel.

You ask around for a referral for an intellectual property law firm in the Bay Area, and you get the names of three possible lawyers, but no

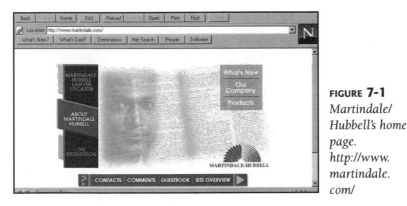

FIGURE 7-1
*Martindale/
Hubbell's home
page.
http://www.
martindale.
com/*

specifics about them or their law firms. So you pull a copy of the latest Martindale-Hubbell off the shelf (or on your screen—it's now on the Internet at *http://www.martindale.com*).

With Martindale, you find the three candidate law firms. But, let's face it—it's not much more than name-rank-serial number, which doesn't tell you if they're right for this case and this client. Martindale says that all three firms do commercial litigation for name-brand clients, so they all look qualified. Wouldn't it be nice to know a little more about the firms' cultures? You certainly don't want to hook this client up with someone who, in addition to submitting patent applications to the PTO, spends his nights sleeping in the local ERs hoping to stumble upon a client.

A Web page says a lot about a firm. You get online, and quickly discover that one of the firms doesn't yet have a Web page, so you don't know anything more about it. Fortunately, the other two lawyers are on the Web. For example, compare Figures 7-2 and 7-3.

Now, how do you make your decision? Well, you still don't know anything about the lawyer who didn't have a Web site, so your finicky client won't even hear that name. It's just too risky. The remaining two look qualified, but which one fits better with your client? If your client is a conservative, button-down type of banker, who wore a tie the last time you went golfing with him on a muggy Saturday morning, you may conclude that the first firm may be more appropriate. On the other hand, if your client is young and brash, he may be more comfortable with Dennis Kahane's style.

This is a "feel" you just can't get from Martindale or even a brief phone call. With the added information you get from a Web page, you're going to feel more comfortable about picking a lawyer across the country.

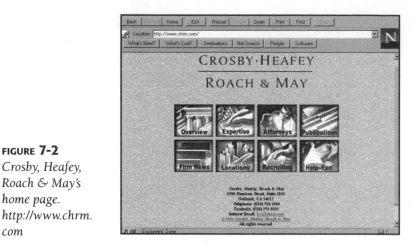

FIGURE 7-2
*Crosby, Heafey,
Roach & May's
home page.
http://www.chrm.
com*

And if this is how you are going to find other lawyers to help your clients with referrals, other lawyers will be doing the same. For example, at one time lawyers who couldn't be reached by telephone missed referrals from other lawyers. Soon, the same will be true of those without Web pages.

PERSONAL ACCOUNT

Barry Levinsky

Inland Steel Legal
Department
blevinsk@counsel.com

It's not only those in private practice who may be looking for your name on the Internet, but in-house counsel who need to hire a lawyer in your area. Barry Levinsky, in-house counsel for Inland Steel in Chicago, says that a Web page is an important element in how he evaluates a firm he's thinking of hiring:

> *While I believe a good Web page can become part of the matrix of reasons I have for hiring a firm, I think it unlikely that I will find myself at a partic-*

FIGURE 7-3
*Dennis Kahane's
home page.
http://www.
kahane.com*

ular firm's Web page because I am looking for firms on the Web. There are simply too many Web sites to begin an effective search. I suspect that I will look at a firm's Web site (and I will definitely check to see if there is a site) because I found the firm in Martindale, or someone has recommended it, or the firm's name is well known, or some other reason that has caused me to specifically look at the site.

But what am I looking for? It's not primarily that the firm is a good firm with good people. I've gotten that far already! I really don't care about the firm's mission statement either. I do want to find out something more than can be contained in a pre-packaged brochure. In large part, I want to see what the firm thinks I want to see and how good that information is from a qualitative perspective.

A Web site can tell other lawyers more about your practice than can a directory, a phone call, or even a four-color brochure. In the next chapter, we'll hear what legal professionals say are the important elements of a good Web site. But before we move on, let's see what role Web sites play with existing clients.

THE BEST NEW CLIENT IS AN EXISTING CLIENT

If I got anything out of those boring marketing seminars, it was that your existing clients are the best source of new legal work. "Cross-selling" and other buzz words are mouthed by the marketing gurus. Now a new phrase will be added to their vocabularies: "Web sites." If the Web may become the key ingredient to getting referrals, it may also soon be necessary in order to keep your current clients.

Now you've gone too far, you say—why in the world do my *existing* clients expect me to have a Web site? They already know more about me than they'll ever get on a computer monitor.

But ask yourself, why did you buy a fax machine fifteen years ago?

Did you buy it to get new clients? Or to serve your existing clients better? I remember when fax machines were still a rare commodity, and many law firms didn't own one. (But they had "telex" numbers— what in the world were *those* for?) I know some of those firms resisted the (then substantial) expenditure for their first fax machines. "We have U.S. mail, Fed Ex, and messengers—why do we need a fax?"

But the wallet opened after hearing the key question from *the* big client. "What is your fax number?" the client said when he needed a contract looked at before the end of the day. "It's not running now, but it will be in the afternoon," the lawyer said as she made a note to go buy a fax machine over her lunch hour.

Today that same client expects to reach you by email or connect to your Web site to peruse the résumé of the new associate you assigned to handle his case. Like a fax machine in the early '80s, a Web site says you are keeping up with technology to serve your clients. Bruce Hake says:

> *A site on the Web demonstrates that you are keeping up with current developments. It also allows you to communicate quickly, efficiently, and conveniently with your current client base. Do you think that makes an impression? You bet it does.*

Like a fax machine, a Web site is another tool to serve your clients and is becoming a necessary piece of your technological arsenal. We can wish it were the old days, when all a lawyer needed was a typewriter, a phone number, a mail box, and maybe an ad in Martindale-Hubbell to have a complete law office. Now, on top of the list you need faxes, computers, email, and Web sites. The reasons aren't new or unique; a Web site is just another supplement to everything else out there.

PERSONAL ACCOUNT
Don MacLeod
Editor-in-chief, "Internet Law Researcher"
dunvegan@panix.com

Don MacLeod, a law librarian and author of *The Internet Guide for the Legal Researcher*, when asked why lawyers should have a Web site, wrote the following:

> *Why have a Web page? It's for the same reason that one has a published telephone number, an entry in Martindale-Hubbell, an ad in the yellow pages and fancy letterhead: so people can get in touch with you. And a Web page is a singularly inexpensive and flexible way for clients and colleagues to find you.*
>
> *A Web page is not a magic wand that creates billable hours from thin air— nothing does that— but it is a very good way to demonstrate your expertise in your practice area. It also works as a display ad that can be changed at will. A Web page is a combination business card, biography, point-of-contact and marketing brochure. As the Web becomes a standard feature in the landscape of legal practice, indeed, a basic business tool, a Web page will be an everyday accessory to a practice the way a business card and a phone number are today. It's happening already.*

In other commercial contexts, the test of an advertising medium (and I think Web pages as used by law firms are fundamentally advertising media) is whether or not the page either moves the goods or attracts enough gawkers to make the site valuable to a paying advertiser. The "advertiser" in this case is the attorney or firm seeking the greatest number of visitors to a page in hopes of landing some retainers. This may turn out to be the weakest argument for a Web page. Better to think of a Web page, as I said before, as a new-fangled way to present yourself and your firm to the public. It does electronically what ads in the yellow pages or other publications did (and still do).

The arguments in favor of a page outweigh the not-inconsiderable criticisms leveled at them. Web pages don't replace face-to-face contact or personal referrals or having your mug on the 6:00 news as good ways to drum up clients. But they provide a perfect supplement—and I stress supplement—to the marketing efforts already underway.

And as Don stressed, a Web page is an effective supplement to other marketing efforts, as it's "a combination business card, biography, point-of-contact, and marketing brochure." When viewed in this context, it's simply another way to get your name in front of clients.

Susan Ross, an attorney with InterLegal Services in Arizona, added an appropriate touch when asked why a lawyer should bother with a Web page:

Not meaning to be cynical, but does this mean that you feel you should not be listed in the yellow pages either?

There are several reasons a law firm should have a Web page. Having a Web page gives your firm another means of getting its name out to the public. For example, if you have a Web page and your URL is listed on your business card, then a potential client to whom you give a card can simply look up your firm on the Internet. This is not to say that you cannot follow up with a marketing letter, but having a Web page can supplement these marketing efforts. In addition, you can easily communicate new announcements about changes or additions to your firm, a new location, or new areas of practice. Think of the information that you send to potential and existing clients, such as your firm résumé and new developments in your area of practice. Why not have it on the Net? Millions of people browse the Web all the time for information.

PERSONAL ACCOUNT
Susan Ross
InterLegal Services
intrlegl@netzone.com

Maybe it isn't a pleasant thought realizing that you must add (yet another) element to your firm's marketing efforts. Many of us didn't like the idea that we'd have to print expensive brochures when that became popular several years ago. And when the postal service became universal, I'm sure lawyers resisted consulting with clients by mail instead of in person. Things change, and it's just another way we must keep up with the changes we need to stay competitive.

But looking at a Web page as simply another drain on your time isn't the whole picture.

SAVING TIME AND OTHER IMPOSSIBLE DREAMS

Creating a Web site may be seen as just another time-eater. Just as you had to spend time designing the new firm brochure, you now must spend time designing your Web page. But unlike the brochure, your Web page can save you time, once it's up and running.

For example, one California patent attorney says that he can refer clients and potential clients to his Web page to answer routine questions about patents and copyrights. Instead of taking non-billable time answering those questions, his clients can look at his Web page. And on that page they'll see his name over and over again. He'll probably get a call or email when they have some paying work.

PERSONAL ACCOUNT
Jeffrey Kuester
Attorney with Louis T. Isaf, P.C.
http://www.kuesterlaw.com
kuester@kuesterlaw.com

And once you become familiar with the legal research possibilities on the Net, you will certainly save time. Recall Peter Krakaur's story about researching cattle sales—he could have saved days of time if the Internet had been available then. If you have certain favorites sites on the Internet, you can create a Web page with hypertext links to those sites. Jeffrey Kuester, a patent lawyer in Atlanta, ended up creating his own Web page to house all of his bookmarks:

> *After browsing for a while, my bookmark list became too large and unmanageable, so I decided to create a simple HTML page for my own use as a directory. Before long, it became fairly large, so I thought other IP attorneys might find some of the information useful. Consequently, I placed the information on the Web, requested a few links from other people, and soon others began requesting to be added to my page.*

With his Web page, Jeffrey Kuester has created a customized source for research on the Net. And he didn't just keep it for himself, but opened it to the world at his Web site (*http://www.kuesterlaw.com*). In

FIGURE 7-4
Kuester uses frames to make his page easy to navigate.

the process of saving time, he also created a highly regarded Web page that is an excellent source for referrals. While saving time, he's doing some marketing on the side.

Attorney Christina Johnson called the Internet the "Great Equalizer." No matter how small your law office, the Internet gives you the same ability as the largest firm to get your name in front of the world. Once your site is up, it isn't hard to add more and more pages of useful information at little or no cost. This simply isn't true of print advertising, the yellow pages, or Martindale-Hubbell.

BUT I STILL DON'T SEE THE NEED

Well, maybe you will come to that conclusion. There are a million different ways to spend time and money on marketing, and a Web page may not be at the top of the list. For example, a personal injury attorney said there was no reason to be on the Web because his clients had neither the professional background nor the finances to own a computer. His potential clients weren't on the Web, so why should he be there?

But Susan Ross didn't agree with his logic:

> Let me pose the opposite question. Why not have a Web page? Why not make yourself available to people other than actual clients, such as other attorneys? Actual clients are not your only target. Isn't it worth getting your name and info to anyone that could potentially refer a client to you? For example, some attorneys may search the Web to find out information about

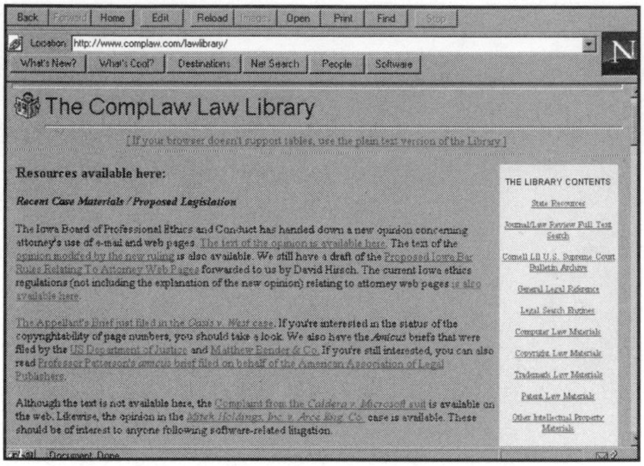

FIGURE 7-5
*CompLaw's
Online Law
Library page.
http://www.com
plaw.com/*

an attorney they met at a conference, or for potential referrals for out-of-
state services for friends or family of clients. Why not make information
about your practice as available as possible?

This personal injury attorney isn't the only lawyer who has questioned the need for a Web page. One lawyer already on the Internet
(because he was participating in a listserv discussion group) thought
that if he created a Web page for his firm, it would be "merely throw-
ing a stone into the ocean."

PERSONAL ACCOUNT
Samuel Lewis
Romanik Lavin Huss & Paoli
http://Complaw.com
slewis@CompLaw.com

Samuel Lewis, a lawyer in Hollywood, Florida, barely could contain
himself when he disagreed with the lawyer's statement:

*You're right, there's no need for a Web page! In fact, you should probably
have your firm withdraw its ad from Martindale and make sure that you're
not listed in West's Legal Directory, as there are certainly too many attorneys listed there, too! ;-) [...serious laughter from the peanut gallery...]*

*Seriously, it may not be a matter of actually needing one right now, but
eventually, your firm will probably have one. Most firms will have a Web
site (and quite a number already do). Look at television commercials and
see how many companies are concluding their ads with Web addresses as
well as or instead of telephone numbers. As the use of the Internet grows,
having an existence on the Web, no matter how small or insignificant, will
be as important as having your telephone number listed in the telephone
book or firm listed with one of the legal directories.*

*As a friend of mine concluded in response to my amazement at seeing so
many television advertisements with Web addresses, the Internet Web address and email address is the telephone number of the 90s. I suspect more*

and more this will be true as we approach the end of the century (at least for email addresses, if not both).

Of course, this is only my two cents' worth...

Sam's two cents' worth sums up the belief of those lawyers who have already set up Web sites. But clearly not every lawyer or law firm needs one—at least right now. It's simply another element of how a lawyer presents himself or herself to the public. If you believe that you need to make yourself visible in every way possible, a Web site is another way to do it. It will probably not cause a rush of new clients, especially now that so many law firms are already on the Web. But without a Web site, you may be like a lawyer with an unlisted phone number—if a potential client can't find you, they'll simply call another lawyer.

Compared to traditional marketing efforts, a Web page can be a much more efficient way to get your name out. If you can get someone to your Web site (which we discuss in the next chapter), it's an incredibly easy means to provide information about your firm. The more someone knows about you, the more likely you will become his or her lawyer.

If you've decided you need a Web site, the next chapter shares the advice of other legal professionals on how to make a site effective.

Creating Your Own Web Site

8

Depending on your computer literacy and free time, some of you may choose to HTML code your own Web pages. But even if you're like most lawyers and hire someone else for the nitty-gritty, you won't have an effective Web site without becoming personally involved in its design. In this chapter, we discuss the creation of a Web site.

► Planning a Web Site

► If You Build It, Will They Come?

► The Home Mechanic ... Or Hire a Handyman?

► You Don't Need a Call From The State Ethics Board

PLANNING A WEB SITE

Planning a site is the most time-consuming part of the process. But without planning, your efforts will be wasted.

Would you prepare a Supreme Court brief without planning? Of course not. You would chart out on paper the key elements of the case and how they will be linked in your brief. And no less effort should go into a Web site. Your Web pages will be there for millions of people to see worldwide, not just nine black-robed jurists.

To effectively plan a site, you must ask yourself: What is the *purpose* of my Web site? Unfortunately, the question is a moving target in the current legal market. Today's answer may be different from the one you supply a year—or even six months—from now. Fortunately, because Web sites can be easily modified, keeping up with changes is not an insurmountable problem.

Begin by asking a very important question: What do you want to accomplish with a Web site? Is your goal to attract new clients to your firm? If so, how are you going to get them to your site? How will you get the word out that your site even exists? And once they visit your site, how will you get them to make that key initial contact with you?

Or do you want your Web site to primarily provide service to your existing clients? If so, how are you going to make the site useful? Is your goal simply to increase goodwill? Or will it provide a new way for clients to use your services, thereby increasing your billables? Is your Web site's *purpose* to increase your legal work from existing clients?

The planning process is the essential first step in answering these questions. The Internet is already littered with lawyers' sites that lack focus, because the lawyers who set them up didn't know why they were creating a Web site. Many sites contain little more than the name and address of the law firm. If your only purpose is to say you have a Web page, the creation process will be short and the results even shorter. Unless someone accidentally stumbles across your site no one will ever see it. But you probably have higher hopes than that.

In planning a Web site, you must remember that the technology is passive. Potential clients must make their way to your Web site by design, not by accident. A Web site doesn't actively place itself in front of a viewer, like a television commercial or even a newspaper ad. It's more like a yellow pages ad: no one's going to see it unless they're looking for it. And a Web site might be even more passive than that. Unlike the yellow pages, all of the "attorney" listings are not located in some "lawyer" section on the Internet (a scary thought, indeed!). Except for a few directories linking the sites together, attorneys' Web sites are scattered around the cyberworld.

Even though a Web site is relatively passive, some lawyers have successfully figured out how to get people to see their Web sites. But again, the key element was a sense of mission and purpose. The successful ones knew the *purpose* of their Web sites before they built them. In the process, they built Web sites that accomplish their goals, whether they be to attract potential clients or create referrals from other lawyers.

For example, Mark Welch urges lawyers to consider a number of questions before building a Web site:

> Think about why you are doing it, what you want to do, and how you will do it. Will you provide substantive information that your potential clients can use? Will you post a firm brochure or a business card? Can you devote adequate resources to keep the Web site current? Will all people who represent your firm on the Internet check their email daily? Do you need to hire someone else to design the Web site?

> Don't be a lemming, chasing other lawyers over a cliff, only to drown in the vast ocean of the Internet. A lot of lawyers grab the first opportunity to create a Web presence, and end up with a very limited home page that costs a lot to update or expand. Other attorneys create flashy pages with lots of graphics or special effects, but no substance. Think about how people will find your site. I doubt anyone will find my Web site because they searched for "Mark Welch." Instead, they search for "probate" or "trust" or "estate planning" or "guardianship" or "conservatorship," and they are looking for answers that will help them decide what to do next. It's not helpful for most people to find an attorney site that simply says "Mark J. Welch represents clients in estate planning, probate, trusts, guardianships, and conservatorships." Instead, they want to know what those things are, and how an attorney can help them.

PERSONAL ACCOUNT
Mark Welch
Attorney at law
http://www. caprobate.com/

markwelch@ca- probate.com

Mark's questions are appropriate, because a Web site cannot be viewed in isolation from the rest of your legal practice. What type of law do you practice? And how will a Web site fit into your marketing plan?

PERSONAL ACCOUNT
Steve Bowles
Vice President,
Great Communicators
http://www.greatcom.com
73173.2347@CompuServe.
com

Steve Bowles, a vice president with Great Communicators, recently contributed to a discussion about whether lawyers need Web sites. Steve knew the issue was only part of the broader subject of marketing:

> We've been reading with fascination the many responses to why a law firm should have a Web page. There have been many great responses from "Why not have a Web page?" to lengthy explanations of Web page benefits.

> The question, though, is narrowly focused. It should read: "Why should a law firm market itself?"

> Most of you know that answer. The business of law is more competitive now than ever. Clients who were once fiercely loyal to a firm will change attorneys at a moment's notice if they perceive their lawyer is not jumping through enough hoops, or if they feel they can cut fee expenses. So marketing is essential to maintain a competitive edge and improve the firm's bottom line.

> Web pages may be the "fad du jour," but are only one ingredient needed to complete a successful marketing recipe. We feel that while Web pages provide a new and exciting means of marketing, law firms should not ignore already tried and true methods of attracting new business. Web pages have actually awakened many firms to the value of marketing. Firms that once shied away from any sort of visibility are amazed that simple efforts can solicit responses. Think what can be accomplished if a firm has in place a well thought out plan, designed specifically for its business, that maps specific goals, strategies, and actions to attract and maintain business. Many firms recognized this fact long ago and have in place an in-house marketing staff, an outside public relations firm, and sometimes both.

> And before anyone raises the question, I'm not talking about advertising. There are effective ways to market a firm without violating each state bar's rules on advertising. While many state bars already have developed rules on Web pages as advertising, firms also should recognize that there are other means of using the Internet for marketing other than Web pages.

> Marketing a law firm, just like any business, should be the responsibility of everyone in the firm, from the most senior partner to the receptionist. But the firm members should not be solely responsible for developing the marketing methods. That should be the job of a public relations/marketing professional. There are many out there who understand the business of law and the rules and regulations that govern law firm behavior. Most PR/marketing people also understand that it takes a complete, all-encompassing effort to effectively deliver a message to any business's audiences.

So, although Web pages can provide a firm with instant visibility and credibility, the Web is no panacea. Once the glow of a new venture into the Web fades, the firm may become disenchanted and ask itself, "Was it worth it?" when expectations aren't fulfilled.

But if the Web is incorporated into a detailed marketing plan, one that encourages activity on all fronts, the firm will gain long-term satisfaction through an ever-improving bottom line.

Mark's and Steve's views suggest that the purpose of a Web site is largely to generate new legal work. But other lawyers create Web sites without the "advertising" focus. Like a TV show, the purpose of their Web site is simply to get people to tune in. Maybe clients will eventually result from that use and maybe they won't. Or maybe they are seeking to increase their presence in the legal community which, long term, may help the bottom line.

Florida attorney Samuel Lewis decided early in the process that he did not want his Web site to be just another Internet ad:

I made a decision very early on that the Web site I created wasn't going to be an advertising tool. This was a conscious decision I made from the beginning, and is perhaps one which many attorneys putting together Web sites should attempt to make. There are attorneys who have gone so far as to put together Web pages which do little more than ask the visitor to fill in a form telling the attorney about their legal problem. The lawyer to which I refer actually includes a blank on the form where the visitor is asked for a credit card number which will be charged directly. From what I understand, the attorney has already made some money off the Web page. This approach, however, was one I chose to avoid.

PERSONAL ACCOUNT

Samuel Lewis
Romanik Lavin Huss & Paoli
http://Complaw.com
email:
slewis@CompLaw.com

FIGURE 8-1
Complaw's home page
http://complaw.com

The question of how much of an advertisement the Web page should be is not a minor one, but it is not the most important question you must ask when designing a Web site. Perhaps the single most important question to be asked is, "Why will people come back to my page once they've seen it?" I know that when I look at a Web site I find interesting, I'll add a bookmark for that site in my Web browser. If I go back to that site, and nothing's changed, chances are good I'll be disappointed. A few such visits, and I might even consider removing the bookmark. A colleague of mine put it this way: Content is king!

So when considering how to design a Web site, I started by answering the first question. Rather than have the Web site exist as an advertisement, I wanted the site to exist as a reference library or a general source of information for other attorneys. In essence, this helped resolve the second question at the same time. Since the site would serve as a source of information, it would be very easy to change or add to the information available on the site. This would keep the site changing frequently, and keep visitors' interest as a result.

For Sam Lewis, once he knew the *purpose* of his Web site, the rest of the planning process was easy. So, before you take even the first step, decide what you want to do with your Web site. It'll make the rest of the process that much easier.

But before your plan is cast in concrete, make sure you've considered the unique aspects of your legal practice. You may recall that Tennessee attorney Gregory Siskind was able to generate two-thirds of his firm's legal practice from the Internet, and you'd love to emulate those results. But ask if this purpose fits in with your firm's practice. His law practice concentrates in immigration law, which naturally fits with a national and international presence created by the Internet.

Immigration law is certainly not the only practice area that fits well with a Net presence. San Francisco attorney Christina Johnson believes that her intellectual property law practice "lends itself to the Internet." Law practices that focus on representing high-tech clients may also have better success on the Internet. In fact, these law practices probably *have* to be on the Internet, because their technology-savvy clients *expect* their lawyers to understand and participate in the world of technology. The growth of the Internet has renewed old arguments and raised entirely new intellectual property issues, so Christina's instincts are right on the mark. But even if your practice isn't uniquely suited to the Internet, it will have its place if you give it some thought.

Finally, before you determine your Web site's purpose, look around at other Web sites. Spend time surfing the Net, seeing what other lawyers have done. Ask yourself what sites hold your interest and how they do this. Learn from those that don't capture your interest. Learn from their mistakes and get an idea of how you're going to make your presence heard above the growing din of the Web.

Samuel Lewis did precisely this before he designed his first Web page:

> *When you decide you're going to create a Web site, take the time to look around first and develop a plan. See what other attorneys or firms are putting on their Web pages. Determine what you want the Web site to do for you, and how you want others to see you through that site. Also pay attention to how the sites are designed, and make a list of the things you like and don't like. Once you've done this, you'll have a better idea of how to go about designing a Web site, or instructing someone else to design it.*

In the end, deciding the purpose of your Web site will not guarantee success, but it will provide a solid foundation upon which you can proceed to build a successful site. Also, it's easy to get off track and lose focus while building a Web site. If you determine your *purpose* before you start it's easier to stay on track. If your purpose is to attract new clients, then your Web page must be designed to not only get the attention of potential clients, but be calibrated to attract the type of clients you want. If your purpose is to get other lawyers to refer you business, then the site will have to be calibrated to resonate with fellow professionals and to project an image that will encourage referrals.

Even if you don't get a single new client or referral from your Web site, it may be wildly successful. Samuel Lewis didn't intend to build his site to get referrals and new legal business. Instead, he did it to get his feet wet in the world of the Internet so that he could demonstrate his computer and Internet expertise. Since his purpose was clear, his Web site has become a "complete success" for him, even though it hasn't *directly* generated *any* legal business:

> *In the end, I consider my Web site to be a complete success. While it hasn't brought referrals, it has brought requests for me to speak at CLE seminars, to write articles for a variety of publications, and has put me in direct contact with many other attorneys around the country who help to shape computer and Internet law. This is still such an unsettled and unwritten area of law that contacts such as these are critical. I would not be able to keep up*

with all of the different changes to state law regarding this technology if I didn't have attorneys in those states sending me email about the latest change (it's hard enough keeping up with the changes in Florida alone). The site has also encouraged people to submit opinions or to at the very least, drop me an email telling me that some new opinion has been released or that a new suit has been filed dealing with my area of law. So perhaps the message to leave you with is this: if you're going to build a Web site, be sure your expectations of that site are clear. I have realized everything I wanted to accomplish with my Web site. Even though the Web site has not generated any referrals, what it has brought me is infinitely more valuable.

Since Sam focused on the purpose of his Web site, and achieved that purpose, his site is a success. Eventually the site will also lead to legal work, even though that wasn't his initial goal. Secondary and unanticipated benefits are the cherry that tops the Web site sundae. They are not the reasons you set up the site, but you're happy to have them. For example, Sam is now speaking at CLEs and writing articles because he has established himself as an expert in this emerging field. It probably won't be long before other attorneys refer Internet legal work to him because of his expertise.

So before you jump into creating a Web page, decide its purpose. That purpose can be modest, like Sam's, or ambitious. But it's the first and most indispensable step in the process. Besides keeping your Web site focused, it also serves to give you a benchmark by which to gauge the success or lack of success of your site. If you build a site without clear and realistic expectations, how will you ever measure its success? When that's done, you're then ready for determining what the site is going to look like. We cover that issue next.

IF YOU BUILD IT, WILL THEY COME?

Too many businesses, from law firms to pet shops, have jumped on the Web without defining their purpose. As a result, they have posted nothing more than an electronic billboard. Such billboards only obscure the view for Net users and irritate them in the process. I suppose these billboard-creating law firms believe that if their billboard, like a yellow pages ad, is seen enough, the Net surfer will remember their name and call when they need legal services. But on the Net a visitor *won't* look at a "billboard" Web site more than once—unless given a reason to do so. Remember, on the Internet no one will see your site unless they point their mouse in your direction.

So if *you* build a Web site, will they come? Not just because you built it.

In the real estate business the old saying goes that the three most important things about a piece of property are location, location, and location. In all the discussions about constructing effective Web sites, the three most important elements are content, content, and promotion. We'll discuss these concepts, along with other hints from lawyers who have created effective Web sites—sites that clients and lawyers want to repeatedly visit.

CONTENT IS KING

Successful Web site operators will be the first to tell you that on the Internet "content is king." The content will depend on your type of practice and what other lawyers are already offering on the Net. For example, there are already many sites that seek to provide comprehensive links to legal materials (see the MegaSites discussed in Chapter 5). Unless you've got a new twist or subject, or think you can do it dramatically better, creating another MegaSite will do little to provide content.

This is when you appreciate having clearly defined the purpose of your site. Now's a good time to check it. If it's to attract potential clients, try to figure out what they will be looking for on the Net. Michael Olenick gives an example of what a family law practitioner could do while emphasizing the primacy of content:

> The reason to build a Web site is to attract clients and build prestige. The problem with all the lawyers' Web sites you've probably been looking at is that they fulfill neither of these functions.
>
> Lawyer's Web sites—like most Web sites—are uninspired, unoriginal, boring pages that offer nothing but a lawyer's name, areas of expertise, photos of the office art, etc.
>
> But a law office that builds content will both show off the expertise of their staff, which builds prestige, and will attract clients.
>
> For example, a firm that specializes in family law might place an FAQ on family-law onto the Web. Maybe they even want to make it searchable. Their chances of a distressed client looking for help and calling them is much higher than a firm that just drops a print ad in the newspaper or puts up a Web page listing the names of the partners.

Michael's suggestion is a good one if your purpose is to attract clients. Try to imagine what a potential client is looking for when she gets on the Internet. If you're a construction lawyer who represents owners of defective buildings, maybe your site should include links to articles discussing warranty claims against builders. If you represent policyholders in insurance coverage litigation, maybe a glossary of insurance terminology will grab the search engines and attract a client's attention. You know your practice better than anyone else, so you already know what kinds of information clients are seeking when they contact your office. Make it easy for prospective clients to access some of this information before they pick up the phone and call. First, it will weed out those who don't really need your services. And, second, it will make that first client interview much more rewarding since the client will have already covered the routine material on your Web site.

And when you provide quality content, keep in mind the unique Internet subculture. First, don't even think about charging for content on your site. The client knows why you have a Web site—to promote your practice. Asking them to pay for what amounts to an ad is a sure-fire way to drive them away. When someone seeks information on the Net, they expect that information to be free. You can complain that such an attitude is unreasonable, but it's a fact and ignoring it courts disaster. Providing free information to visitors of your site fits with the Net's free-information philosophy. You may not be earning money, but you will be earning goodwill—which is more often than not a prelude to earning money.

Mark Welch discusses how giving away information not only makes for an interesting Web site, it's also good business:

> My law practice has thrived based on a policy of generously giving away information that clients can use to evaluate their own estate planning needs, and I had developed a number of written materials to disseminate basic information about estate planning. Since those materials were already on my computer's hard disk, and since I quickly recognized that a Web page is nothing more than a text document coded the same way as most word processor files, I knew it would be relatively easy for me to create a Web site using existing materials. Equally important, I knew I could maintain and update my Web site, keeping it current.

So giving Web site visitors free information generates goodwill, just as if you had sponsored a program on PBS or spoken at a Chamber of Commerce function. But giving potential clients free content also generates legal work in a more direct way. You may tell them just enough that they realize a need for (your) legal services. Bruce Ward, a Kansas attorney, says that good Web sites "offer some general way for clients and potential new clients to get answers to some of their basic questions, yet leave them hungering for more, which requires them to contact the law office for more information." In other words, once your content has brought them to your doorstep, the next step —hiring you to do legal work—may be an easy step for the person to take.

But how do you get them to your doorstep?

You must find out what they need. Surf the Net and look for gaps in your legal area. What isn't yet being offered that you could offer? Or how can you offer something better than what's already out there? And what will make clients or lawyers want to come back to your site?

Seattle lawyer Bob Cumbow explains how he figured out the content he would offer on his Web site:

> One day one of my email correspondents asked me for a list of U.S. cases re-lating to the Internet. I said I didn't have one, but I was sure I could get one in a hurry, and I confidently posted to two listservs a request for such a list. I got back half a dozen replies along the lines of: "No, I don't have one, but when you find one, could you send me a copy, too?" So another light bulb came on, and I decided there was a need for this. I compiled as thorough a list as I could of published opinions and filed cases that have some implication for Internet Law, and posted it to my firm's Web site (http://www.perkinscoie.com) where, periodically updated, it remains today.

PERSONAL ACCOUNT

Bob Cumbow
Perkins Coie
http://www.perkinscoie.com/
cumbr@perkinscoie.com

In a similar way, Gregory Siskind realized that his potential clients were seeking information in the ever-changing area of immigration law. His firm decided to create content by putting together an immigration newsletter, along with hypertext links to related resources on the Internet:

> Glitzy graphics and lots of information on your firm are nice, but they won't get you much business. Content is the key. And not just a few little articles or a handful of links to some generic legal resources. Your Web site needs to be hit (visited) repeatedly in order to build up name recognition. The only way to do that is to have something worth coming back to see. For us, our newsletter is the heart of our site. We also complement our newsletter with a document collection of the complete text of new bills, cases, and laws as well as an ex-tensive page of links on immigration resources all over the Internet.

PERSONAL ACCOUNT

Gregory Siskind
Siskind, Susser, Haas & Chang
http://www.visalaw.com/
gsiskind@visalaw.com

People know that Siskind's newsletter will regularly have new articles, so they repeatedly visit the site. It's designed to cause repeat visits, and it's very successful in doing so. The site gets more than 60,000 hits per week!

You now know that content is king. Your site, if its purpose is to attract clients or other lawyers, must have content that will interest them. But, you may think, legal stuff is so BORING. A Web site should be fun—do I have to make it as stuffy as a law library?

No.

Net publishing is the most flexible and diverse medium you'll ever encounter. Some lawyers have gone so far as to include pictures of their friend's miniature schnauzer on their site (an AKC-registered schnauzer, no less). This may not be your style, and probably runs counter to the image you're trying to project. But if you're creative, you can probably come up with something that relates to your law practice and is interesting at the same time.

Estate planning lawyer Mark Welch, knowing the importance of content, was able to have some fun on his Web site *and* generate traffic:

> *I keep hearing about the importance of content in an Internet Web site as the best way of generating results (often defined in terms of generating hits, but of course most of us measure "results" by the number of clients or amount of fees collected).*

> *A couple of months ago, a student wrote to me asking if I knew where he could find some actual wills on the Internet for a class project. I initially brushed him off by just pointing him to my search page (http://www. ca-probate.com/search.htm), but my curiosity was triggered, so I ran a search and sent him the URLs for wills I found. A few days later, I had some spare time and decided to create a Web page for links to "Wills on the Web" and initially posted it with about eight famous wills (Nixon, Onassis, Burger, Lennon, Presley, etc.). Since then, in my spare time I have collected more and updated the page so now it has about 40 wills, going back to the year 1615!*

> *I always viewed this page as a pleasant diversion, and perhaps a useful research tool for students.*

> *But after moving my entire Web site and reviewing the statistics, I have discovered that this simple, basic page of links has become the single most popular page at my Web site, excluding the index/home page. I am getting*

about 80 hits daily at the "Wills on the Web" page (of an average 750 hits total per day at my site). In addition, I am finding that the "Wills on the Web" page is being linked from many sites that weren't interested in adding links to my home page.

As I noted in my first paragraph, the importance of this observation depends on how you measure "success" for a Web site. However, I think the page represents content that will draw people to my site, and creates an opportunity for them to jump to my other pages, which creates an opportunity for some local folks to eventually discover my site and perhaps retain me.

Mark created traffic with his "Famous Dead People's Wills" site. (Does Elvis' will *really* belong?) I'm sure you, too, can think of content for your site that is interesting or fun.

But even if it isn't "fun," there must be content you can provide that will attract clients or other lawyers. For example, the San Francisco law firm of Brobeck, Phleger & Harrison does it with their filing service for EDGAR SEC filings *(http://www.brobeck.com)*. The site not only makes it easy to find out information about EDGAR and other SEC matters, but also makes it very easy to contact the firm for legal advice. As another example, the law firm of Arent Fox has the "Advertising Law Site" *(http://www.advertisinglaw.com)*, maintained by partner Lewis Rose. The site is recognized as one of the best places to get information about advertising law on the Net.

Come up with good content, and you've jumped the first hurdle. But now you've built it. Will they come?

Only if they hear about it.

PROMOTION

Unfortunately, just building a Web site with great content is not enough to make it a success. For example, when I first started practicing, I thought the only ingredient to being a successful lawyer was to be a good lawyer—do good work, and the rest would fall into place. But this plan ignored the other main ingredient: promotion. It doesn't have to be overt, like commercials during the noontime soap operas. But you have to get your name out, by writing articles, speaking at seminars, or networking with other lawyers. In one form or another, it is promotion, and it is necessary to a successful law practice.

Likewise, a successful Web site needs promotion. Some of the tools are the same, and some are quite different.

BAIT THE SEARCH ENGINES

In Chapter 5 we discussed the different search engines available on the Web. Some of those search engines will find your site without any effort by you, but others need you to give them your address. All of the search engines are more likely to find your site if you give them some help.

Lawyer Mark Welch explains what he did after he finished creating his Web site:

> Since I wanted the world to know about my Web site, I spent a weekend submitting information about my Web site to a variety of indexes, search engines, and other Web resources. Most of these are listed in my links page in the section describing Web search engines and directories. While some of the search engines need nothing more than your URL (Web page address), many directories request detailed information, and I had to spend some time reviewing the existing materials in those directories before deciding how to word entries, and to figure out which category to use.

Although this effort will take time, it shouldn't cost you anything. Mark again comments:

> I did not pay anyone to publicize my site, and I did not pay anyone for a listing. My impression is that the various directories that limit listings to paying customers all have a very limited pool of listings, and no reasonable consumer will rely on those listings anyway.

Getting on these search engines has been made easier by a Web site called SubmitIt (*http://www.submit-it.com*). It allows you to conveniently send your URL to most of the big search engines through one entry at its site. But remember that because the search services are swamped with new Web sites, it may take many weeks to actually get listed.

As we discussed earlier, there are different kinds of search engines and indexes. Some roam the Internet and create indexes of keywords. How are you going to make sure that the search engine indexes your site?

There was a recent discussion on a listserv about how to "bait" the search engines so they find your site. One person was surprised to find one document at a law site being hit more often than any other file. The mystery was solved when he realized that it contained the definition of a sexual act. He suggested that others should let their imaginations run wild and hide sexually oriented words on their Web pages so they'd be found by the search engines.

Mark Neely, an Australian lawyer and author of *The Australian Beginner's Guide to the Internet*, responded to the suggestion:

> *I really wouldn't encourage people to lace their HTML code with references to sexual-related materials or, for that matter, include keywords that are not related to the materials on their site.*
>
> *The power of Web search engines such as Yahoo and Lycos are their ability to accurately (within reason) catalog and index Web-based information resources.*
>
> *With current technology, a lot of the cataloging done to date is inaccurate. For example, you might think a site with details of Charlie Chaplin's movie career should be cataloged as an entertainment site, whereas others might consider it more appropriately listed as a media (or even cultural) site.*
>
> *As such, some fairly arbitrary decisions are made regarding site listings. This is even more so when the examination and categorizing of a site is achieved without human intervention through the use of a Web robot, a program designed to scan HTML files and select key words and appropriate index categories.*
>
> *Because Web indexing is an inaccurate art, using Web search engines is often a frustrating experience for many users. If everyone started lacing their HTML files with "choice" keywords, the whole system would become unworkable.*
>
> *Yes, in the short term you may increase your hits, but it will lead to a number of problems for you:*
>
> - *If it becomes an acceptable practice, then the prospect that your site (even with its extra keywords) will find its way to the top of the list becomes less likely. You may well be listed, but toward the bottom, many screens away (and this also applies to your legitimate listings) as searches turn up thousands of hits.*
>
> - *In the event that you do manage to lure someone to your site who was in fact looking for your competitor, you are more likely to alienate them than befriend them. You shouldn't lose sight of the fact that the customer is spending his money (as well as his time) being lured to your site under false pretenses. I'm certain that trade practices legislation will have something to say about that.*
>
> *It might not be considered unethical, immoral, or even illegal, but it certainly does undermine the usefulness of the Web.*

PERSONAL ACCOUNT
Mark Neely
Attorney and Internet consultant
http://www.ozemail.com.au/~accessnt
accessnt@ozemail.com.au

And finally, given recent moves in the U.S. and abroad, lacing your HTML with saucy words might even backfire. Your site will not only be inundated by connection requests from a bunch of socially challenged adolescents, but you might even find yourself running afoul of the Communications Decency Act (in whatever form it emerges from the appeals process) or many other similar pieces of legislation in force around the globe.

Not only does it undermine the Web's usefulness, it won't accomplish your purpose. Are "socially challenged adolescents" your potential clients? (Well, if you do juvenile defense work, maybe, but they won't be on the Net when they need your services).

Mark Welch discusses the proper way to bait the search engines and keep the search directories updated:

I continue to resubmit my new and updated Web pages to the search engines, to make sure they update information about my site. I have also made changes to some of my pages, especially the home page (index page, at http://www.ca-probate.com/index.htm), *so that my page will hopefully be more likely to appear in response to a relevant query. I learned the importance of choosing the right title for a Web page so that it makes sense when it appears in a list of responses from a search for a phrase like "estate planning" or "California probate attorney."*

Now, if you're planning to hire someone else to code your Web page, you may think the whole idea of baiting the search engines is not your problem. But who is going to tell your designer what to put on your page? You know best the type of person you want to visit your site. *You* are going to have to decide what types of titles will get people to visit. So, even if the letters "HTML" make you shiver in fear, you are the one who must figure out how to get people to find your site.

GET LINKED TO SIMILAR SITES

Your efforts should not stop at baiting the search engines. Contact the webmaster of similar sites and ask to link their site to yours (most pages contain a link to the site's webmaster or author). For example, Mark Welch's estate planning site might be successfully linked to a site catering to the elderly. A construction lawyer would probably love to have his site linked to the American Institute of Architects' Web site.

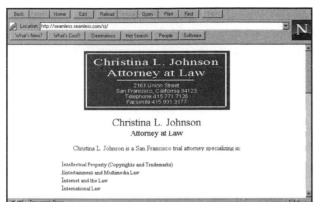

FIGURE 8-2

Christina Johnson's home page http://seamless.seamless.com/cj/

By accident, attorney Christina Johnson learned the importance of getting linked to other sites:

> *Unbeknownst to me, my page has been linked up to several other sites, including Thompson and Thompson (a trademark search firm) which has generated even more business in the area of trademark law. I recently received an inquiry from a man in New York who indicated that he had seen my page in connection with Thompson and Thompson and said I was the only law firm (out of at least twenty firms) to have a telephone number listed. He also said he was impressed that I called him so quickly following his email to me. I am now working with him on a trademark for his company.*

PERSONAL ACCOUNT

Christina Johnson

Attorney at law
http://seamless.seamless.com/cj

cjohns08@reach.com

The whole point is to get people to visit your site. It doesn't matter how they get to your site, whether it be by search engine or through another site. Either way, they are now through the front door. If you have good content, they will stay and learn about you and your firm.

NETWORK ON THE NET

We've now discussed the importance of getting your site found—either by search engines or by being linked to other sites. But there are many more ways to promote your Web site, most of which are "traditional" in nature. If your head has been spinning from the technology of the Internet and an overdose of words like "search engines" and "links," the rest of this section will be comforting.

All attorneys know the importance of networking with other attorneys. It's a good way to get referrals. Networking also occurs on the Net (a redundancy?), but with a little cybertwist. Gregory Siskind gives suggestions to promote your Web page by joining mailing lists or newsgroups:

You need to promote your Web page in as many places as possible. I partic-
ipate in a newsgroup in my practice area. Mainly, I just answer questions.
But my Web site's address and subscription info for my mailing list are in-
cluded in my signature. I also post the table of contents of my newsletter in
the newsgroup a few days before the newsletter is released. I always notice
increased activity on my site after I have answered a newsgroup question.
(By the way, be careful about including appropriate disclaimer language in
any posting.)

And once you have a Web site, there are other ways you can network
with your colleagues. If another attorney has a similar site, ask to be
linked to it. He, in turn, will ask you to return the favor. You now
have created another node on your lawyer network

PERSONAL ACCOUNT

Rein Nomm

Rein Nomm & Associates,
Inc.
http://users.aol.com/netir/
rna-ir1.htm

reinman@oeonline.com

You don't have to be a professional marketer to successfully promote your
Web page. Marketing on the Internet is just a different flavor of the marketing lawyers have been doing for years. Yet, it does help to have the advice of
a professional at times to focus the task. Rein Nomm, from Plymouth,
Michigan, *(http://users.aol.com/netir/rna-ir1.htm)* advises professionals how
to promote their Web site. He effectively summarizes the two key elements
of an effective site:

As a marketer of professional services, my experience has repeatedly shown
that the difference between a successful Web site (one that generates regular
traffic) and a run-of-the-mill site (one that even you wouldn't visit if it
weren't your firm's site) can be summed up in two words: content and pro-
motion. Give the cybercitizens a reason to visit your site (content) and then
let them know how to find your site (promotion).

Content could be as simple as providing links to sources of relevant infor-
mation or as complex as including a search engine to locate information in
a topical database created by your firm.

Promotion should be more than just listing your site with online search en-
gines (Yahoo et al), which is a good first step. To ensure that your site is
brought to the attention of prospective clients, you need to first identify (by
industry, profession, or geographic market) whom you are seeking to reach.
Then research the Internet for discussion groups (i.e., mailing lists such as
net-lawyers) and newsgroups that reach these target audiences. Next, be-
come an active participant on the list, contributing items of genuine worth
rather than overt self-promotion. If you are seeking to make contact with
corporations, run a search for their Web site and pay them a visit. Assum-
ing that your site includes information of value, send the company an email

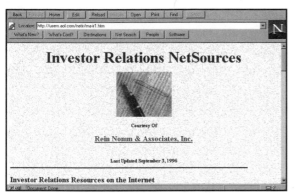

FIGURE 8-3
*Rein Nomm's page
clearly states the
firms focus.*

*message requesting them to visit and partake of the valuable informational
resources to be found on your Web site.*

*Although this approach requires more time than putting up a site and waiting
for the world to visit, it works. I've done it and I'm doing it again, right now.*

In addition to content and promotion, there are several other spices
that can improve the taste of your Web creation.

K.I.S.S. (KEEP IT SIMPLE, STUPID)

Lawyers have the reputation of taking the simplest transaction and
complicating it beyond all recognition. Deserved or not, don't let that
reputation apply to your Web site. If you don't make your Web site
accessible, it will not be visited.

What do I mean by accessible? Of course, every Web site is accessible
once it's on the Internet. But if your layout is so confusing that no
one can immediately make heads or tails of the page, a visitor will
quickly leave it. Content will mean nothing if no one spends time
looking at your page.

San Francisco attorney Christina Johnson has some very basic advice:

*My advice to any law firm or sole practitioner who is thinking of putting up
a home page is to keep it simple. I know the conventional wisdom is to constantly update your page and add substantive material for potential clients
to peruse. I have found, however, that the simplest content is the most approachable.*

Keeping a site simple also means that its layout must not overwhelm
the viewer. Although it may make the site pretty, the overuse of
graphics scares people away. In a small survey of lawyers conducted

in the fall of 1995, Lex Mundi's Steve McGarry asked lawyers what would improve the information available on the Internet. The third top suggested improvement was making access faster by including fewer graphics on Web pages.

What is "fast" access versus "slow" access? In Chapter 2, we discussed the various ways people connect to the Internet. For the vast majority of people, it's probably through a modem connection, although more and more people are getting high-speed connections (ISDN lines, T1 connections, and the like). But even with the fastest modem connection, too many graphics can be a concern.

Using the most common modem speed at the time, test your site. Samuel Lewis realized he was too heavy on the graphics once he started doing some testing:

> *Testing helped streamline the pages tremendously. More importantly, some of my best testing was done through my standard dial-up connection at home. The reason is quite simple. At the office, I had a direct network connection to the Web server, and so pages loaded incredibly fast. I started putting complex graphics on the pages, and the pages looked great. From home, through a modem, I saw how the pages loaded for anyone using a 14.4k or 28.8k modem. I reasoned that if I couldn't stand the wait for the page to load, then neither could anyone who might visit my Web site. Very quickly, the complex graphics were pulled out of the pages in exchange for simpler images or no images at all.*

Everyone has his or her own level of patience—for me, more than 10 or 15 seconds of waiting and I'm planning where to go next. Web surfers are impatient by nature. Don't make them wait, or they may visit some other lawyer's more accessible site.

Besides graphics, there are other fancy techniques that can backfire on a Web site. For example, more sites are incorporating frames, which break up the Web site into different units. It's a handy way to immediately throw a lot of content in front of the viewer. But done incorrectly (which is easy to do), it can chase the viewer to another site.

Just use your common sense. And remember the modem advice? Likewise, view your site from the most common size of monitor. The frames may look great on some 21-inch monitor at your Web designer's office, but how does it look on a basic 14-inch monitor?

Another way to make your home page load faster is to keep it short. Use it only as an introduction to your firm and as a directory to the other content at your site, which can then be accessed through links. Samuel Lewis discusses how he learned to keep his home page simple:

> *At first, my style included the text placed in tables, and horizontal lines broke each page into many different sections. It was only a matter of time until the tables almost completely disappeared, and the lines were used sparingly. Information on pages was split up into smaller pages rather than placing everything on one page; there's nothing more annoying than trying to load a Web page and having to wait for a huge page to load, when all I wanted was a little bit of information at the end of the page.*

Keeping a page simple is just a corollary of the keyword of Web page design: content. If a page is too complicated, a viewer will not be able to find the content. Kansas attorney Bruce Ward sums it up from his experience:

> *I look at literally hundreds of Web pages every month. Truthfully, most of them I see fail in my eyes for two reasons: (1) they lack interesting content, and (2) their design is so poor that either I can't get to the content provided or it is so distracting that I quickly lose interest and move on to another page.*
>
> *The design of a Web page needs only to be sophisticated enough to be reasonably pleasing to the eye and allow easy and sensible navigation to its various parts and sections. Anything else is counterproductive. Remember, content is everything.*

PERSONAL ACCOUNT

Bruce Ward

Attorney at law
http://www2.southwind.net/ ~bward/
bward@southwind.net

Don't be stupid. Keep your design simple, so the content can reach your site's visitors.

COMMUNICATE WITH THEM

As lawyers, we're all supposed to know the importance of communication. But by looking at some Web sites, you'd think otherwise. I've often searched Web sites trying to find a way to email a lawyer, and left in frustration without success.

One of the easiest tools is to have an email link at your Web site. With the link, the viewer only has to click on the link to open up an email box, already pre-addressed to you. Email links make it very easy for a viewer to contact you for legal work. And for most lawyers, that's the purpose of their Web site—to get new legal work.

Barry Levinsky, an attorney with Inland Steel in Chicago, says that if "nothing else, such a link suggests that the firm and the lawyer know how to use email." And in Gregory Siskind's opinion, you can't overdo it. At his firm's

Web site, they have made it easy for clients to contact the firm in numerous ways:

> You need to make it easy for people who find you to make contact. We have email links located at key places throughout our site: our front page, our bio page, our contact page. We have a consultation questionnaire form which makes conducting a telephone consultation much easier. We have an 800 number. We offer consultations using Internet Phone and CU-SeeMe.

But remember that if you have email links, you must regularly check your email—at least once a day, and probably more. This isn't a problem for lawyers who are already using email, but it may be for others.

PERSONAL ACCOUNT
Carl Middlehurst
Marketing and trademark attorney
Carl.Middlehurst@Corp.
Sun.com

Carl Middlehurst was surprised at how often this advice is ignored:

> One important thing to remember is that the Web is a two-way street. So while it is great to see a number of firms on the Web they have to remember that it will be interpreted as a sign that they use the Web. So if I send email to a big conservative firm via its Web site, I expect that someone will actually read it and respond. We did a random survey (while working with a journalist on another project—our email address looks like we might be a client) and found that some firms did not reply to email sent via the Web server. Some partners didn't ever read email, some didn't know how to respond, some were too busy, some didn't use it unless they knew who was sending them mail. On the other hand, some firms were great, and responded promptly. The basic message is if you set up a site and you know you have people in your firm who don't use email, have email from the site sent to an alias for a secretary or other postmaster. That way, at least in-house counsel who send email asking for information about a firm will get a response. Non-response sends a worse message than not having a Web site.

It's common sense that you must respond to email, but you must also have a working email link. I randomly tried email links on a number of Web sites. Although a pre-addressed email box came up on the screen, 5 to 10 percent of the messages were returned to me as non-deliverable. This, too, sends a worse message than not having a Web site at all. Make sure your email link works. Test it once in a while.

Another tool used by Net-savvy lawyers is to request that visitors sign a guestbook. Of course, many won't, but with the ones that do, you'll have created a mailing list of those interested in your legal services.

Maybe you'll have to give them an incentive to sign your guestbook. Siskind's law firm offers to send their immigration newsletter (by email, of course), if you'll give them your name and address. Gregory Siskind discusses the advantages of this approach:

> *Use your Web page to sign people up for your mailing list. Our Web site contains a free subscription form for our newsletter. Once a person is on your list, you don't have to worry about whether they visit your site. I know that every month, thousands of people are going to get my newsletter and see my firm's name. I typically hear from new clients who let me know that they have been reading my home page or getting my email newsletter for a year or more. By the time they contact us, they feel like they already know us pretty well. If I had to list any item as the most important part of our Web page, the subscription form would have to be it.*

Remember: once you have a potential client on your mailing list, the rest can be done the old-fashioned way. You can send them printed newsletters, firm brochures, or any other familiar marketing tools. And, in addition, you can keep them informed by email. You will soon learn that a Web page, tied in with email, is a great way to expand communications—and create legal work—with clients or potential clients.

TELL THEM WHAT YOU DO

If you stay in contact with potential clients, they can get to know you and, hopefully, will contact you when they need legal help. When you communicate with clients through your Web site, make sure they leave the site knowing something about you and what you do. Clients like to hire lawyers they know. Use your Web pages to let people get to know you.

I've heard people complain about boring Web sites that go on and on about "who" a lawyer is, but not "what" he does. Sure, that lawyer graduated from Harvard or this lawyer won some award. But can he solve my legal problem? Has he dealt with it before? For example, if a lawyer posts an article about a legal issue instead of just her résumé, she'll show that she can actually *do* something about a problem.

Telling a client what you do is giving an active picture of who you are, instead of a passive summary of your past accomplishments. Wichita attorney Bruce Ward developed his first home page in the summer of 1995. He says that if he were redesigning the page today, he'd do it differently:

> *I would de-emphasize the research part and better emphasize that part devoted to the nature of my office and practice. In other words, I would try to*

showcase those things that make my office special and that would entice an existing client to stay with us and a new client to come on board.

This could be done by highlighting the type of things I know and do in my practice. Yes, it is a tooting of my own horn, but so what? It can be done tastefully and effectively. These are the very things I used to do through my quarterly newsletter, which I have not had time to publish in the last two years.

Bruce's last comment is important. He wishes he had designed his Web page to be more like his newsletter, where he provided content that clients wanted to read. It suggests that an effective Web site will have many of the same elements as an effective newsletter. In newsletters, you give substantive information that tells clients what you *do* in your practice. Use the same tools for an effective Web site.

KEEP THE PAGE CURRENT

This final tip is more of an admonition. Don't let your site get out of date. A two-year-old firm brochure may be current, but a similarly aged Web site is a Model A Ford. Because an electronic Web page can be easily updated, there is little reason not to keep the page fresh and new.

The popular Web wisdom is that you must tell your viewers when you last updated the page. Take a look at a few Web pages, and most will have a "Last Updated" box somewhere on the page. Erika Penzer, former executive editor at *Counsel Connect*, says that "frequent updating is a very, very key element to a successful site." And she says that you should make it very obvious that you've done so: "You have to make it abundantly clear to everyone who visits it, right at the top, when you've updated it last, what is new, and if possible when the next update will be."

By frequently updating your site, the idea is to get repeat visits by the same viewers—if they like your site, they'll come back to see if you've added anything new and interesting. By a quick glance at the "Last Updated" reference, viewers will know whether they should stay at your site.

Of course, a lawyer doesn't need to do the updating himself, as it can be done by your Web site consultant. But a legal professional must provide the information for the update. You must expect a Web site to take some of your time. It could be as time-consuming as writing a new article every few weeks, or as little work as adding a link to a new court decision in your area of the law.

If you don't expect to change your site, you may not want to include any reference to the last time it was updated. But recognize that it won't take long for viewers to learn that nothing changes on your page. Unless you provide them with a unique resource that changes without your involvement (e.g., a link to another database), your repeat visits will dwindle to nothing.

Finally, even if you don't update your Web site's substance, make sure people can still find you. I used law firm directories, like the one at Washburn University School of Law, to find many law firms while writing this book. I was amazed at how many links led to non-existent sites. Assuming the directory had the correct URL, this meant that either the law firm had shut down its site or had moved without a forwarding address. This was much worse than not creating a Web page in the first place: my first impression of the law firm was negative. It had almost the same impact of receiving a letter stamped "Addressee Unknown." Would you retain that law firm in the future?

If you shut down your Web site, get it off the directories. If you move it to another server resulting in a new URL (which is not infrequent), maintain your old site for up to six months so that you can provide a forwarding link to your new site. Then notify every webmaster of sites that have links to your page and give them your new URL so they can update their link to you. No webmaster likes dead links on his or her page, and they may not go out of their way to find you, but rather may simply delete the link.

THE HOME MECHANIC... OR HIRE A HANDYMAN?

This book won't try to tell you how to properly code a Web page. In Chapter 3, we introduced HTML coding and gave a list of places where you can find software that lets you easily create your own Web pages. And there are dozens of good books out there that teach HTML coding, in addition to HTML software packages

But this book *will* try to raise some of the issues pertinent to whether you want to even try to code your own Web site or should leave it to an expert. Now, some lawyers have trouble turning their computers on and off, while others could have been sitting in Bill Gates's seat but for wasting time in law school. This is a personal thing, based solely on your "tech-tolerance" level.

If your tech-tolerance level is either very low or very high, then answering this question is easy. But if your level is anywhere in the middle, you'll want to listen closely to the professionals' advice in this section.

The first question is, of course: Is coding a Web page that difficult? As we discussed in Chapter 3, a Web page consists of coding in HTML, which works when your Web browser interprets the code and reveals a page according to the browser's interpretation. As a result, a Web page opened in Netscape's browser may look different than a Web page opened by Mosaic's browser.

You can view the coding of your favorite Web sites and learn from them how to do it yourself. Samuel Lewis relates his experience in getting his first Web page up and running:

> I started my crash course into HTML layout by finding a demo version of a Windows-based HTML editor. There are many different HTML editors available, including add-ins for Microsoft Word or WordPerfect which allow you to create a Web page in much the same way that you create and format a document. Still, having the editor didn't give me everything that I needed to know. So I went back to the source, literally. While browsing Web sites, I would start looking at the source code for those sites (Document Source is a menu option in Netscape). From this, I started to get an idea of what commands needed to be used where. Within a very short time, I had Web pages up for everyone in the world to see.

California attorney Mark Welch started with a free site on America Online, and used their software to create his first home page. He quickly graduated from AOL's basic setup and began using other software available on the Internet. After a couple of long weekends, his site was on the Internet:

> I started by downloading several HTML editors from various Web sites, and quickly learned that HTML coding (used in Web pages) is quite simple and easy to learn if you're familiar with older word processors that use special codes for formatting text (similar to WordPerfect's "reveal codes" mode).

> I created most of my Web pages using WordPerfect (without the "Internet Publisher" extensions), and the rest with text editors (including PC-Write and Windows Notepad). Most of the work was simply formatting the pages and adding links to other pages.

> It took about 20 hours in a single weekend to convert about a dozen newsletter articles and the 20 chapters of my booklet into Web pages, and to

upload them to America Online. (Other attorneys with comparable sites have spent much more time, apparently because they have less computer experience.)

I probably spent another 10-20 hours enhancing and revising pages since then, just for basic information and formatting. In addition, I have spent a lot of time "surfing the Internet" and as I do so, I frequently update my "Web Links" page (http://www.ca-probate.com/links.htm) to reflect new and newly discovered sites. As I write new newsletter articles, I add those to the Web site. Likewise, as I discover relevant articles elsewhere on the Web, I add links to those articles on my newsletter-articles page (http://www.ca-probate.com/news_idx.htm).

For computer-savvy attorneys, creating your own Web page will not be overly difficult. However, if word-processing software still drives you nuts or if you're already missing too many of your kid's ball games, you may want to hire a professional for the job.

Glynn Fluitt, Executive Vice President of MJM Communications in New York City, doesn't deny that a lawyer could code his own Web pages. But Glynn makes a case why lawyers are better off hiring a professional to design a Web site:

Yes, HTML is pretty simple. The concept, though, is garbage-in-garbage-out. Coming from a photography background, I can state it in this manner:

Anyone can buy a camera today and take a technically correct photograph this afternoon. As a photographer, I can take that same camera, apply a studied eye of composition, adjust an exposure, compensate for a mood, anticipate an audience, understand the chemistry at my lab, compensate for the shortcomings (color, saturation, hue, grain) of my film that I have stored in bulk and tested exhaustively, alternate between multiple formats of cameras, film, and end product to fit the usage, enhance a subject, diminish blemishes, and maintain quality control. Uncle Harry can photograph a wedding for the cost of a roll of film. I can photograph it for $1,200 plus the cost of the rolls of film. In the end, you'll be happier with the end product that I give you (unless Uncle Harry is an advanced photographer, in which case even he would not do the wedding for just the cost of a roll of film!).

Same thing applies to graphic design. I understand more of the psychology of composition, the impact of graphics, the intended impact on an audience, the general desired effect of a graphic end product, the resources that are available, the maintenance of an end product, and on and on, drawing on the years of experience that I have as a graphic designer. I have purchased additional software that allows me to enhance the products I design and in-

PERSONAL ACCOUNT

Glynn Fluitt
Executive Vice President,
MJM Communications
*http://catalog.com/mjm/
welcome.html*
gfluitt@ix.netcom.com

vested heavily into computer equipment on which to run that software. Certainly, you can pay me an hourly wage of $10/hr for my time, for which I will simply insert HTML tags into your pre-prepared text document, or you can pay me for the experience, background, and expertise that I bring to the table.

I am sorry to get a little windy on this, but client-education is one of the most aggravating aspects of an arts industry. Very few people look up from the operating table and ask the doctor why it costs hundreds of dollars for an injection when they can buy the syringe at the drug store themselves for fifty cents and the drug probably costs less than five cents/ml to produce.

The major point for a client to understand is that background and experience counts for something. If an artist is charging $1,000 per page and has nothing in a portfolio to show you, then you are overpaying. If an artist has a dynamic portfolio and only charges you $150 for "simple HTML insertion," then his/her true artistic capabilities will not be available to you and s/he will probably breed a resentment for you as an underpaying client who doesn't understand the complexities of this type of work.

Glynn's argument is probably persuasive to any lawyer who's been asked why it costs a thousand bucks for a "simple" contract. Experience isn't cheap, and you often get what you pay for.

But Mark Welch, who felt comfortable coding his own Web pages, disagrees, and feels that lawyer-created sites are superior:

I could have spent a lot more for the same (or worse) results. In an article in The Recorder, *a San Francisco legal newspaper, several law firms quoted costs as high as $500 per month and thousands of dollars in startup costs to create Web sites. Based on my evaluation of many other law firm Web sites, especially in my field, I think that the attorneys with the best Web sites are the ones who spent the least.*

The key to hiring a consultant, then, may be to stay close to the design process. Who knows your legal practice better than you? And who knows your potential clients better than you? If your consultant is not given any direction, it truly will be a "garbage-in-garbage-out" process. Don't forget: content is the key, and no consultant (even one with a lawyer background) knows better than you the type of content that will attract *your* clients.

Bruce Ward suggest lawyers should be "wary of page design consultants who will stress the razzle-dazzle of design over content." He suggests that you devote 90 percent of your time to the Web page's content and only 10 percent to its physical design. This means, of course, that no matter how you look at it, you—not a consultant—will do most of the work creating your Web site.

If you're simply curious about what your home page could look like but don't want to spend money on consultants quite yet, there are Web page generators that you can use for free on the Net. For example, Home Page Generator (*http://counsel.net/sampler*) will ask you a series of questions and then create a sample home page for you. I tried it and the finished product was extremely boring, being not much more than a business card. But with it and space on a Web server, a lawyer can have a Web presence in less than ten minutes.

YOU DON'T NEED A CALL FROM THE STATE ETHICS BOARD

The development of new technology moves much faster than our legal system. It often takes years for the law to catch up with the blazing pace of technological innovation. Since attorneys were first regularly found on the Web only as recently as 1994, very few jurisdictions have issued any statements on the ethical implications of this technological frontier.

With the law changing monthly, even daily, I won't attempt to explainhow to design and maintain a Web page that meets your jurisdiction's rules. By the time you read this, any definitive advice would be outdated. But it isn't an insurmountable problem. Attorneys from virtually every state are now on the Web, so you aren't the first lawyer to face this issue. Give your state bar a call, and I'm sure they can give you some guidelines to follow.

Although it's impossible to give any specific guidelines, there are several issues to consider. First, because the Internet goes everywhere—and I mean *everywhere* (not the moon, yet, but give it time)—do you have to comply with the advertising rules of every state? Every country? Of course, taken literally, this is impossible; you're not going to concern yourself with Ugandan laws. But what about those of Iowa? Despite the uniqueness of the Internet, the issue isn't entirely new. For example, existing print and broadcast advertising crosses state borders. But the rules concerning it may not apply to Web pages.

Second, all jurisdictions prohibit the unauthorized practice of law. If you provide legal advice over the Internet to a person residing in a state in which you aren't licensed, are you illegally practicing law in that state? Again, this issue isn't entirely new, but the Internet's ignorance of borders exacerbates the problem.

Third, if your Web page only provides information and doesn't solicit legal business, is it even advertising? Must it comply with the advertising rules of the ethics codes?

To address these questions, you should look at several rules of the ABA Model Rules of Professional Conduct (or whatever similar rules have been adopted in your jurisdiction). In particular, look at Rules 7 and 8.

In addition to these general rules, some states (such as Iowa, Texas , and Florida) have imposed specific new rules on Web pages. The new rules, some of which are quite restrictive, have caused some lawyers to not publish Web pages.

If you build a Web site, you should consider the use of several disclaimers to avoid creating an attorney/client relationship with someone who is not yet a client. Peter Krakaur, who runs the *legalethics.com* Web site, presented these draft disclaimers for discussion purposes only in May of 1996 at the Second Annual Statewide Ethics Symposium in California. Because the law is changing quickly and the rules of every jurisdiction vary, you should check with your state bar for guidance and not rely on these draft disclaimers to meet your jurisdiction's rules:

- Home Pages: [Attorney/law firm] is licensed to practice in the State of ___. Our principal office is located in ____, __. [We have attorneys who are also licensed to practice in the State(s) of ___.] The information provided in this Web Page Set is offered for informational purposes only; it is not offered as and does not constitute legal advice. [Attorney/law firm] does not seek to represent you based upon your visit or review of this Web Page Set. This Web Page Set may be considered advertising under the rules of _____. You should not make legal hiring decisions based upon brochures, advertising or other promotional materials. This Web Page Set was reviewed by [attorney].

- Email Fill-in/Response Forms: Please feel free to send us email with your thoughts about our Web Page Set or to request more information about us. The transmission of an email request for information does not create an attorney-client relationship, and you should not send us via email any information or facts relating to your legal problem or question. If you are not a client of [law firm/attorney], your email may not be privileged or confidential. If you are a client, remember that email may NOT be secure. There is a risk that your communication may be intercepted illegally. There may also be a risk of waiver of attorney-client and/or work-product privileges that may attach to your communication.

But disclaimers alone are not going to address the ethical rules of your Web site. To give you an overview of the current status of the law, Susan Ross, an attorney and founder of the Internet consulting firm InterLegal Services, published an article in the May 1996 issue of *The Internet Lawyer* (*http://www.internetlawyer.com*). The entire article is reprinted below:

PERSONAL ACCOUNT
Susan Ross
InterLegal Services
intrlegl@netzone.com

If It Walks and Talks Like an Ad: Web Pages, Advertising, and Ethics.

You have convinced members of your firm and yourself that the firm needs to develop a Web page. It will provide marketing for the firm, information to the general public, and a presence on the Internet. Is this advertising? If it proposes a commercial transaction, then the answer is yes. Now, have you thought about whether and how your state's ethics rules on advertising may apply?

Many states have adopted the Model Rules of Professional Conduct. These rules permit a lawyer to advertise legal services through public media provided the lawyer refrains from making false or misleading statements, the lawyer retains a copy or recording of the advertisement for two years, and the ad includes the name of at least one lawyer responsible for its content. The rules also restrict a lawyer's payment of referral fees and solicitation of prospective clients.

Just as states have adopted these or similar rules and applied them to television, radio, and print ads, now states are assessing how these rules apply to the unique features of the Internet, including Web pages. Although several states are currently evaluating how their ethics rules apply to the Internet, Florida and Texas have led the pack by putting guidelines into place. In Florida, the state bar issued a statement on the regulations of Web pages in the January 1, 1996, issue of the Florida Bar News. In that statement, the Florida bar concluded that attorney Web pages are advertising, that the current ethical rules apply to all computer ads, not just Web pages, and that attorneys must submit hard copies of their Web pages for review along with a $50 filing fee.

In Texas, the state bar has issued interpretive commentary for Internet advertising. Texas attorneys must submit copies of their home pages and any material changes to the state bar along with a $50 filing fee. The commentary also gives examples of information that generally do not constitute solicitation, such as attorney biographical information, news articles, and announcements of personnel changes. However, all of the material on the Web site must comply with the Texas Disciplinary Rule of Professional Conduct. Although Florida and Texas have taken these initial steps, both states are still looking at additional issues of lawyer advertising on the Internet.

Several other states, including Arizona, Kentucky, and New Jersey, are evaluating whether and how their current advertising rules apply to the Internet. New Jersey is expected to issue a report in May. Arizona is looking at how the current rules apply and whether new rules are necessary.

Meanwhile, Arizona attorneys must comply with the current advertising rules when designing a Web page. Kentucky's state bar has stated that attorneys should submit Web pages to the Attorneys' Advertising Commission, and that each Web page must contain a statement indicating an advertisement.

Although current rules can easily address some issues, such as labeling Web pages as advertising and ensuring that none of the information on the Web page is false or misleading, some issues are more complex. For example, if your state requires approval of advertising before publication, does that mean that you must submit your weekly updates to your Web page for approval? Not only could such a process be onerous for the bar, it also could delay your firm's ability to get information out on a timely basis.

How do states handle retention requirements for sites that are constantly updated or collecting information? Tennessee, for example, requests a print copy of marketing material on the Web site as launched and on a monthly basis. Other states are still looking at these issues.

Keep in mind that current state rules may not be sufficient. The Internet knows no state boundaries, and therefore, choice of law becomes a major issue. A potential client in Iowa looks up an Arizona attorney's Web page, and although the Web page complies with Arizona's rules, it violates Iowa's rules. Which state's rules control? This issue also affects firms located in multiple states or with attorneys licensed in multiple states.

For those issues that fall into the gray area of whether and how the current rules apply, formal ethics opinions may be necessary. Some issues may require new rules. Unfortunately, getting a formal ethics opinion or new rule in place can take several months—and you are looking at putting up a Web page now. What do you do in the meantime? Ask. Contact your state bar.

Most likely, you are not the first attorney in the state to ask about applying ethical rules on advertising to Web pages.

For more information on ethics and the Internet, check out Kuesterlaw at http://www.kuesterlaw.com. Jeff Kuester, an attorney in Georgia and chair of the state's NetEthics Committee, has an award-winning site that addresses ethics and the Internet. The ABA/BNA Lawyer's Manual on Professional Conduct has recently published a two-part article on advertising, email, and other ethical issues that face attorneys on the Net. You can reach this article at Kuesterlaw or through the BNA's site at http://www.bna.com. For an update of what is happening in your state, check out http:///www.legalethics.com, a site maintained by Peter Krakaur, an attorney and Internet consultant in California.

In addition to Susan Ross' article, there are several other ethics articles that can be found on the Internet. For example, at *http://www.legalethics.com/articles.htm* you can find the following:

- "The Ethical Boundaries of Selling Legal Services in Cyberspace," by William E. Hornsby, Jr., staff counsel to the American Bar Association Commission on Advertising

- "Analysis: Ethics of Advertising on the Internet," Joan C. Rogers, legal editor of the *ABA/BNA Lawyers' Manual on Professional Conduct.*

If you're interested in the ethical rules governing Web pages (do we have a choice?), regularly check Peter Krakaur's site at *http://www.legalethics.com* for the latest in legal ethics issues. In addition, the School of Communications at California State University, Fullerton, has an ethics site at *http://www5.fullerton.edu/les/ethics_list.html*. Legal ethics is only one of several subjects included, as it also has links for business ethics, movie ethics, and military ethics, to name just a few.

Legal Trends on the Internet

9

In the world of electronics, the future arrives faster than a printed book can make it to the shelf. Visionary predictions risk missing the obvious. For example, attorney Eugene Volokh wrote about the risk of trying to predict the future in *Technology and the Future of Law*[1]:

> *The slide rule was a marvelously elegant mathematical device, and it earned its manufacturers millions. In 1967, one such manufacturer, Keuffel & Esser Co., commissioned a study of what life would be like in a hundred years. The study predicted 3D television and domed cities, but it didn't predict that within five years the electronic calculator would be the slide rule's death. Beware, the slide rule story says—if you don't foresee technological changes, you're in trouble.*

With the assistance of other legal professionals, this chapter attempts to identify what the Internet will do to the practice of law in the future. Most of the changes are already in play, and not wild predictions of domed cities or intergalactic travel.

▶ Cultivating Class Actions

▶ Virtual Law Firms

▶ Worldwide Law Networks

▶ Electronic Service and Filing

▶ Widespread Public Legal Information

▶ Teleconferencing

[1] 47 Stan. L. Rev. 1375 (1995)

CULTIVATING CLASS ACTIONS

In the introduction, we talked about how the Internet excelled in the quick and inexpensive distribution of information. It only seems natural, then, that as the Net's reach expands, it will be used for finding members for class actions.

PERSONAL ACCOUNT
Brian Hufford
Pomerantz Haudek Block & Grossman
http://seamless.com/ pomlaw
DBH1959@aol.com

For example, an owner of a Dodge Caravan tapped into an Internet newsgroup in March of 1995 after she spent several months trying to draw attention to the braking problems she experienced with her minivan. Once on the newsgroup, a flurry of emails and postings resulted. Soon, the owner of a problem Chrysler created a Web site devoted to Chrysler anti-lock brakes problems. New York attorney Brian Hufford writes about how the Internet helped build his class action:

> In the summer of 1995, I was contacted by a friend whose brakes had failed on his Jeep Cherokee. When he learned that an acquaintance of his had also had problems with his brakes, he called me, asking me to investigate to determine whether there might be a defective part involved. I immediately used available legal databases to determine whether there had been any news reports about the problem and found out that, in fact, there had been numerous complaints about the anti-lock braking system (ABS) in certain Chrysler vehicles, in particular the Bendix 10 ABS system that was used in the 1991-1993 minivans and various other models. At this time, I had joined America Online and also used CompuServe, but did not rely on them much for my practice.

> One news story changed all that, however. It reported that Charlene Blake was leading a movement on the Internet to focus attention on the Chrysler ABS problem, and it gave her email address. So I sent her an email explaining who I was and asking if she could help me with my investigation. Charlene responded soon after and, within a short period of time, provided me with the email addresses of many other people who had had similar problems. In addition, Charlene directed me to certain newsgroups on the Internet where people discussed problems with their automobiles. I then searched —and found—the same thing on AOL. In short, these newsgroups permitted individuals with a particular problem to explain what had happened and ask if other people had experienced the same thing.

> By reviewing the messages left on the newsgroups, I identified many people who apparently had the same problem with their ABS and I sent them an email explaining my investigation. Nearly all of them replied, and most of them immediately asked if they, too, could participate in the action. By Oc-

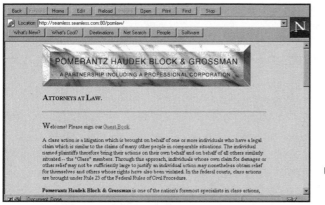

FIGURE 9-1

tober 1995, I had 34 named plaintiffs (as well as many other contacts) and filed suit against Chrysler on behalf of a class of all current and former owners or lessees of the Chrysler vehicles (representing more than 350,000 consumers). It does not stop there, however. While I knew that there was a substantial problem with the Chrysler brakes, and had identified many people who had suffered as a result, we still had no idea exactly what was the defect that caused the failure of the ABS systems.

Through the Internet I began to inquire as to whether anyone had any ideas. I received a number of very helpful responses from people who happened to have above-average experience with automobiles who were able to explain to me how brake systems work and what their theories were about the problem. Through these ideas, I was able to begin putting together an amended complaint which spelled out the details of the defect. Then I was contacted through the Internet by a former Chrysler mechanic, who told me that he worked on the ABS systems and had received from Chrysler what is called a "Master Tech"—a manual that Chrysler issues periodically to help its mechanics deal with persistent problems. This manual, which the mechanic sent me, addressed the diagnosis and repairs of a "typical" problem in both the Bendix 10 ABS as well as the Bendix 9 ABS used in the 1989-1991 Jeep Cherokees.

In sum, that problem consisted of a leak in the master cylinder seal which caused the ABS pump to run continuously in order to build up the necessary pressure in the accumulators. Because of its overuse, the pump would eventually fail, leading to a loss of both the ABS as well as all power-assisted braking —causing a substantial loss of braking power. When I compared this analysis with the reports I had received from my plaintiffs (including information contained on repair records they had maintained with respect to their ABS systems), it was clear that this was the defect that had caused their brake systems to fail. Moreover, through other Internet contacts, I was able to obtain copies of certain Technical Service Bulletins (TSBs), which Chrysler disseminates over time to its dealers. These TSBs can actually be located through resources on the Internet itself, suggesting that Chrysler had been aware of the problem for quite some time but had failed to acknowledge it publicly.

With the new information in hand, I filed an extremely detailed amended complaint in March 1996, this time with more than 100 named plaintiffs. Barely a month later, in mid-April, Chrysler announced that it was doing a "safety recall" of the ABS systems because of the persistent leak in the master cylinder seal. In short, Chrysler finally conceded the defect and agreed to take action to correct it. In my opinion, this action was largely influenced by our lawsuit, which laid out the nature of the defect and Chrysler's knowledge of it. As of this date (August 1996), our litigation is still pending, and Chrysler has not conceded anything, including the effect of our case on its decision to recall the brakes. Nevertheless, the case shows just how powerful the Internet can be. Without it, I would have been limited to a very small number of people with the problem and with virtually no way to identify the cause of the problem without getting discovery from Chrysler.

With the Internet, however, I was able to contact numerous affected Chrysler consumers all across the country (and the world for that matter, as I also was in contact with people in Canada, South America, and Europe who had had Chryslers with similar problems), while at the same time exploring the cause of the problem through many experts who are on the system. The Internet has now become a daily part of my practice. I sign on to it several times a day and use it on a regular basis to investigate cases.

Currently, I am pursuing several cases against health maintenance organizations (HMOs) for, among other things, the failure to disclose the financial incentives they pay to their participating physicians to encourage them to reduce the level of care they provide to their patients. Through the Internet, I have developed contacts across the country who are interested in the same issues and are quite willing to help me with such cases. Because of my experience, I have now arranged for my firm to upgrade its computers so that everyone can have easy access to the Internet, and I also have arranged for our firm to have its own Web page.

The Internet represents the future. It provides a unique means for a single person, whether in a small town or a metropolis, to contact like-minded people across the world and to raise issues and concerns that affect them. It provides a means for people who have suffered similar damages or injury to contact one another, to find out how to deal with their problems, and to seek solutions. In short, it is democracy at work—and the best tool the "little guy" could ever have.

Brian's experience is not all that unique. For other lawyers, the Net has also played a supporting role for class actions. At the "Consumer Law Page," sponsored by the law firm of Alexander, Rapazzini & Graham (*http://consumerlawpage.com/*), you can link to a page regarding General Motors' ABS brakes and the problems alleged with its ABS braking system. If you've had problems, the page asks you to fill out a questionnaire relaying your experiences, thus using the Web site as a way to build a class action lawsuit.

California attorney Mark Thierman writes how he used the Internet to quickly find the evidence necessary to support a class action:

> *The story starts after my wife was subjected to a sudden "declaration" of being surplus by a new manager who didn't like her, after she had a record of more than ten years of great service and wonderful reviews in the company. She was the right-hand person, and a major executive mover and shaker, so the new "boy" on the block didn't like her. Fifteen days after being her boss, without a meeting or any review, my wife was surplus. I filed a wrongful termination lawsuit, and put a small (five-page) memo in an email to all the company's managers (there were approximately 12,587 of them), inviting them to furnish information of "similar" instances and asking if they wanted to join as named plaintiffs in the lawsuit. When the class members responded, we had more than fifty boxes of information all showing that the company was lying when it declared surplus, since it hired back twice as many as it declared surplus, 20 percent of them former company employees without benefits. We now have more than 120 named plaintiffs, the class is about 1,600 former employees, and cross-motions for partial summary judgment are pending.*
>
> *Now my whole practice has changed, as we filed a second multi-million dollar wage hour overtime case for 450 low level "managers" who don't manage people, just things.*

PERSONAL ACCOUNT

Mark Thierman
Thierman Law Firm
http://www.tvlf.com/
thiermn1@tvlf.com

The experiences of Mark Thierman, Brian Hufford, and others demonstrate the Net's power to quickly and cheaply garner information. As information is often the key to creating and supporting a class action, expect to see many more class actions birthed on the Internet.

VIRTUAL LAW FIRMS

The word "virtual" is already suffering from overuse—virtual reality, virtual corporations, and yes, virtual sex. The promise of virtual law firms may be less titillating, but no less exciting.

But what is a virtual law firm? There are probably as many definitions as there are such firms in existence today. Just as there are many forms of law firms (partnerships, corporations, of-counsel arrangements, affiliations, and associations), there are many variants of virtual law firms. One defining feature of a virtual law firm is what it's *not*: it's not a bunch of lawyers planted in the same office, sharing the same conference rooms and the same secretaries. Instead, it's a group of lawyers tied together by only electronic means. Today, that electronic tie is usually email, but it will increasingly involve more sophisticated variants such as teleconferencing and the like.

Being in its infancy, the virtual law firm (VLF) of today has met only partial success and works better in theory than in practice. For example, the founder of a California firm that touts itself on the Net as "The Virtual Law Firm" admits that he has only received a small amount of work as a result of his VLF. Given its uniqueness, he has had problems with things such as malpractice insurance. Without his traditional practice, his VLF may not have continued.

In the near term, the future may not be so bright for VLFs that don't also exist in some traditional form. But this doesn't mean that other variants of VLFs aren't working. In fact, variants of VLFs are very successful today. These VLFs are more like the traditional associations of law firms to create referral networks among the members.

PERSONAL ACCOUNT
Harris Tulchin
Harris Tulchin & Associates
http://www.laig.com/law/intnet

EntEsquire@aol.com

In California, entertainment lawyer Harris Tulchin has created an association of law firms held together by a Web page. In the summer of 1995, he conceived and developed the International Entertainment and Multimedia Law and Business Network (*http://www.laig.com/law/intnet*). He writes about how he has used the Net to create a lucrative group of attorneys unified around his Web page:

> *Essentially, I am a sole practitioner involved in the practice of entertainment, multimedia, and intellectual property law but, having been in practice for 17 years, I have developed positive relationships with attorneys around the world who have agreed to become affiliates, of counsel, or simply colleagues of the firm, thereby building a worldwide network of entertainment law firms in a dozen of the top film and television producing nations around the world. I've encouraged the members to contribute articles and outlines of helpful information regarding pertinent legal and business issues in the entertainment and multimedia industries. We now have a number of excellent articles and outlines up on the Web. We also provide direct links to the major film festival Web sites around the world along with a calendar of events in the multimedia business. Other staples of the site in-*

clude direct links to copyright and trademark laws, other useful legal and business Web sites, a description of our services, and bios of the affiliates. There's a considerable amount of content on the site. While a lot of other sites have glitzy graphics, we have none. In order to keep the initial set up cost relatively low, we chose not to include graphics. We've also found that visitors don't have to wait long to get the content. As the technology improves we may change this strategy, but right now it seems to work.

From an initial investment of $500, we have generated substantial actual revenue from clients around the world whom we would never have reached. The time invested along with the maintenance has definitely been worth it. I do spend about 45 minutes to an hour a day monitoring mail and responding to inquiries along with sending letters and email...it's a regular part of my day now and I enjoy it.

In New Jersey, lawyers Parry Aftab and Nancy Savitt have created the "Virtual Law Firm Network." Because they practice domestic and international law matters, they needed support in complex legal specialties, such as international tax, environmental law, and intellectual property. Rather than hiring lawyers to meet those needs, they created a network of other practitioners to help on a case-by-case basis.

CONTACT
Parry Aftab
Aftab & Savitt, P.C.
http://www.aftab.com
paftab01@counsel.com

Using a private online room, the VLF Network members share announcements, new legal developments, and marketing ideas, just like they would during a firm meeting. And they also use the Internet to transmit all of their documents back and forth among members working on a case. Corrections and comments can be made online in their private rooms. This VLF has permitted Parry and Nancy to simultaneously harvest the best aspects of a large and small firm.

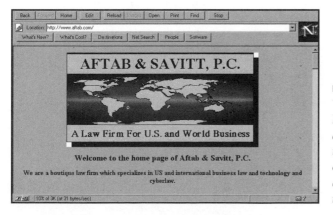

FIGURE 9-3
The Internet knows no borders, a fact that AFTAB & SAVITT exploit at their site.

Thousands of other lawyers use the Internet to join their practices together. As the technology becomes more familiar, we'll see more variants of virtual law firms on the scene. Certainly, the traditional law firm—bound by common walls—will not soon pass away. But virtual law firms—bound by electronics—will grow and mutate, expanding the ways for you to practice law in the future.

WORLDWIDE LAW NETWORKS

It isn't too hard to see the practical uses of email for a lawyer. But take this mundane technology and integrate it into a system, and the uses are limitless. The Internet will be used as the primary means of tying lawyers together around the world.

PERSONAL ACCOUNT
David P. Berten
Bartlit Beck Herman
Palenchar & Scott
David.Berten@
bartlit-beck.com

When time is short and there's a lot of work to do among many lawyers, only a technology that is easy and instantaneous will get the job done. Lawyer David Berten explains how email was used by a trial team, spread all over the country, to prepare for trial on short notice:

Six months ago, two of my partners and I were contacted by a new client with a serious problem. The client's motion for summary judgment in a patent case had just been denied. Trial started in six weeks, and the client wanted an experienced jury trial lawyer to try the case. The trial team included one lawyer from our Denver office, two from our office in Chicago, a law student, patent counsel from another Chicago law firm, local counsel in Minneapolis, and the client in Miami.

Within days, all seven of these people had established secure email connections with each other. As the trial lawyers poured over depositions and documents to learn the basic facts of the case, email inquiries were fired off to the client and patent counsel. Answers would circulate almost instantly. Within a week, a detailed theory of the case and a draft opening statement were emailed from the trial counsel for extensive input and corrections from the client and patent lawyers.

Lawyers who don't use email might find little remarkable about that story. Phones and fax machines would seem to allow the same level of communication. The truth is, though, they don't. As anyone who has tried it knows, just scheduling a conference call among seven people is a major juggling act. Actually pulling one off, with every lawyer there at the appointed hour, is the full circus.

The fact is, no one undertakes such a big production to address routine questions. The routine questions are never asked, or the person who really needs to know—the trial lawyer—rarely hears the answer directly from the horse's mouth. The fax machine's best use is fast communication of formal written documents, not informal communications. Just getting it out takes many hands: the lawyer, the secretary, the person who takes it to the fax room, and the person who faxes it out. On the receiving end, the process gets repeated in reverse.

For David Berten's case, secure email was the only way to get the job done. Without email, the lawyers would have all packed up and moved into a Minneapolis hotel so that they could jointly prepare for trial. Instead, they could just as efficiently remain in their own offices, until trial forced them to physically relocate to Minneapolis to try the case (and this may change in the future, too, as we'll discuss later).

Faced with tying lawyers together for more than one case, lawyer Michael P. Curreri created a product known as "TrialNet" (*http://www.trialnet.com*) for his insurance clients. He explains the problem and how they used the Internet as part of the solution:

PERSONAL ACCOUNT
Michael P. Curreri
Wright, Robinson, Osthimer & Tatum
http://www.trialnet.com
mcurreri@trialnet.com

Our contact with our insurer and corporate clients over the last few years has reflected a common theme among them. Market pressures have required their companies to continue to reinvent themselves to stay competitive. Greater efficiencies inside each company have been accompanied by significant efforts to bring legal expenses and fees under control. The difficulty, of course, has always been in finding ways to reduce those expenses without inordinately increasing indemnity pay-outs. Over the last year, we have completed development of a litigation management network which can be implemented at almost no cost to insurance companies (or other self-insured "sponsors"). By coordination and collaboration of the efforts of outside counsel, this system achieves both the goals of increased quality and decreased cost. That networked system is now made available to our clients through a separate company called TrialNet for which I act as president.

We realized early on that carriers were concerned about the expense of defending their insureds in technically complex litigation where the "learning curves" for individual counsel could be substantial. There appeared to be considerable potential for increasing quality and decreasing costs associated by coordinating outside counsel. Until recently, the most effective tool for that coordination was the use of electronic bulletin board systems (BBSs). While the BBS software of the 1980s had the capability of providing these

FIGURE **9-4**
*TrialNET provides an information sharing resource for member trial lawyers
http://www.trialnet.com/*

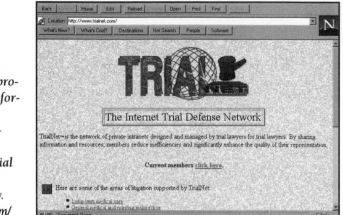

benefits, they tended to be difficult to use, somewhat limited in scope, required long distance charges to access, and generally were much less user-friendly than the networking applications of 1996.

In an effort to take full advantage of the emerging technology originally developed for the Internet, we created TrialNet. TrialNet is a system of software, hardware, and business methods for collecting, organizing, and disseminating litigation information among the participants in civil litigation. The network electronically connects law firms and their mutual clients using current networking technology and the original programming of Trial-Net itself. It is the only such service available in the nation.

TrialNet permits member defense counsel to share information relating to defense litigation in ways that were not technically possible only a year ago and can be customized for the particular client, subject matter, or geographic region. Some of the functions currently available on this system include:

- *Collections of materials regarding plaintiff's experts, including full-text transcripts, curriculum vitae, information regarding utilization of the experts and effective opposition to them, authored literature, prior rulings, etc.*

- *Logic-driven word search engines (similar to that used by Lexis or Medline) for searching and retrieving testimony from expert depositions and trial transcripts, medical literature collections, legal briefs, etc.*

- *Similar collections and search engines for defense expert witnesses, organized using methods that are particularly useful to defense counsel.*

- *Information regarding opposing counsel, including standard discovery, pleadings, objections, adverse rulings, tips from other defense counsel and "standard expert witness information."*

- *For corporate sponsors, standardized client-approved discovery responses, custom designed tools to reduce in-house repetitive functions, information regarding common discovery issues, internal personnel directories, and information about potential corporate fact witnesses and standard corporate exhibits.*

- *Graphic catalog of trial exhibits and an automated system of sharing the exhibits.*

- *Key pleadings, motions, and memoranda samples, with information regarding prior rulings.*

- *Links to all federal government agencies, many courts, dozens of law libraries (with services such as fully searchable C.F.R., U.S. Code, and state codes), daily updates of Congressional and agency actions, NIH library connection, and hundreds of other time- and cost-saving information sources.*

- *Fully automated uploading and indexing of data, using methods designed specifically for litigators and litigation/claims managers.*

- *Links to daily-updated industry news summaries. Communications "center" for counsel-to-counsel postings, queries, and automated email communications.*

- *Home page for in-house litigation counsel or claims managers to allow for effective communication of topical issues and concerns to all counsel with email simplicity.*

- *Unlimited use of Medline as a "bundled" service in addition to the other services noted above.*

All of this information is maintained on secure server computers that are owned by TrialNet, Inc. Data is transmitted over regular telephone lines (rather than requiring expensive special hardware), but is fully encrypted during transmission for security. Information that is client-specific is only accessible by designated counsel for that client. Otherwise, information is available to all designated counsel who have access to the system through the use of frequently changed passwords. Because certain generic information is made available to all members with similar interests (e.g., engineering expert witness information), a sponsor's outside counsel gets the full benefit of not only their own combined work product, but the experience and information available from all other similarly situated defense counsel throughout the system.

TrialNet networking is a very tangible method by which defense costs can be significantly reduced while meaningfully increasing the quality of represen-

tation by outside counsel. It is a method of efficiently and effectively coordinating the efforts and information of all counsel for the mutual benefit of our clients.

As lawyers discover the Internet's potential, expect to see more and more systems like TrialNet using the Net's global reach.

ELECTRONIC SERVICE AND FILING

My local court first allowed filing by fax in the 1980s. At first, I was surprised, because the clerks and judges had to read dot-matrix-like print on curly paper. But I learned that the courts were willing to adapt to the way lawyers practiced law.

Likewise, expect the courts to adapt to lawyers using the Net. More so than the fax, electronic document transfer holds many advantages for the courts. Don't expect the Internet to kill paper-based court systems, but in this era of tight public budgets, expect the courts to demand electronic documents instead of paper when it saves time and money. As Washington attorney John Maxwell states:

> *It seems only logical that the next step is to have all of the filing done electronically so the clerk does not have to deal with any papers. This will save the taxpayer a lot of money and the large spaces dedicated to storing paper files would be eliminated. Most judges, like most attorneys, like to read from paper rather than from a computer screen. Those parties who want a paper copy of motions and affidavits can still print whatever they want to read.*

And the federal courts in the Northern District of Ohio are leading the way in this transition. The Electronic Filing and Attorney Docketing Service has been operating since January 1, 1996. This system allows attorneys to electronically submit pleadings and docket entries over the Internet, eliminating the need for court staff to handle paper documents or make docket entries. The system manages the thousands of maritime asbestos cases that it receives each year. These asbestos cases involve approximately 400 attorneys who create approximately 500,000 docket entries per year. All filings must be electronic and the service permits attorneys to electronically view and obtain all case documents and dockets from their offices.

Patti Smith, a paralegal with Vorys, Sater, Seymour and Pease of Columbus, Ohio, writes about the Ohio system:

PERSONAL ACCOUNT

Patti Smith
Paralegal, Vorys, Sater,
Seymour and Pease
smithpa@vssp.com

> We were part of a pilot group which tested the beta (and now continues to use) the current version of the Electronic Filing System (EFS) written for the Northern District Federal Court for Maritime Asbestos Litigation in Cleveland, Ohio. This system allows lawyers to actually file their pleadings via the Internet directly with the court and thus reduce costs from paper, postage, copying, and the like.
>
> The EFS was written because of the volume of maritime cases in the Northern District Court (approximately 20,000) and the fact that the court personnel were literally months behind in processing. It was recognized that everyone could benefit by having an avenue to directly file pleadings (with the formatting used in any word processor rather than simply uploading an ASCII file as an attachment to email, etc.). The Administrative Office of the U.S. Courts (Technology Enhancement Office, or TEO) became involved and began to create such a system. The TEO pointed us toward the court's home page, including a comment board so we could post any difficulties and share our knowledge in working through the initial quirks of a new system. In addition, the pilot group members and the court officials all traded email addresses and telephone numbers so we could communicate easily.
>
> Our first "live" experience began with cases filed in 1996. Plaintiffs file their complaints via the EFS; however, service of the summons and complaint on the defendants is still done according to the Rules. Once our clients are served and our answers prepared in our word processor, we log onto the EFS using the pre-distributed attorney log-on name and password provided by the court when we registered our attorneys. The "act" of this log-on is the "official signature" from the attorney authorizing the pleading to be filed.
>
> Thereafter the system is written to be very user-friendly in that it acts as a form with fill-in blanks and browser ability. At the initial log-on there is a one-time procedure to "soft link" an attorney with his/her client name for future identification. We are taken through a series of questions; i.e., case number, pleading type, etc., and the pleading file is sent and the filing accomplished. We are given a transaction number so we can verify that our filing was received and accepted.
>
> There are also report-writing programs to see what pleadings are still due and what has already been filed, as well as the ability to access a docket of a case and then download any pleading. Once again, everything is accessed and accomplished by a fill-in-the-form type action. At the current time, there are no monetary fee charges by the court, although this may change in

the future. However, it is still anticipated that costs can be held to a minimum by using the Internet.

Once electronic filing systems become more common and the legal system becomes more familiar with their workings, we can expect to see more courts using electronic filing systems. Because of the potential cost savings (ease of filing, less storage space), in the not-too-distant future we may find courts *requiring* electronic filing. Paper filing may never disappear, but it may eventually take second chair to electronic documents.

There are more than just cost-saving advantages to electronic pleadings. Stanford law professor Joseph A. Grundfest demonstrated this when he filed a copy of a Supreme Court brief on the Web because it gave the justices hypertext links to all of the cited materials. "This is the future," he predicted. "The legal system will initially learn about the Internet through supplemental postings that don't replace paper. Gradually, we may evolve to an environment where hypertext postings on the Net are the rule, not the exception." Professor Grundfest's brief can be found at *http://www-leland.stanford.edu/group/law/reckless*. Although I don't predict the Supreme Court to soon be reading their briefs on a laptop, I'm sure even the most senior justice can see the utility of hypertext links to all citations.

In addition to Internet filing of pleadings and briefs, expect to see the Net used to serve process in certain situations. Currently, many states allow service by fax, especially for motions when time may be of the essence. In England, at least, one court has already allowed the service of an injunction by email. California attorney Harris Tulchin relays the story:

> *The law firm of Schilling and Lom (an affiliate of the International Entertainment and Multimedia Law and Business Network) successfully served a High Court injunction by email. The order was obtained by Justice Newman after a threat was issued by an individual who evidently sought to distribute libelous material about one of Schilling and Lom's clients over the Web. One of the partners in the firm, Jonathan Coad, claimed that this was a case of first impression in the U.K., where normally writs or orders are served by hand and it can take days to locate the individual, and the costs and expenses can be substantial. The action was also a major break in tradition for U.K. courts, where writs are still issued in leather-bound documents by hand. In this case the restraining order was issued over the Net for the cost of a local telephone call.*

It is only a matter of time before email is regularly used as one of the means to serve process. Technology is already available to prove that an email was sent, received, and opened by a recipient. This makes it similar to return-receipt certified mail, which is already used for service in some cases. And the law profession and the courts quickly adapted to the use of faxes to serve some papers. Once the courts and the public become familiar with email technology, expect to see the word "email" mentioned in your local Rules of Procedure.

TELECONFERENCING

It's been predicted for decades that we'd all be talking to grandma over a videophone. Only in the past few years has its sister, teleconferencing, become common, but it's still not cheap. It's certainly not in every home or even every law office.

The Internet may finally change that, although it's still a few years off because of technological restrictions. Lawyer John Maxwell, Jr., writes:

> The teleconferencing software is interesting, but the current demand for bandwidth makes the video too choppy, and the software is not as ubiquitous and easy to operate as the telephone. If the demands for speed can be met by 28.8 modem speeds or ISDN installation everywhere, I can see a lot of court hearings occurring by teleconferencing. Client meetings could also occur that way. I have represented clients for years just knowing them as a voice on the phone.

> Teleconferencing will add the ability to see the client's non-verbal demonstrations, documents, and photos without having to schedule a meeting or having materials mailed in advance.

PERSONAL ACCOUNT
John Maxwell, Jr.
Meyer, Fluegge, & Tenney, P.S.
http://www.wolfenet.com/ ~maxjd/genmft.html
maxjd@wolfenet.com

Lawyer Jeffrey Kuester believes that "technology will continue to improve the interface and backbone of the Internet so that real-time audio/video conferencing will soon be possible, as well as convenient, with easy-to-use wireless access. Thus, as the quality and convenience of Internet communication increases, more and more people will use the Internet in their day-to-day lives."

Currently, voice and video over modems is rough, but Intel is supposedly developing new voice communication software that is useable over a 14.4 modem. If (and when) Internet connections go through cables, we will see a huge explosion in using the Net for voice and video conferencing.

And the software won't stop at simply allowing plain old voice communication over the Internet—you'll be able to *encrypt* your voice, too. PGP (the encryption software developed by Philip Zimmermann) now also has available PGPfone. PGPfone can turn a PC or Macintosh into a secure telephone. To get it, go to the PGPfone home page at *http://web.mit.edu/network/pgpfone*.

These technological advances will accelerate the current trend of decentralizing where lawyers work. Law school professor Eugene Volokh, in the article "Technology and the Future of Law," 47 Stan. L. Rev. 1375, 1398 (1995), writes about how computer networks and videoconferencing will change where lawyers work:

> *Used together, the technologies may finally make it feasible for lawyers to spend much of their work week at home, office politics permitting. All case materials will be on the computer at the office, available via modem from a home computer. …And the videophone will let lawyers talk face-to-face to partners who need to give them assignments, or to associates who need to be given directions, or even to friends at work with whom they want to chat.*

> *Obviously, video conversations aren't the same as face-to-face ones. Even with video, much body language and personal warmth gets lost, as does the ability to look over a paper document with another person. But despite these drawbacks, business is already often transacted by telephone. As video becomes more functional, it will add a substantial level of realism to such long-distance communications. And if a document is available on the computer, it should be no problem for both people to read it and have a video conversation about it at the same time.*

> *The advantages for the law firm are substantial. Lawyers are already unhappy about working 10- or 12-hour days. An extra hour or two of daily commuting only makes things harder. Letting lawyers avoid the commute might make them more willing and able to put in the work time.*

The changes aren't only about lawyers spending more time at home. They're also about spending less time traveling to court. Eugene Volokh continues at page 1400:

> *Videoconferencing also raises the possibility of video court arguments. Imagine that every law firm would have a conference room with a video camera and two large screens, one to see the judge and one to see the opposing lawyer. A judge's chambers would have a similar arrangement. Motions would be argued by videoconference; the lawyers would save traffic time (and flight time) as well as time waiting in the courtroom.*

The savings could be dramatic, once the technology gets cheap enough. Again, something will be lost through video, but some courts already allow telephone oral arguments. Moreover, what will be lost—the personal magnetism of the lawyers—perhaps ought not to play a big role in the first place, at least from the perspective of the judicial system.

Professor Volokh admits that there are structural roadblocks to video court hearings, but predicts at some point the lower costs and efficiencies will win out. "At some point, lawyers may find it hard to justify to a client why they spent a day, or even a few hours, traveling for half an hour of oral argument." The courts will also see the advantages of having greater scheduling flexibility when lawyers aren't pacing outside of their chambers.

Once Internet technology makes video conferencing workable—and very affordable—you'd better get accustomed to talking into a camera.

In this chapter, we looked at just a few ways the Internet will transform the practice of law. And by now, your head may be spinning thinking about the technological changes ahead. You may sigh in frustration, pondering how the legal profession just survived the PC revolution and now must tackle the Net revolution. But as you can see from the experiences in this book, these changes should not cause your shoulders to sag in weariness. Instead, the changes—fed by the Internet at the vortex's eye—should energize you with the possibilities inherent in the technology. Think of the Web resources available at your fingertips! Imagine the ways you can use email to make your practice more efficient!

With the Internet, lawyers can practice law more effectively than ever before. This thought shouldn't make you nervous, but instead excite you with the possibilities. Get online and start exploring what this new world can do for your law practice!

Glossary

anonymous FTP

A site that lets you log on without a secret password and lets you move files between that computer and yours.

application

(a) Software that performs a particular useful function for you ("Do you have an electronic mail application installed on your computer?").

(b) The useful function itself (e.g., transferring files is a useful application of the Internet).

bandwidth

The size of a network and its ability to carry data. The more bandwidth or larger the network, the more data that can go through the network at once.

baud

When transmitting data, the number of times the medium's "state" changes per second. For example, a 2400-baud modem changes the signal it sends on the phone line 2400 times per second. Since each change in state can correspond to multiple bits of data, the actual bit rate of data transfer may exceed the baud rate. Also see "bits per second."

BBS (Bulletin Board System)

Used in networking to refer to a system for providing online announcements, with or without provisions for user input. Internet hosts often provide them in addition to Usenet conferences.

beta

A test version of a software application.

bits per second

The speed at which bits are transmitted over a communications medium.

bounce

Email that can't get delivered for whatever reason bounces back to you. The bounced email message (bounced by an ominous computer character called a daemon) often describes the reason for the bounce.

bridge

Hardware used to expand the capability of a LAN by selectively forwarding information to another part of the LAN.

browser

A software program that allows you to view, search, and download items from the Internet. Common browsers are Netscape and Mosaic. Also known as a Web browser.

BTW

Common abbreviation in mail and news, meaning "by the way."

Chat (Internet Relay Chat or IRC)

A service that allows large group conversations over the Internet.

client

A software application (q.v.) that works on your behalf to extract a service from a server somewhere on the network. Think of your telephone as a client and the telephone company as a server to get the idea. For lawyers, clients are quite a different creature. Lawyers are supposed to work on behalf of the client, instead of the other way around.

commercial networks or service providers

Companies such as America Online, Prodigy, and CompuServe support private networks. These networks now provide access to the Internet in addition to their own content. Because of their additional content and ease of use, they are often more expensive than going to an ISP.

cyber

Often used as a prefix to anything relating to the electronic world, especially the Internet, such as the cyberworld, cyberspace, etc. The word "cyberspace" was created by William Gibson in the novel Neuromancer.

dial-up access

A type of connection to the Internet that allows you to call a computer directly on the Internet, staying connected only during the time you are online. Dial-up access is cheaper but slower than direct access.

direct access

A permanent connection to the Internet that continues even if you are away from your computer. Direct access is faster and more expensive than dial-up access.

distribution list

A mailing list that sends out a newsletter or bulletin to its subscribers. This may be the list's sole purpose.

discussion group

A term including mailing lists, newsgroups, and chat groups.

DNS (Domain Name System)

A distributed database system for translating computer names (like ruby.ora.com) into numeric Internet addresses (like 194.56.78.2), and vice versa. DNS allows you to use the Internet without remembering long lists of numbers.

download

To move a file from a remote computer or server onto yours.

email

One of the most popular tools on the Internet. With email software, you can send messages, documents, and graphics to other people connected to the Internet.

emoticons

A combination of the words "emotion" and "icon." Used to express emotions in email, such as the sideways smiley face :-). Here's a list of some of the most common ones:

:-) humor, smile, it's a joke

;-) wink

:/) not funny

:-} grin

:-] smirk

:-(unhappy

'-) wink

;-) sardonic incredulity

8-) wide-eyed

:-o shouting

:-w speak with forked tongue

:-T keeping a straight face (tight-lipped)

:-# censored

:-? licking your lips

FAQ (Frequently Asked Questions)

Either a frequently asked question, or a list of frequently asked questions and their answers. Many Usenet newsgroups, and some non-Usenet mailing lists, maintain FAQ lists (FAQs) so that participants don't spend time answering the same set of questions. (Pronounced "fack" or spelled out F-A-Q.)

firewall

A software program on a host computer that blocks access to unauthorized entry.

flame

A virulent and (often) largely personal attack against the author of a Usenet or mailing list posting. Flames are unfortunately common. People who frequently write flames are known as "flamers."

frame relay

A data communication technology which is sometimes used to provide higher speed (above 56 Kb and less than 1.5 Mb) for Internet connections. Its usual application is in connecting work groups rather than individuals.

Freenet

An organization providing free Internet access to people in a certain area, usually through public libraries.

FTP

(a) The File Transfer Protocol; a protocol that defines how to transfer files from one computer to another.

(b) An application program that moves files using the File Transfer Protocol.

FYI

A common abbreviation in mail and news, meaning "for your information."

gateway

A computer system that transfers data between normally incompatible applications or networks. It reformats the data so that it is acceptable for the new network (or application) before passing it on. A gateway might connect two dissimilar networks, like DECnet and the Internet, or it might allow two incompatible applications to communicate over the same network (like mail systems with different message formats). The term is often used interchangeably with router (q.v.), but this usage is incorrect.

GIF (Graphical Interchange Format)

Developed by CompuServe online services, this graphic file format allows images to transfer over telephone lines more quickly than other graphic formats.

Gopher

A menu-based system for exploring Internet resources.

hit

The number of times someone accesses a Web site.

home page

The introductory page to a Web site. You may start with this page or you may start elsewhere on the Web site depending on how you entered.

hostname

That portion of a URL that defines who the host is, i.e., *ibm.com* or *apple.com*.

hotlink

A color-coded portion of text displayed on a Web site that, if clicked on, takes you to another site or document. Also known as hyperlink.

HTML (HyperText Markup Language)

The language in which World Wide Web documents are written.

HTTP (HyperText Transfer Protocol)

The language computers use to speak to each other to transfer World Wide Web data.

hypermedia

A combination of hypertext (q.v.) and multimedia (q.v.).

hyperlink

A color-coded portion of text displayed on a Web site that, if clicked on, takes you to another site or document. Also known as a hotlink.

hypertext

Documents that contain links to other documents; selecting a link automatically displays the second document.

IAB (Internet Architecture Board)

The "ruling council" that makes decisions about standards and other important issues.

IETF (Internet Engineering Task Force)

A volunteer group that investigates and solves technical problems and makes recommendations to the IAB (q.v.).

image

A picture or graphic that appears on a Web page.

IMHO

Common abbreviation in mail and news, meaning "in my humble opinion."

Internet (or Net)

(a) Generally (not capitalized), any collection of distinct networks working together as one.

(b) Specifically (capitalized), the worldwide "network of networks" that are connected to each other, using IP and other similar protocols. The Internet provides file transfer, remote login, electronic mail, news, and other services.

intranet

Private portions of the Internet set up mostly by companies that want to use the powerful networking features of the Net for their own company networking purposes.

IP (Internet Protocol)

The most important of the protocols on which the Internet is based. It allows a packet to traverse multiple networks on the way to its final destination.

IRC

(See Chat)

ISDN (Integrated Services Digital Network)

A digital telephone service. With ISDN service, phone lines carry digital signals, rather than analog signals. If you have the appropriate hardware and software, if your local central office provides ISDN service, and if your service provider supports it, ISDN allows high-speed home or office access to the Internet (56 Kbps).

ISOC (Internet Society)

An organization whose members support a worldwide information network. It is also the governing body to which the IAB (q.v.) reports.

ISP (Internet Service Provider)

An organization that supplies users with access to the Internet.

Java

A program produced by Sun Microsystems that allows for a higher degree of interactivity, motion, and sound on Web pages.

jpeg/jpg

A graphic (pictures) format that compresses an image and makes it easier to transmit.

keyword search

An electronic search that allows you to find more information than a subject search because the computer looks at words in the titles and content of a source as well as the subjects. It also allows you to find more specific information, because each source yields many more keywords than subjects. The challenge in using keyword searching is to refine your topic so that the search yields an adequate number of useful citations.

kill file

A list of newsgroup users whose postings you do not want to read. You can create a kill file and include email addresses of people whose messages you don't wish to read.

LAN (local area network)

A network that connects computers and other peripherals in a small area, such as a building or classroom.

leased line

A permanently connected private telephone line between two locations. Leased lines are typically used to connect a moderate-sized local network to an Internet Service Provider.

link

The text or graphic you click on to make a hypertext jump to another page.

listserv

(See mailing list)

lurk

What one does in a newsgroup or mailing list when one listens to the discussion, but doesn't participate. Unlike the real world, it is considered polite, and in fact proper netiquette, to lurk in a discussion group before participating.

mailing list

A conference/discussion group on a specific topic where all messages are sent to one email address and then redistributed to the email boxes of the list's subscribers. If the list is moderated, someone will review the messages before redistributing them.

modem

A piece of equipment that connects a computer to a data transmission line (typically a telephone line of some sort). Most people use modems that transfer data at speeds ranging from 1200 bits per second (bps) to 28.8 Kbps. There are also modems providing higher speeds and supporting other media. These are used for special purposes, for example, to connect a large local network to its network provider over a leased line.

moderated

A newsgroup or mailing list that has a person screening the messages coming in before he or she posts them to subscribers.

Mosaic

One particular browser for the World Wide Web; supports hypermedia.

multimedia

Documents that include different kinds of data; for example, plain text and audio, text in several different languages, or plain text and a spreadsheet.

netiquette

Etiquette for the Internet.

Netscape

The most well-known and commonly used browser.

newbie

A newcomer to the Internet.

newsgroup

A conference/discussion group where people post and read messages at the newsgroup site rather than in a mailbox. Reading the messages requires your ISP to subscribe to the newsgroup and for you to use a newsreader. Newsgroups are organized by subject area (i.e., *alt.politics.clinton*).

newsreader

A software program that allows you to read and post messages to newsgroups.

packet

A bundle of data. On the Internet, data is broken up into small chunks, called packets; each packet traverses the network independently. Packet sizes can vary from roughly 40 to 32,000 bytes, depending on network hardware and media, but packets are normally less than 1500 bytes long.

port

(a)   A number that identifies a particular Internet application. When your computer sends a packet to another computer, that packet contains information about what protocol it's using (e.g., TCP or UDP), and what application it's trying to communicate with. The port number identifies the application.

(b)   One of a computer's physical input/output channels (i.e., a plug on the back of the computer).

Unfortunately, these two meanings are completely unrelated. The first is more common when you're talking about the Internet (as in "Telnet to port 1000"); the second is more common when you're talking about hardware ("connect your modem to the serial port on the back of your computer").

post

An individual article sent to a newsgroup or to a mailing list.

PPP (Point-to-Point Protocol)

A protocol that allows a computer to use the TCP/IP (Internet) protocols (and become a full-fledged Internet member) with a standard telephone line and a high-speed modem. PPP is a newer standard, which replaces SLIP (q.v.).

protocol

A definition of how computers will act when talking to each other. Protocol definitions range from how bits are placed on a wire to the format of an electronic mail message. Standard protocols allow computers from different manufacturers to communicate; the computers can use completely different software, providing that the programs running on both ends agree on what the data means.

real time

Synchronous communication. For example, talking to someone on the phone is in real time, whereas listening to a message someone left on your answering machine is not (asynchronous communication).

router

A system that transfers data between two or more networks using the same protocols. The networks may differ in physical characteristics (e.g., a router may transfer data between an Ethernet and a leased telephone line).

scanner

A piece of computer equipment that converts photos and other hardcopy into graphic computer files.

search engine

A Web-based tool that finds Web pages based on terms and criteria specified.

server

(a) Software that allows a computer to offer a service to another computer. Other computers contact the server program by means of matching client (q.v.) software.

(b) The computer on which the server software runs.

service provider

An organization that provides connections to a part of the Internet. If you want to connect your company's network or your personal computer to the Internet, you have to talk to a service provider.

shareware

Software made available, usually over the Internet, for free on a trial basis. The developer asks those who keep and use it to pay a nominal fee.

shell

On a UNIX system, software that accepts and processes command lines from your terminal. UNIX has multiple shells available (e.g., C shell, Bourne shell, Korn shell), each with slightly different command formats and facilities.

signature

A file, typically about five lines long or less, that people often insert at the end of electronic mail messages or Usenet news articles. A signature contains, minimally, a name and an email address. Signatures usually also contain postal addresses, and often contain silly quotes, pictures, and other things. Some are elaborate, though signatures more than five or six lines long are in questionable taste.

SLIP (Serial Line Internet Protocol)

A protocol that allows a computer to use the Internet protocols (and become a full-fledged Internet member) with a standard telephone line and a high-speed modem. SLIP is being superseded by PPP (q.v.).

smiley

Smiling faces used in mail and news to indicate humor and irony. The most common smiley is :-). You'll also see :-(meaning disappointment, and lots of other variations. See emoticons.

snail mail

Mail sent via the post office or express delivery service.

spamming

The frowned-upon practice of sending large amounts of junk email to people who have not requested it.

subject search

An electronic search based on the traditional method of categorizing books and other materials by subject. These subjects are usually fairly broad, general topics established by an authority such as the Library of Congress.

subscribe

Joining a mailing list or newsgroup to read and send messages to the group.

surf

To mindlessly click from link to link on the Internet looking for something interesting.

TCP (Transmission Control Protocol)

One of the protocols on which the Internet is based. TCP is a connection-oriented reliable protocol.

telecommuting

Working from home using a computer over an online network.

Telnet

(a) A terminal emulation protocol that allows you to log in to other computer systems on the Internet.

(b) An application program that allows you to log in to another computer system using the protocol.

tiff file

A graphic format for pictures.

timeout

What happens when two computers are talking and one computer, for any reason, fails to respond. The other computer will keep on trying for a certain amount of time, but will eventually give up.

UNIX

A popular operating system that was very important in the development of the Internet. You do not have to use UNIX to use the Internet. There are various flavors of UNIX. Two common ones are BSD and System V.

upload

To move a file from your computer to another computer or server.

URL (Universal Resource Locator)
The combination of letters and numbers that uniquely identifies a Web resource.

Usenet
An informal, rather anarchic, group of systems that exchange news. Usenet is essentially similar to bulletin boards on other networks. Usenet actually predates the Internet, but these days the Internet is used to transfer much of the Usenet's traffic.

username
The name you receive from your service provider to identify your account on the host computer. Generally, your user name is created from your real name, such as your first name and last initial. Your user name is to the left of the @ symbol in your email address.

WAIS (Wide Area Information Service)
A powerful system for looking up information in databases or libraries across the Internet.

Web
(See World Wide Web)

Web browser
A software program that allows you to view, search, and download items from the Web. Common browsers are Netscape, Mosaic, and Microsoft Explorer.

Web page
A file accessible by a Web browser. Web pages can contain text, sounds, pictures, movies, and hypertext links to other Web pages.

Web server
A computer directly connected to the Internet that responds to requests from browsers to send Web pages.

Web site
A set of Web pages for a person or organization.

Webmaster
A person who maintains a Web site.

World Wide Web
A hypertext-based system for finding and accessing Internet resources. Also known as WWW, the Web, or W3.

WWW
(See World Wide Web)

Index

More Titles from O'REILLY™

Songline Guides

NetLearning: Why Teachers Use the Internet

By Ferdi Serim & Melissa Koch
1st Edition June 1996
304 pages, ISBN 1-56592-201-8

In this book educators and Internet users who've been exploring its potential for education share stories to help teachers use this medium to its fullest potential in their classrooms. The book offers advice on how to adapt, how to get what you want, and where to go to get help. The goal: To invite educators online with the reassurance there will be people there to greet them. Includes CD-ROM with Internet software.

NetSuccess: How Real Estate Agents Use the Internet

By Scott Kersnar
1st Edition August 1996
214 pages, ISBN 1-56592-213-1

This book shows real estate agents how to harness the communications and marketing tools of the Internet to enhance their careers and make the Internet work for them. Through agents' stories and "A day in the life"scenarios, readers see what changes and what stays the same when you make technology a full partner in your working life.

NetActivism: How Citizens Use the Internet

By Ed Schwartz
1st Edition September 1996
224 pages, ISBN 1-56592-160-7

Let a veteran political activist tell you how to use online networks to further your cause. Whether you are a community activist, a politician, a nonprofit staff person, or just someone who cares about your community, you will benefit from the insights this book offers on how to make the fastest-growing medium today work for you. Includes CD-ROM with Internet software and limited free online time.

NetResearch: Finding Information Online

By Daniel J. Barrett
1st Edition Winter 1997
240 pages (est.), ISBN 1-56592-245-X

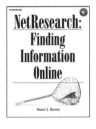

Whatever your profession or avocation, NetResearchteaches you how to locate the information you need in the constantly changing online world.

Whether you're using the Net to research statistics for a report, to find free software, or to locate an old college roommate, it pays to locate online information rapidly. But the Net is a very big, disorganized place, and it can be difficult to locate just the information you want, when you need it. In *NetResearch,* you'll learn effective search techniques that work with any Internet search programs, present or future, and will build intuition on how to succeed when searches fail. Throughout the book, the author offers quizzes that allow you to practice your own research skills or that you can use as a teaching tool to help others.

Covers the Internet, America Online, CompuServe, Microsoft Network, and Prodigy.

NetTravel: How Travelers Use the Internet

By Michael Shapiro
1st Edition Winter 1997
225 pages (est.), ISBN 1-56592-172-0

NetTravel is a virtual toolbox of advice for those travelers who want to tap into the rich vein of travel resources on the Internet. It is filled with personal accounts by travelers who've used the Net to plan their business trips, vacations, honeymoons, and explorations. Author and journalist Michael Shapiro gives readers all the tools they need to use the Net immediately to find and save money on airline tickets, accommodations, and car rentals. Includes CD-ROM with Internet software.

Software

WebSite™ 1.1

By O'Reilly & Associates, Inc.
Documentation by Susan Peck & Stephen Arrants
2nd Edition January 1996
Four diskettes, 494-pg book, WebSite T-shirt
ISBN 1-56592-173-9; UPC 9-781565-921733

 *WebSite 1.1* makes it easier than ever for Windows NT 3.51 and Windows 95 users to start publishing on the Internet. WebSite is a 32-bit multi-threaded World Wide Web server that combines power and flexibility with ease of use. *WebSite 1.1* features include: HTML editor, multiple indexes, WebFind wizard, CGI with Visual Basic 4 framework and server push support, graphical interface for creating virtual servers, Windows 95 style install, logging reports for individual documents, HTML-2 and -3 support, external image map support, and Spyglass Mosaic 2.1 Web browser.

WebSite Professional ™

By O'Reilly & Associates, Inc.
Documentation by Susan Peck
1st Edition June 1996
Includes 3 books, ISBN 1-56592-174-7

 Designed for the sophisticated user, *WebSite Professional*™ is a complete Web server solution. *WebSite Professional* contains all of *WebSite*'s award-winning features, including remote administration, virtual servers for creating multiple home pages, wizards to automate common tasks, a search tool for Web indexing, and a graphical outline fo Web documents and links for managing your site. New with *WebSite Professional:* support for SSL and S-HTTP, the premier Web encryption security protocols; the WebSite Application Programming Interface (WSAPI); Cold Fusion, a powerful development tool for dynamic linking of database information into your Web documents; and support for client and server-side Java programming.

WebSite Professional is a must for sophisticated users who want to offer their audiences the best in Web server technology.

WebBoard ™

By O'Reilly & Associates, Inc.
1st Edition February 1996
Includes 3 diskettes & a 98-pg book, ISBN 1-56592-181-X

 *WebBoard*™ is an advanced multi-threaded conferencing system that can help attract users to your Web server. With *WebBoard,* people can use their Web browsers to participate in online discussions about any number of topics. *WebBoard* is ideal for use in business environments and in legal or educational organizations or groups—anywhere online discussions can help groups communicate and keep track of ongoing decisions and issues.

PolyForm™

Documentation by John Robert Boynton
1st Edition May 1996
Two diskettes & 146-pg book, ISBN 1-56592-182-8

 *PolyForm*™ is a powerful 32-bit Web forms tool that helps you easily build and manage interactive Web pages. *PolyForm*'s interactive forms make it easy and fun for users to respond to the contents of your Web with their own feedback, ideas, or requests for more information. *PolyForm* lets you collect, process, and respond to each user's specific input. Best of all, forms that once required hours of complicated programming can be created in minutes because *PolyForm* automatically handles all of the CGI programming for processing form contents.

Statisphere™

By O'Reilly & Associates, Inc.
1st Edition Winter 1996
2 diskettes & a 135-page book, ISBN 1-56592-233-6

 *Statisphere*™ is a Web traffic analyzer that provides precise, graphical reporting on your Web server's usage. Easy-to-read, browser-based reports deliver real-time profiles and long-term trend analysis on who's visiting your site and what they're reading. Whether you're tracking traffic rates for advertising, or steering Web development efforts to where they'll have the most impact, Statisphere gives you the answers you need to make the right decisions about your Web site.

shopPBS

from the comfort of your own computer chair

http://www.pbs.org/shop

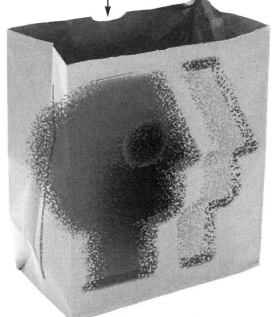

Now your favorite PBS videos and products are just a mouse click away with shopPBS.

At this special cyber shop you'll find a video collection with more than 200 titles, a bookshelf that includes the acclaimed book *NetLearning: How Teachers Use the Internet* and other fun items like the lovable Wishbone doll. Best of all, ordering is done online with secure credit card transactions!

For a fun-filled shopping adventure, make your next online stop shopPBS.

http://www.pbs.org/shop

PBS ONLINE® (http://www.pbs.org) is the premier choice for unique and compelling interactive content developed specifically for the Internet.

IF PBS DOESN'T DO IT, WHO WILL?   http://www.pbs.org/shop

Stay in touch with O'REILLY™

Visit Our Award-Winning World Wide Web Site

http://www.ora.com/

VOTED

"Top 100 Sites on the Web" —*PC Magazine*
"Top 5% Websites" —*Point Communications*
"3-Star site" —*The McKinley Group*

Our Web site contains a library of comprehensive product information (including book excerpts and tables of contents), downloadable software, background articles, interviews with technology leaders, links to relevant sites, book cover art, and more. File us in your Bookmarks or Hotlist!

Join Our Two Email Mailing Lists

LIST #1   NEW PRODUCT RELEASES: To receive automatic email with brief descriptions of all new O'Reilly products as they are released, send email to: **listproc@online.ora.com** and put the following information in the first line of your message (NOT in the Subject: field, which is ignored): **subscribe ora-news "Your Name" of "Your Organization"** (for example: **subscribe ora-news Kris Webber of Fine Enterprises)**

List #2   O'REILLY EVENTS: If you'd also like us to send information about trade show events, special promotions, and other O'Reilly events, send email to: **listproc@online.ora.com** and put the following information in the first line of your message (NOT in the Subject: field, which is ignored): **subscribe ora-events "Your Name" of "Your Organization"**

Visit Our Gopher Site

- Connect your Gopher to **gopher.ora.com**, or
- Point your Web browser to **gopher://gopher.ora.com/**, or
- telnet to **gopher.ora.com** (login: **gopher**)

Get Example Files from Our Books Via FTP

There are two ways to access an archive of example files from our books:

REGULAR FTP — ftp to: **ftp.ora.com** (login: **anonymous**—use your email address as the password) or point your Web browser to: **ftp://ftp.ora.com/**

FTPMAIL — Send an email message to: **ftpmail@online.ora.com** (write "help" in the message body)

Contact Us Via Email

order@ora.com — To place a book or software order online. Good for North American and international customers.

subscriptions@ora.com — To place an order for any of our newsletters or periodicals.

software@ora.com — For general questions and product information about our software.
- Check out O'Reilly Software Online at **http://software.ora.com/** for software and technical support information.
- Registered O'Reilly software users send your questions to **website-support@ora.com**

books@ora.com — General questions about any of our books.

cs@ora.com — For answers to problems regarding your order or our products.

booktech@ora.com — For book content technical questions or corrections.

proposals@ora.com — To submit new book or software proposals to our editors and product managers.

international@ora.com — For information about our international distributors or translation queries.
- For a list of our distributors outside of North America check out: **http://www.ora.com/www/order/country.html**

O'REILLY™

101 Morris Street, Sebastopol, CA 95472 USA
TEL 707-829-0515 or 800-998-9938 (6 A.M. to 5 P.M. PST)
FAX 707-829-0104

Titles from O'REILLY™

INTERNET PROGRAMMING

CGI Programming on the
    World Wide Web
Designing for the Web
HTML: The Definitive Guide
JavaScript: The Definitive Guide
Learning Perl
Programming Perl, 2nd Edition
Regular Expressions
WebMaster in a Nutshell
Web Client Programming with Perl
    (Winter '97)
The World Wide Web Journal

USING THE INTERNET

Smileys
The Whole Internet User's Guide
    and Catalog
The Whole Internet for Windows 95
What You Need to Know:
    Using Email Effectively
What You Need to Know: Bandits on the
    Information Superhighway

JAVA SERIES

Exploring Java
Java AWT Reference (Winter '97 est.)
Java Fundamental Classes Reference
    (Winter '97 est.)
Java in a Nutshell
Java Language Reference (Winter '97 est.)
Java Threads
Java Virtual Machine (Winter '97)

SOFTWARE

WebSite™ 1.1
WebSite Professional™
WebBoard™
PolyForm™
Statisphere™

SONGLINE GUIDES

Gif Animation Studio
NetActivism
NetLaw (Winter '97)
NetLearning
NetResearch (Winter '97)
NetSuccess for Realtors
Shockwave Studio (Winter '97 est.)

SYSTEM ADMINISTRATION

Building Internet Firewalls
Computer Crime:
    A Crimefighter's Handbook
Computer Security Basics
DNS and BIND, 2nd Edition
Essential System Administration,
    2nd Edition
Getting Connected:
    The Internet at 56K and Up
Linux Network Administrator's Guide
Managing Internet Information Services
Managing Usenet (Spring '97)
Managing NFS and NIS
Networking Personal Computers
    with TCP/IP
Practical UNIX & Internet Security
PGP: Pretty Good Privacy
sendmail, 2nd Edition (Winter '97)
System Performance Tuning
TCP/IP Network Administration
termcap & terminfo
Using & Managing UUCP
Volume 8: X Window System
    Administrator's Guide

UNIX

Exploring Expect
Learning GNU Emacs, 2nd Edition
Learning the bash Shell
Learning the Korn Shell
Learning the UNIX Operating System
Learning the vi Editor
Linux in a Nutshell (Winter '97 est.)
Making TeX Work
Linux Multimedia Guide
Running Linux, 2nd Edition
Running Linux Companion
    CD-ROM, 2nd Edition
SCO UNIX in a Nutshell
sed & awk, 2nd Edition (Winter '97)
UNIX in a Nutshell: System V Edition
UNIX Power Tools
UNIX Systems Programming
Using csh and tsch
What You Need to Know:
    When You Can't Find Your
    UNIX System Administrator

WINDOWS

Inside the Windows 95 Registry

PROGRAMMING

Advanced PL/SQL
Applying RCS and SCCS
C++: The Core Language
Checking C Programs with lint
DCE Security Programming
Distributing Applications Across
    DCE and Windows NT
Encyclopedia of Graphics File
    Formats, 2nd Edition
Guide to Writing DCE Applications
lex & yacc
Managing Projects with make
Oracle Performance Tuning
Oracle Power Objects
Oracle PL/SQL Programming
Porting UNIX Software
POSIX Programmer's Guide
POSIX.4: Programming for
    the Real World
Power Programming with RPC
Practical C Programming
Practical C++ Programming
Programming Python
Programming with curses
Programming with GNU Software
Pthreads Programming
Software Portability with imake,
    2nd Edition
Understanding DCE
Understanding Japanese Information
    Processing
UNIX Systems Programming for SVR4

BERKELEY 4.4 SOFTWARE DISTRIBUTION

4.4BSD System Manager's Manual
4.4BSD User's Reference Manual
4.4BSD User's Supplementary
    Documents
4.4BSD Programmer's Reference
    Manual
4.4BSD Programmer's Supplementary
    Documents

X PROGRAMMING
THE X WINDOW SYSTEM

Volume 0: X Protocol Reference Manual
Volume 1: Xlib Programming Manual
Volume 2: Xlib Reference Manual
Volume. 3M: X Window System
    User's Guide, Motif Edition
Volume. 4: X Toolkit Intrinsics
    Programming Manual
Volume 4M: X Toolkit Intrinsics
    Programming Manual,
    Motif Edition
Volume 5: X Toolkit Intrinsics
    Reference Manual
Volume 6A: Motif Programming
    Manual
Volume 6B: Motif Reference Manual
Volume 6C: Motif Tools
Volume 8 : X Window System
    Administrator's Guide
Programmer's Supplement for Release 6
X User Tools (with CD-ROM)
The X Window System in a Nutshell

HEALTH, CAREER, & BUSINESS

Building a Successful Software Business
The Computer User's Survival Guide
Dictionary of Computer Terms
The Future Does Not Compute
Love Your Job!
Publishing with CD-ROM

TRAVEL

Travelers' Tales: Brazil (Winter '96)
Travelers' Tales: Food (Fall '96)
Travelers' Tales: France
Travelers' Tales: Gutsy Women
    (Fall '96)
Travelers' Tales: Hong Kong
Travelers' Tales: India
Travelers' Tales: Mexico
Travelers' Tales: San Francisco
Travelers' Tales: Spain
Travelers' Tales: Thailand
Travelers' Tales: A Woman's World

TO ORDER: **800-889-8969** (CREDIT CARD ORDERS ONLY); **order@ora.com**; **http://www.ora.com/**
OUR PRODUCTS ARE AVAILABLE AT A BOOKSTORE OR SOFTWARE STORE NEAR YOU.

International Distributors

Customers outside North America can now order O'Reilly & Associates books through the following distributors. They offer our international customers faster order processing, more bookstores, increased representation at tradeshows worldwide, and the high-quality, responsive service our customers have come to expect.

EUROPE, MIDDLE EAST AND NORTHERN AFRICA (except Germany, Switzerland, and Austria)
INQUIRIES
International Thomson Publishing Europe
Berkshire House
168-173 High Holborn
London WC1V 7AA, United Kingdom
Telephone: 44-171-497-1422
Fax: 44-171-497-1426
Email: **itpint@itps.co.uk**

ORDERS
International Thomson Publishing Services, Ltd.
Cheriton House, North Way
Andover, Hampshire SP10 5BE,
United Kingdom
Telephone: 44-264-342-832 (UK orders)
Telephone: 44-264-342-806 (outside UK)
Fax: 44-264-364418 (UK orders)
Fax: 44-264-342761 (outside UK)
UK & Eire orders: **itpuk@itps.co.uk**
International orders: **itpint@itps.co.uk**

GERMANY, SWITZERLAND, AND AUSTRIA
International Thomson Publishing
Königswinterer Straße 418
53227 Bonn, Germany
Telephone: 49-228-97024 0
Fax: 49-228-441342
Email: **anfragen@oreilly.de**

AUSTRALIA
WoodsLane Pty. Ltd.
7/5 Vuko Place, Warriewood NSW 2102
P.O. Box 935, Mona Vale NSW 2103
Australia
Telephone: 61-2-9970-5111
Fax: 61-2-9970-5002
Email: **info@woodslane.com.au**

NEW ZEALAND
WoodsLane New Zealand Ltd.
21 Cooks Street (P.O. Box 575)
Wanganui, New Zealand
Telephone: 64-6-347-6543
Fax: 64-6-345-4840
Email: **info@woodslane.com.au**

ASIA (except Japan & India)
INQUIRIES
International Thomson Publishing Asia
60 Albert Street #15-01
Albert Complex
Singapore 189969
Telephone: 65-336-6411
Fax: 65-336-7411

ORDERS
Telephone: 65-336-6411
Fax: 65-334-1617

JAPAN
O'Reilly Japan, Inc.
Kiyoshige Building 2F
12-Banchi, Sanei-cho
Shinjuku-ku
Tokyo 160 Japan
Telephone: 81-3-3356-5227
Fax: 81-3-3356-5261
Email: **kenji@ora.com**

INDIA
Computer Bookshop (India) PVT. LTD.
190 Dr. D.N. Road, Fort
Bombay 400 001
India
Telephone: 91-22-207-0989
Fax: 91-22-262-3551
Email: **cbsbom@giasbm01.vsnl.net.in**

THE AMERICAS
O'Reilly & Associates, Inc.
101 Morris Street
Sebastopol, CA 95472 U.S.A.
Telephone: 707-829-0515
Telephone: 800-998-9938 (U.S. & Canada)
Fax: 707-829-0104
Email: **order@ora.com**

SOUTHERN AFRICA
International Thomson Publishing Southern Africa
Building 18, Constantia Park
240 Old Pretoria Road
P.O. Box 2459
Halfway House, 1685 South Africa
Telephone: 27-11-805-4819
Fax: 27-11-805-3648

O'REILLY™